Praise for J
Go with Go

MW00582090

"Hogan dug one of the greatest golf swings ever out of the Texas dirt. He, clearly, had the fundamentals down pat, as presented in his system: *Five Lessons: The Modern Fundamentals of Golf.* You'll enjoy reading J. Mike's stories of his life, of Hogan, Palmer, Nicklaus and others that he has met, while traveling the fairways of life."

Curt Byrum | PGA Professional and Golf Channel Commentator

"Steer Horns, Harleys, Helicopters, Hot Air Balloons… and Golf? Oh, yes! And Hogan, Palmer, Nicklaus and others, too! All entwined to give the reader a view of a personal life and way of living, all in the pursuit of Excellence… Systematically."

Joseph F. Wyzkoski, Jr. | IBM, Xerox

"J. Mike has written about the fairways of life, being in and out of the rough, out of bounds, and rebounding to live a lifestyle of faith. Funny and real!"

Alice Cooper | Shock Rock Musician, Rock 'n Roll Hall of Fame

"J. Mike's stories of legendary Titanic Thompson and his personal experiences with Ben Hogan, Tommy Bolt, Arnold Palmer, Dan Jenkins, Jack Nicklaus and others are just part of this delightful read on golf and life's journeys."

Sam F. Casano | MD and Golf Buddy

"The pictures alone are worth the price of this book. The stories, lessons, and wisdom… priceless."

Ricky Barnes | PGA Tour Player

"Here are some hilarious stories, on Golf, God, and Greater inner happiness, throughout a lifetime, producing even greater capacity for life while living in such a screwed-up mad, mad, world."

Michael S. Hyatt | Senior VP UBS Financial

"Have you got an old man for a friend? If not, J. Mike's your guy! Through some 70 odd years of living, not every well he's drilled has gone dry (metaphorically). Here's a great read on Golf, Life, Love for the Game, Relationships and God's plan for one's own life."

Reed Day | MD, DMD, FACS

"Starting with the principles formed in the corporate culture of IBM, J. Mike provides an enjoyable, fascinating, and often very funny read on the matters of Golf. Wonderful perspectives, too, on living the Christian Way of Life."

Jeff Moore | Executive Director, Alice Cooper's Solid Rock

"J. Michael Meadows has always had a clear sense of purpose: to place a great emphasis in the pursuit of things he loves. He is an extraordinary story teller and nowhere is his magic more evident than in his imaginative and deeply entertaining stories."

Patrick Gallagher | JD

"From boyhood into manhood; since 1959 I have known and played golf with J. Michael Meadows, meeting on The Meridian Golf Course, in Oklahoma City. Greatly influenced from and guided by parents of character, faith and grace, he writes good stuff: I know, for I was there."

J. Malcolm Haney | Xerox, Kodak

GO WITH...
GOD, HOGAN,
AND THE HYBRID

[signature]

TRAVELING LIFE'S FAIRWAYS
STORIES | TRUTHS | WISDOM

J. MICHAEL MEADOWS

LZ

Published by Learning Zone, LLC, an imprint of Brisance Books Group LLC
The publisher is not responsible for websites or their content that are not owned by the publisher.

Learning Zone LLC
3219 E. Camelback Road #355
Phoenix, AZ 85018

Printed in the United States of America
First Edition October 2018

ISBN: 978-1-944194-39-0

Cover design: PCI Publishing Group

102018

DEDICATION

for Jim and Bobbie Meadows
Kristin and Courtney
My Diane

FOREWORD

More than golf connects J. Michael Meadows and me. Together, we have more than 100 years in the game: his 60 plus years of golf, including his 40 years as Tournament Chairman of The United States Screen Door Open International-Invitational Golf Championship (that I was fortunate to win in 2011), and my 40 plus years in golf. That has allowed us to share many special stories and experiences.

I have been fortunate to have played competitive golf at the university level (University of Arkansas) as well as on the PGA Tour. J. Mike's 25 years of experience has been in golf tourism (China, South Africa, and primarily, throughout all of Scotland) along with 25 years as President of ProFundWest, a national organization providing a system of fundraising for non-profits and worthy causes.

Our higher level of connection is in our shared principles of faith, knowing that the biggest problem in our life has been solved and in knowing that as long as we are alive, God has a purpose for our lives, and a system for us to follow.

We will never have the level of difficulties and hardships on the golf course that we will encounter in life. So, while a hybrid golf club may be your "best chance" to get you out of a particular lie on the golf course, there is no such thing as an unplayable lie in life. Utilizing the Hybrid Power System (Divine Resources) that God has for you, you will cease trying to solve your own problems apart from Him, giving you a relaxed mental attitude – and a peace of mind in the middle of everything that is going on around you.

J. Mike delivers a very human and delightful read with some hilarious stories throughout this book, a book about an Oklahoma boy, without a serious care in the world. Later he delves into some of his own personal struggles in adulthood and the legacies of being part of the human race and the impossibility of living the "Wrinkle Free Life." He shares the history of the "Screen Door Open" and his experiences with the legends of the game... you won't want to miss it!

Here's an amusing, very poignant, and entertaining read. The personal encounters with Hogan, Palmer, Nicklaus, and others, you will enjoy.

Mike Swartz
PGA Professional

U.S. Open 1988
U.S. Open 1992
U.S. Open 1996
U.S. Open 1997
U.S. Screen Door Open Winner 2011

INTRODUCTION

IN QUEST OF THE MERIDIAN

The Meridian Golf Club, circa 1956

I was about nine or ten years old when I first came upon The Meridian. I didn't understand much about it then. For that matter, I don't fully understand it today. It is still revealing itself to me.

The Meridian Golf Club was located along the way of my older brother Steve's paper route, just down the street from our house in Oklahoma City. I was drawn to The Meridian, as I still am today, drawn to its meaning anyway. The Meridian Golf Course, as I first saw it, was a vast expanse of field upon which I could play.

The first thing I did on The Meridian Golf Course was fill milk cartons with water from the creeks and ponds. Then I'd pour the water down ground squirrel holes until one of those critters came up for air and then—zap—I'd catch me one of those squealing little varmints with their gnashing teeth. Gee, what fun!

The summers were so hot while "squirreling" that I started spending most of my time, while on The Meridian Golf Course, in the creeks and ponds, wading and swimming, getting relief from those sweltering days of June, July, and August. In the water, I found what seemed to be hundreds of balls… golf balls. I was finding bags of balls (literally—as I was filling Steve's paper-carrier bags) and taking them home. I couldn't believe how plentiful they were.

I had quite a collection of various brand names and numbers of golf balls, all in different conditions. Some seemed brand new, while others were badly stained, green and brown, from being on the bottom of The Meridian's big lake, no doubt, for a long time.

That's when the enterprise began. Dad said, "Mike, you could sell these good ones (those without the gashes in them) back to the golfers."

Sell golf balls back to the golfers? Hmm… Better than a lemonade stand, I thought!

I quickly learned that "the golfers" would buy back the good balls and even those I had scrubbed and soaked in bleach. Twenty-five cents, fifty cents, even as much as seventy-five cents—for one golf ball. I had found my first sales territory! And what a bonanza it was.

Toward the end of that long hot summer, sales were dropping off as many of "the golfers" acted angry with me and told me that I wasn't supposed to be on The Meridian. I was chased off the golf course several times and once I was practically dragged out of the lake, while I was diving for golf balls, by some old man driving a scooter. He took me to the house where all the golfers met. From there, he called my dad.

Dad came and talked to the man for what seemed like forever, while I sat on the porch of the so-called clubhouse. I was scared.

We drove home in silence. I didn't know what was going to happen to me or what I had done wrong. After all, it was Dad who helped me get started in this new entrepreneurial venture.

Finally Dad said, "Mike, you shouldn't pick up a lost golf ball until it stops rolling." This is still a good lesson, today. And that is just one example of the many lessons I learned—with humor included—from Dad throughout the time I lived under the roof of Jim and Bobbie Meadows.

In our garage there was a door in the middle of the ceiling with a rope attached. Pull on the rope and it brought down a staircase, going up to where all kinds of stuff was stored. As kids, we were strictly forbidden from going up into the attic. The attic was off limits. Mom and Dad had warned us that we were sure to fall through the sheetrock ceiling.

When we got home from the Meridian that day, Dad climbed up into the attic and brought down a dusty old tan canvas bag containing two wooden mallets; one had *Driver* written on it, the other *Spoon*. There were also metal sticks numbered 3, 5, 7, 9, and a putter. The leather wrappings on the grips were frayed and peeling. The threads around the wooden club heads were unwinding. I looked at these in wonderment and awe. On all of these clubs was written "Johnny Bulla Signature."

When I looked up at Dad, he was smiling and said, "Son, when you go back to The Meridian Golf Course, you'll need these. They belonged to your granddad." And I absolutely wanted, for sure now, to go back to The Meridian and play golf.

Those Johnny Bulla clubs have long since vanished but, oh, how they had thrilled me! The Meridian Golf Course isn't there anymore either. It is now all covered with houses and the Windsor Hills shopping center… a Crest Foods store, dd's Discounts store, a Laundromat, Gopuram Taste of India, a Dollar Tree, and Chen's Chinese Buffet.

Dad's been gone since 1990, and I certainly miss him the most!

But from all this—my first set of golf clubs, The Meridian Golf Course of Oklahoma City, and my wonderful parents—came great memories, wisdom, and guidance that have impacted my entire life. The Meridian, after all, means "the highest point or stage of development… Excellence."

And, for that, we all should continue IN QUEST OF THE MERIDIAN.

As a skinny kid in Oklahoma, I had no idea how the game of golf would be instrumental in directing my career, give me the best friends I would ever have, and reinforce my faith and spiritual growth.

I have accepted the encouragement from friends and associates to take up my pen (OK, I'm really on my computer, typing this Word document) to write of subjects very difficult to capture in detail, but simple in the fundamentals. (Oh, no! Right now, I'm terrified that when I exit out of Word and it asks me if I want to save the changes to my 280-page draft that I swear I did not make...)

I do this with the following admissions, and these initial statements of fear:

I am not a writer, and have never been published.

I am not a psychologist by any stretch of the imagination.

I am not a professional golfer or instructor, but have loved and played golf forever.

I am not a theologian, though I am not unfamiliar with the Bible or Biblical Doctrine.

I am not a philosopher, although I think of myself as a deep thinker and a questioner.

So, then...who am I?

That is a scary question, but I guess it's partly the subject matter of this book.

What I am, I'm guessing here, is an Entrepreneur, Raconteur, and Outdoorsman, plain and simple. However, if you are reading this book, then I can put a check mark on the first admission above, as I have become a published writer, an author.

Folks coming into my home invariably walk around the place and often make comments regarding the two pictures (one autographed) of British Prime Minister Tony Blair.

My own Hogan's Alley

I have a "billiards" room (fancy word for having a pool table) that I call Hogan's Alley, with its four pictures of Mr. Hogan (those three very famous ones and one, a personal treasure of mine, with two great friends and Mr. Hogan, taken at Shady Oaks Golf Club, Ft. Worth, Texas). There is a full wall-mount set of Hogan golf clubs, the irons from many years ago that have never once hit a golf ball, and are priceless... if you ask me.

Old Tom

There is an oil portrait of Old Tom Morris that I obtained from an antiquities shop in St. Andrews, Scotland (The Happy Hacker), hung above the famous print of *The Golfers,* one of the greatest art icons of the game, by Charles Lee, 1874.

There are pictures of Arnold Palmer, Jack Nicklaus, and a trophy case filled with various memorabilia, along with bookcases on golf and baseball (including autographed baseballs and pictures of Willie Mays, Ernie Banks, Gaylord Perry, Lefty Gomez, Hank Aaron, Bob Feller, Eddie Robinson, Greg Maddux, and Mickey Mantle).

Upon strolling into my bar area, with its tartan wallpaper, one will find several fine single-malt Scottish whiskies, flasks, jiggers, and glasses from famous golf venues. The walls are full of pictures of great Scottish golf courses: The Old Course, Carnoustie, Turnberry, Royal Dornoch, Prestwick, Muirfield, and others.

My Bar

I have scorecards and pictures of my best rounds of golf taken with the best of friends with whom I have traveled—globetrotting near and far to play the game of golf.

Affixed to another wall, is my own personal "green jacket," won (in the Masters tradition...) in 1987, at the 10th Annual Screen Door Open, played at Pierre Marques Golf Club, Acapulco, Mexico. The jacket is framed in glass, with the Screen Door Open logo on the left breast pocket.

The Green Jacket

That's right, but it is now known as The United States Screen Door Open International Invitational Golf Championship—the USSDOIIGC! This is the only major individual golf win of my life. You see, I had to invent my own golf tournament, then win it. I did win the Potato Skins Classic in 2000, which is kind of like winning the Toledo Open. I was also named Participant of the Decade, from 1990-1999.

1987 10th SDO

There has always been an element of surprise associated with the USSDOIIGC...

For the 10th Annual event, in 1987, a passport was required. We flew to Acapulco, Mexico and the Las Brisas Resort where our accommodations were the Villas, high on the mountain above the resort. It featured luxury and first-class service, including self-driven pink jeeps for our local transportation.

Why they allowed us to board the aircraft, I do not know.

Las Brisas Villas   *Our own pink Jeeps*

One evening in Mexico Colin Ferguson, the Screen Door Open's first international participant, was driving one of the "pink jeeps" provided by Las Brisas. "Fergy," as we affectionately called him, was from London, England where they not only drive on the wrong side of the street, but they also drive from the right front seat of a car. You see, they put a steering wheel where the front passenger is supposed to sit. I'm not entirely sure what kind of trouble the ole boy had, but he was arrested and spent the night in the Acapulco "hoosegow" or *carcel* which is Spanish for jail.

Mucho cervezas y tequila resulted in only one missing windshield and a minor front-end dent.

The *policia* had taken all of Fergy's American money and pesos and left him with only his pounds sterling, as they had no idea what that was. They also tried to sell him drugs and tried to fix him up with someone's sister. The Mexican authorities released him the following morning, in time for him to play in the final round of the "10th Annual" at the Pierre Marques resort course. Colin McNee "Fergy" Ferguson's picture is blurred in the photo above to save further international embarrassment.

Walk into my home office today and the first thing you'll see is the picture of the Royal & Ancient Clubhouse of St. Andrews Scotland, signed by friends and presented to me at the 1997 20th Annual Screen Door Open Golf Championship at The Old Course. Another tournament for which passports were needed.

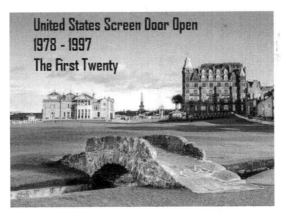

The Old Course, St. Andrews, Scotland

I could start the story there, in Dallas in 1977, some 40 years ago, with talk of hosting the first Screen Door Open Golf Tournament at Tenison Municipal Golf Course and move forward from those days, but that would be skipping some 30 years of my early life, my background, and influences which are all a part of me.

Can't do that!

ONCE IN A LIFETIME

I remember a song by The Talking Heads from the late 1980s. It was a song about finding yourself in a shotgun shack, or in another part of the world, or in a beautiful car, even in a beautiful house, with a beautiful wife, and so forth… then asking yourself the question…

Well, how did I get here?

And let me add two more questions:

Why am I here?

Where am I going?

So, during the passage of time that I have been given so far…

Here's a look at my answers to these questions.

GETTING STARTED ON WRITING THIS BOOK

On most mornings, 6:30 am… if you're like me and most everyone else I expect, you may have a cup of coffee and go to the computer. You go to your Inbox of emails and start deleting… delete, delete, delete, even deleting in mass, clicking on one email and dragging through a lot more. And *click*, they're all gone.

If you have been online and bought something or read something recently you are a target and are probably being inundated with a bunch of stuff regarding whatever the subject was you were interested in. If you've bought a golf book, of any kind, online… you will have received and (will be receiving) emails regarding IMPROVING YOUR GOLF via books, products and promotions.

Today, I have received these emails that I recognize as High-Tech Targeted Marketing:

Subject: New recommendations for you based on your browsing history
Subject: What others have purchased
Subject: Based on what you've purchased
Subject: You're looking for new ways to improve your game
Subject: INSTANTLY shave 5 strokes off your score
Subject: Save 8 shots a round

The computer just went "bing" again, and I got another email:

Subject: A New Breakthrough Approach to Playing Better Golf

Admittedly, I've been online doing research, mainly to see what's out there. And it's a lot of stuff: books and all kinds of products to improve your game of golf. By the way, because I'm a curious guy, which of the above would you click on, if you had only one choice? Look at them again and choose the email you would open. You must decide and open one, only one.

Given a choice, I would click on the one beginning with 'INSTANTLY...' because today we are so driven for *instant gratification*, and I would take an INSTANT five strokes off my score over the "Save 8 shots a round" any time. But, in this case, what did *I* actually do?

Delete, delete, delete, delete, delete, delete, delete... and almost INSTANTLY.

Then I picked up one of the golf instruction books I have lying around. This one says something about an "extra club in my bag." I'm only allowed 14, right? The author is highly paid in the field of sports psychology and counselor to players on the PGA, LPGA, and Champions Tours, (practically flawless golfers—in the eyes of us amateurs). Among his many clients is a list of a most talented group of golf professionals, known to just about everyone who follows golf. The author has been a director of sports psychology at the university level and there is a list of a few highly recognizable corporations to whom he has been a consultant.

He must be good.

The subjects in his book include Self-confidence, Trusting Yourself, Letting Yourself Go, Respect, Never Giving Up, The Mental Side of Golf, Under Pressure, Follow Your Dreams, You Can Play Your Best Golf, The Practice Range at a Tour Event, and Fitness Trainers. All OK, and I am sure that all he has to say on these topics is valuable stuff.

The objective, with his PGA professional tournament golf clients, is to prepare their minds for competition. He has also heard from these professionals that "an earlier book helped them for a while but doesn't seem to work well anymore." The explanation: "It's because those books didn't make it clear enough that—for golfers—having a strong mind in the clutch is part of the process." The author says on the next page, "That's because people want results quick with instant gratification." Bring in Huey Lewis and the News, (you remember the song...) "I want a new *Book.*" (Drug).

I'm sure you've seen most all the TV diet ads for quick results, and even how to remove toenail fungus overnight! Quick and Easy, too! The hope and hype of *instant gratification* sells.

Let's be clear: I am not trying to change people or the world. I'm not seeking to accomplish anything other than to deliver a message of survival in the crazy madness and ups and downs of one's place in this mad, mad world.

I'm writing a book. OK, but what's it about?

I have been in and around golf since 1954, playing the game and making the game practically the *center of my life*. My gosh, that's more than 64 years! Surely I can come up with something to write about involving golf. But what could be written, by me, that hasn't already been written?

Sir Winston Churchill said it all with this quote on golf: "A curious sport whose object is to put a very small ball in a very small hole with implements ill designed for the purpose."

I wanted to write more than an autobiography or a memoir. And what would the title be?

I thought about these titles:

The Metaphysics of the Physics of Golf

Or maybe:

Getting Inside of Your Most Innermost Game

Or

The Spirit of Christmas Future and Golf Past

Or

Here's a lot more Mystery on Golf and Life than You Ought Not Care About

Yeah, that's it! *More mystery on life and golf.* Nope, that isn't it at all.

I remember what my dad told me: "Son, there is an absolute science to all things, even spirituality. And there isn't anything mysterious at all. It is only mysterious according to the level of awareness we have. The higher our level of awareness, the more the mystery is resolved."

CONTENTS

Back in the early 1970s, Hoyt Axton wrote a song, recorded by **Three Dog Night**. It was about never having been to Heaven, but on having been to Oklahoma, being born in Oklahoma, not Arizona, and the question…

What does it matter?

Well, I ain't never been to Heaven…

Oklahoma

…but I been to Oklahoma!

CHAPTER ONE

HOW A MAN LIKE ME
GOT TO BE A MAN LIKE ME

The First 21 Years… from 1946
Background and Early Influences

Life, for me, began at a very early age.

It began in Oklahoma, not Arizona. **And it does matter!**

Well they tell me I was born there… Sept. 3, 1946, but I really don't remember.

I am a post-war Baby Boomer. Of course, I didn't know I was a Baby Boomer in 1946, and didn't hear the term for many years thereafter. It is said, in fact, that I am in the first group of the Baby Boomers, those who were born between 1946 and 1964.

Births hit a record high—and more babies were born in 1946 than in any prior year. This was just after WWII with the demobilization of men and women in the armed forces. More than 12 million people were in the military and eight million soldiers returned home from military service that year. More than 78 million babies were born in the United States during the Boomer Years. And, I am one of them.

The Kiss

My dad (Jim Meadows) wasn't in the military; he had some kind of critical job deferment, so he missed out on all that fun. But this was a time when the future looked comfortable and prosperous. Americans felt confident in being able to provide all the material things that they themselves had done without for many years.

Along came Suburbia, an explosion of home building and development where new houses sprung up on the outskirts of towns and where most women were moms and housewives, like my mom (Bobbie Jean Bills-Meadows), who kept me well fed and in clean clothes. A time of health, security, and comfort like never before. Without the Baby Boomers the ole US of A would certainly not be as prosperous a nation as it is today.

Boomer Sooner was a term that I heard long before I heard the term Baby Boomer. How my dad disliked hearing those words—*Boomer Sooner*—which is Oklahoma University's slogan or (whatever you call their shouts) and the Oklahoma University Fight Song. The whole Boomer Sooner thing actually refers to the Land Run of 1889, and the land on which the town of Norman and the University sit today.

Dad preferred "Hook 'em Horns!" He was a Texas Longhorn fan, and a real loyal Texan, though he lived right smack in the middle of Oklahoma football country. Back then it was Bud Wilkinson, head football coach at OU from 1947 to 1963, who compiled a record of 145 wins, 29 losses, 4 ties, and a 47-game winning streak! Football, to my dad, was Texas vs. Oklahoma, or Oklahoma vs. Notre Dame. That was college football to him in the late '40s and the '50s.

Hubbard, Texas is in East Texas. My mother, Bobbie Jean (pronounced as one word, *bob-e-jean*) was born there and spoke Texas English. In East Texas they speak the most basic level of your "Southern accents with a twist" and a dialect unique to Texas alone—and in which Bobbie Jean was well advanced. It's a really big state y'all, so *y'all* will find many words are spoken differently. Bobbie Jean, when speaking words such as: *might, rice, life, type,* and *like...* well they sounded like *[mat], [ras], [laf], [tap],* and *[lak].*

Many of these Texans pronounce the word *pen* like [lak] the word *pin.* Also other words like [lak] *ten* as *tin, Wendy* as *windy,* and making *a bait,* as in a wager or *a bet.* And, let us not forget *warsh* for *wash.* There are many single syllable words that are often pronounced as a two- or three-syllable word: "*Ma' ak*, how you want your '*eh yags*' cooked?" (She's asking about eggs, just so you know...)

Other rural Texas terms are "*fixin' to*" as in "*I was fixin' to come over to your house.*" "*It don't make no never mind.*" *And* how about this same-verb phrase, "*I might [mat] could do that.*"

The origin of *y'all* is often a debated question. To me, however, it is clearly a contraction of *you and all.* And it is, therefore, a plural meaning of "*you all.*" My mother and other East Texans even have a plural for the plural word *y'all.* And that would be the word *all y'all.*

When my mother wanted to have a serious conversation, like the time she wanted me to hear the difference in the way she was pronouncing the words *all* and *oil,* she would start by saying: "*I tell you what, Ma' kel*" (Michael)... "That's when I knew to listen-up!

She'd say, *"Now listen close, ya hear? There is **all** of us… that is **all**, and then there is the **all** you put in the car – that is **all**, you hear me? You put **all** in the car, Ma' kel and there is **all** of us. Now, you hear the difference, Ma' kel, CAINT CHA?"* I said, "Yes, Ma'am!"

I spent the first 21 years of my life in Oklahoma. As my dad said, "You're a born 'Okie,' son, but more importantly, you're pure-bred Texan and raised as a Texan by Texans!"

You may wonder *why Oklahoma?* and *why Oklahoma City?* when both my parents, J.A. Meadows, Jr. (Jim) and Bobbie Jean Bills-Meadows (Bobbie), were such staunch Texans.

Dad was born in Houston, Mom in East Texas in Hubbard. They met in high school, in Dallas. Mom went to Sunset High (no longer there) and Dad attended North Dallas High, located on Haskell, McKinney, and Cole Avenues. *(Not exactly North Dallas, anymore.)* So, why Oklahoma?

"I tell you what…" Here's the reason: Dad was hired and started his lifelong training career with IBM Corporation, sometime around 1938-39. He was an IBM Customer Engineer, assigned and associated with military installations of IBM tabulating equipment, as in "punch-card technology," in the early days of IBM's Data Processing.

He was a Customer Engineer, always having his IBM office at the client's location and, in Dad's case, always at a U.S. Air Force base. The first IBM DP (Data Processing) military tabulating installation was at MacDill Air Force Base in Tampa, Florida in the early 1940s. This is how my brother, Steve, came to be born in Tampa in 1942. Dad, during his career, was assigned to MacDill AFB, Tinker AFB in Midwest City, Oklahoma, and Kelly AFB in San Antonio, Texas.

IBM is, in and of itself, a great story. The company began in 1911 as the Computing, Tabulating and Recording Company (CTR) of the late 1800s, when they obtained their first large contract to provide tabulating equipment for the 1890 U.S. Census. CTR, the precursor to the modern computer giant, grew rapidly and changed its name in 1920 to IBM, International Business Machines, perhaps the best-known computer company in the world.

When my father was going to be transferred, by IBM (referred to sometimes as I've Been Moved) from Tampa, Florida to some place off the U.S. mainland in 1946, Mom and Dad discovered that I was on the way. Not wanting to send expectant parents outside the United States, IBM transferred Dad and assigned him to the IBM computing installation at Tinker Air Force Base (part of Strategic Air Command), in Midwest City, Oklahoma. So, if you haven't figured it out yet, the fact that my Texan parents landed in Oklahoma was all my fault.

My Igloo
My fault, us being in Oklahoma, but Dad could build anything,
even an igloo, during the cold winter months in Oklahoma.

Speaking of "*back then and when*" and the '40s and '50s (pre-TV), I remember listening to the radio. We still have radio today of course, but not like [lak] back then. Life, [laf] back before the television was invented and introduced, was the home entertainment center known as a radio in the living room. We listened to the old-time-radio news and broadcasts of Lowell Thomas and Edward R. Murrow and radio shows like [lak] *The Lone Ranger*, *The Goldbergs*, *Fibber McGee and Molly*, *Amos 'n' Andy* (masterful wordplay comedy i.e.: "*Let's simonize our watches, Andy*"— instead of *synchronize), Jack Benny* and *Our Miss Brooks*, to name just a few.

And, baseball was on radio too! Like [lak] announcer Mel Allen in 1951, The Yankees Voice and *This Week in Baseball* with Mel Allen and Curt Gowdy in 1946. Curt Gowdy was the radio voice at KOMA radio in Oklahoma City. He was hired primarily to broadcast Oklahoma University football games with the new OU football coach Bud Wilkinson and Oklahoma A&M college basketball games with coach Hank Iba.

I've only had three real sports heroes in my life: Mickey Mantle, Arnold Palmer, and Ben Hogan.

"The Mick," like me, was born in Oklahoma. They said he was born in Commerce, Oklahoma, but truth is, Mickey Mantle was really born in Spavinaw, Oklahoma—population, today, of 437. Spavinaw was too difficult to pronounce, I guess, so it was decided they would say that "The Mick" was from Commerce. What the hey, they're only 46 miles apart. By the way, Will Rogers is said to have been born in Claremore, Oklahoma. Truth is, Will Rogers, preeminent philanthropist, actor, humorist, philosopher, and political satirist of the early 1900s, was born on the Dog Iron Ranch just outside of Oologah, Oklahoma, not Claremore. It was Will Rogers who said: "It's hard to tell whether Americans have become such liars because of golf or the income tax."

Mickey Mantle was my first sports hero. I wanted to play baseball, and it seemed like every kid in the '50s was baseball crazy.

The Mick

People started buying this new entertainment box—called television, TV for short. I certainly thought we waited too long, and that we weren't "keeping up with the Joneses," as it's said. When we finally got our first TV, some time around 1950 or '51, there were only black and white screens, and only two channels. Until the scheduled programming began each day, we would sometimes just stare at the "test pattern" of five black circles with an Indian wearing a full headdress in the middle of the screen. While watching the test pattern, one would have to endure the continual, irritating tone (like the sound made when a golf cart is put in reverse) or turn the sound off. It was a "console TV," on which I got to see Mickey Mantle play baseball in the 1952 World Series. I saw him again and in person 16 years later in 1968 at the old Yankee Stadium in New York City, New York.

The First TV and Test Pattern

Name Calling... "You Butt Hole!"

When I was in the second or third grade, I somehow got into the habit of calling my older brother, Steve, a "butthole." I am sure I learned the term from him. He, unlike me, never let our mother hear him say it, but she heard me...

Big brother Steve and me

"What did I here you say, *Ma' kel?*" She'd heard me. And Mom would send me to my room. I think that's called "Time-Out" in today's child-rearing efforts. That didn't work, as it didn't break me of the name calling. I continued to call my brother a "BH." Mom would cut a switch off a bush or tree and use it on me, "switching my legs" while she held on to one of my arms and I ran in circles around her trying desperately to avoid the switching. That didn't work either. Mom even washed [*warshed*] my mouth out with soap, Ivory soap. I can still taste all those white bars of soap she placed into my mouth. But that didn't break me of the name calling either.

She finally broke me of the habit when, one Sunday morning as we were driving downtown to the First Baptist Church of Oklahoma City, she turned around from the front seat of the car as Dad was driving and announced that during the pastor's sermon that morning she was going to stand up, interrupt the pastor, and march my little bottom down the aisle to the front of the congregation where I would apologize to the entire congregation for calling my brother a "butthole." Now I can still recall the fear I had at what Mom was going to put me through. I cannot help but laugh. I know (as a parent myself) my parents would see me do something wrong, thinking it was funny, suppressing the laughter and putting on the angered look to discourage the continued name calling. I still haven't been broken on the "BH" word, but I do like it better than the "AH" word.

Early Churchin'

We were members of the biggest Baptist church in Oklahoma City, the First Baptist Church, and my dad's parents, James Albert and Lillian Meadows, were members of the First Baptist Church of Dallas. Both of these churches belonged to the Southern Baptist Convention, America's largest evangelical denomination. Both of these churches were all encompassing, having gymnasiums, bowling alleys, kitchens with great food, and all that. We took pity on all those who weren't members of the First Baptist Church. I did anyway, until I went to First Christian Church. They had pool tables!

Some time ago, on my own, I simply made the decision to just… Go with God on this one, and I got saved.

It was simple (too simple for some) and sincere, yet it created a lot of related questions about life's issues in living my own life. I was pretty sure that at this early stage of my life I hadn't done a lot of sinning, not yet.

I asked Mom if calling my brother, Steve, a *butthole* was a sin. She said it wasn't a nice thing to do. "Do you think Jesus would call your brother a butthole?" she asked—then she broke out in uncontrollable laughter.

A couple of weeks later, I was baptized at the First Baptist Church, Oklahoma City, at age eight or nine, by total immersion, in a huge, glassed-in-aquarium-type tank sitting high above the choir for all to see. I remember there were several other people going to be baptized, one by one, on that same Sunday. There were men, women, boys and girls, and we were all barefoot, wearing white robes, lined up and ready to go. I think they waited to get a bunch of people to baptize before warming up the water.

Dad had taken me to the swimming pool at Spring Lake Park to rehearse being baptized. I couldn't float very well on my back and didn't like being pushed under water.

While practicing being baptized, Dad reminded me that this was what the Bible said Jesus had also done. "Jesus was baptized by John the Baptist, and for us it symbolizes the death, burial, and resurrection of the Savior," he told me.

Since I got a lot of ear infections when I went swimming, Mom said, "You're not going to be under water that long '*Ma' ak*', so I'm gonna put some cotton in your ears and goop-'em-up with some Vaseline."

When it was my turn and I walked down the stairs into the water, I noticed that pastor, Hershel H. Hobbs had on rubber waders under his white robe. Maybe he was going duck hunting later.

He then said, "In the name of the Father, Son and Holy Ghost, I baptize you, my brother, James Michael Meadows." I was in and out in no time, didn't mess up my crew cut, and didn't get any water in my ears, either.

After my baptism, Dad said, "You're now equipped with potential, son." I responded, "Huh?" "You'll get it someday," he said. I would eventually learn, through time, what he meant, even how to be *more* equipped.

"Work hard, play hard, Mike, and do everything as unto the Lord." I wondered what that was all about. He said things like, "The harder you work, the luckier you get." But the truth of the matter was that the harder I worked the more I would learn, lessening the need for luck. He said, "The more you put into it, the more you'll get out of it!" Dad's instructions for me were to make Christ the center of everything. But as a kid, I didn't really have any knowledge of how that was done. Both my mother and father took a role in my spiritual development and we shared our faith throughout their lives.

Sunday school was a lot about Bible stories and memorizing Bible verses and getting ready for Sword Drills. This is where the kids stood, shoulder to shoulder in line, holding our Bibles, one hand under and one hand on top. Some adult would call out the name of the book, chapter, and verse. As soon as you found the Bible verse, you took a step forward. We waited. Hopefully, everyone would be familiar enough with the Bible to get to the verse in a timely manner. Ample time was given for all kids to get to the verse and step forward when found. Then someone would be asked to read the verse. I figured out early on, that whoever stepped out first was the least likely to be called on to read the Bible verse.

Everyone thought I was a Bible wizard. I fooled them for a while. Then one observant adult said, "Hey Mike, it appears that you have the New Testament opened, yet the scripture in question is from the Old Testament."

I think Baptist kids put in more church time than the Methodists, or any other denominations. Sunday morning was Sunday school, followed by church service. Sunday night was Training Union (just like Sunday school), followed by church service again. That's at least four hours every

Sunday going to church. Then we had Wednesday Night Prayer Meeting, Thursday Night Visitation… well, you get the picture. And it started all over again, the following Sunday.

In the summers we had Vacation Bible School and Church Camp. The Oklahoma Southern Baptists had their camp down south at Turner Falls. Set in Oklahoma's Arbuckle Mountains, near Davis, it was a great time for kids and outdoor adventure. There was more Sunday school stuff, church services, walking the aisle and accepting Jesus as Savior, and swimming in the clear spring-fed waters and lakes. Only thing was that the Baptist Church had "no-mixed-bathing" rule, meaning boys and girls couldn't bathe together; and they couldn't swim together, either.

We had to learn dancing, cards, dice, liar's poker, and other vices elsewhere, too.

The only negative thing that I remember from the 1950s was a fear of the Communists. They were the bad guys. Otherwise, growing up through those years of prosperity was full of freedom in day-to-day life, as we were, pretty much, allowed to fill in the time with whatever we created. It was a very good, no… it was a great childhood. I'm sure the world was an easier place to understand back then. The '50s and '60s were the decades from which I could see for myself why I do certain things a certain way today, why I have different opinions on certain issues, and why certain things bother me and others don't. I see it as all stemming from my upbringing and education.

When I was in the third grade in 1953, we had a screen door on the back of our house which opened out to the back yard. It was just like the screen door my grandparents had in Dallas. Both houses had a screened-in-porch area where the washing machine was located.

These weren't the aluminum storm door types that you see today. These screen doors were made with a wooden frame having a long spring of about 2-3 feet in length. One end of the spring was attached to the door frame and the other end, attached to the far side of the door itself.

When you opened the screen door the stretching of the spring made a very irritating screeching sound. The next thing heard as the door closed was the very loud *BANG* of the door slamming back against the door frame. This was usually followed by the *slap-slap* as the door came to a final rest. When going out we pushed the screen door open, and pulled it wide open when coming back inside the house. We just let the mechanism do its thing.

Every time one of us kids ran in and out of the back of the house the anger of any grown-up would boil, until Dad finally yelled, "Don't Slam the Screen Door!" I remember Dad taking Steve to the screen door one day and saying, "Now stand here, Steve. You are going to slam that screen door 50 times. Go ahead…get started, now!" I remember laughing at Steve and Steve being mad at me. But, I tell you what, it didn't break either of us from slamming the screen door.

Little did I know how important this would be 25 years later, in the naming of a golf tournament, The Screen Door Open.

But back to my dad. Early memories have me first thinking of him as a very practical, conservative, and basically quiet man. What he said mattered, kind of military-like, though he didn't serve in the Armed Forces of the USA. Born in 1918 he had come through the Depression. He did not have a college education. He said he was educated by IBM into "Systems Thinking." He was actually a lot of fun. He told a good (clean) joke, telling us that the best jokes were without bad language, and that kind of stuff. I strive to abide by this today.

I had a little discomfort sometimes in beginning a conversation with my dad. He liked for me to ask questions *about things*. In hindsight, I wish that I would have asked more. Dad taught "Logics" to me at an early age when I questioned any decision he had made. He would answer, "Because I said so, that's why." He replied with even more "Logic with Irony" when he said, "You keep doing that and I'm gonna kick your ass up and around your neck, so you'll have to wink to sit down."

Through the years, I learned that lots of my classmates, fraternity brothers, and work colleagues would come and go, but Mom and Dad were going be in my life for as long as they or I lived.

Dad was "one helluva practical joker"

Our next door neighbors in Oklahoma City in the early 1950s, were the Shoulers. Phil Shouler was a law student at Oklahoma University at Norman and commuted daily some 70 miles, round-trip. His wife (Sooty) gave me my first introduction to finer tastes in cultural elegance. She was a piano teacher and tried to teach me how to play the French classic Frère Jacques (Are you sleeping, Are you sleeping…) which I can still play today with just one finger. You see, my brother Steve had somehow wound up with an accordion from the music department of our little grade school and had practiced and practiced enough to give a solo recital at some school function where he played *Lady of Spain* on his accordion. I, wanting to be like my big brother and play some kind of instrument, asked my mother, "What can I play?" Mom found the agreeable Mrs. Shouler, next door with her piano, to be my piano teacher. She told my mother that I had fingers like lightning… never striking the same place twice. So, I was back outside playing in the neighborhood. By the way, Dad, for ever after, would cringe any time he heard the tune *Lady of Spain.*

Our neighbor Phil would drive from OKC (that's Oklahoma City) to Norman every day to attend law school. This was in about 1949 or '50, just when the first German VW Beetles came to America. Phil bought one of those little German cars. He was so proud and boastful about "that little German car," as Dad called it, especially regarding the great gas mileage he was getting from his new "bug." "My Bug," he called it. And Phil just couldn't stop talking about it.

Phil's VW

Gasoline was somewhere between .09 cents and .19 cents per gallon. (That's right, 9 cents to 19 cents per gallon, depending upon the "gas wars" in Oklahoma). For several weeks, Dad was bringing home a couple of gallon cans of gas every few days, and in the quiet darkness of night he would carefully, quietly sneak over next door and pour a gallon or two of gasoline into our neighbor's new VW gas tank.

Phil was so proud when he kept telling my dad about the gas mileage he was getting in his new VW. He said to my dad, "Jim, this little car is just fantastic. I hardly ever have to go to a filling station for gas."

Then, after several weeks, the crisis hit. A huge problem had developed with Phil's new VW.

All of a sudden, the gas mileage had dropped to an unbelievable new low. Phil's mileage calculation shifted—to an awful performance in miles per gallon! It was so terrible, and Phil couldn't understand it. No longer was the VW getting tremendous gas mileage. In fact, it was now performing less efficiently than Dad's bigger American-made car, the Pontiac. "What is wrong with this car?" a perplexed Phil wondered. "What the heck was going on here?"

Well, "*I tell you what*" was going on: After weeks of adding gas to Phil's VW, Dad had reverted to siphoning gas, every now and then, out of the prized VW. That was my dad, for you… and his VW caper was one of his best "gotchas" ever played on anyone.

Another time Dad got a few bumper stickers that read 'Built in Texas by Texans' from the Ford Motor Car plant in Sherman, Texas. It was such fun for Dad when every now and then he'd put one of those bumper stickers on the back of Phil's little 'bug,' knowing Phil was driving every day right into the middle of campus at Oklahoma University in Norman with that sticker: Built in Texas by Texans.

Ford Bumper Sticker

Not only was gas 9 to 19 cents a gallon, but eggs were 59 cents a dozen, bread was 10 cents a loaf, and coffee was 34 cents a pound. Some of us are paying $4-$5 for a cup of coffee today. I can hear Dad now saying, "$4-$5 for a cup of coffee? Used to be a nickel, or even free!"

Grandparents

My four grandparents and their families were night-and-day different and somewhat confusing to a kid like me. The Bills/Austin people on my mother's side and the Meadows/Garrett people on my dad's side could not have been more different.

Let me first tell you a little about my mother's side of the family.

First, I learned at an early age that I had to have some clarification on the use of words like *dinner* vs. *supper*. My mom said that in farming/ranching communities like Hubbard, Texas the word *dinner* was the mid-day meal and the biggest meal of the day—so the hands could be fortified and keep working. *Supper* was the evening meal, and "you know, *Ma' ak*, the last meal taken before Jesus' crucifixion is called the Last Supper." Ever the dutiful son, I replied, "Yes, Ma'am."

These things are rooted in cultural traditions. I've been around many people who used the word *dinner* for what is now more commonly called *lunch*. Seems always they are country folk. I remember watching *Hee Haw* on TV in the late '60s where it was always, "Hey, Grandpa, what's for supper?"

As a youngster I loved visiting the relatives in Hubbard. I liked that Mom's folks lived out in the country, had a couple of horses, a cow, dogs, and chickens in the yard ("*yard birds*"), and that they did different things. Actually, they did most everything differently.

Once I watched my grandmother (Roxie Austin Bills) go out in the yard area, grab up a chicken and ring its neck... as we were going to have us some fried chicken for *supper*. She pulled the chicken's head back, stretched its neck, swung the bird around from the neck and dislocated the head. The chicken fell to the ground with a lot of wings flapping and legs kicking. I understand a chicken that has just lost its head is not in pain and the kickin' and flappin' are simply reactions of its nervous system. But that's how the saying came about, "You're running around like a chicken with its head cut off."

These folks—my mom's parents, cousins, uncles, aunts (Bills/Austins), and such—were "country," for sure. They would "saucer and blow" their coffee every morning. Let me explain. Coffee is poured into a cup sitting on a saucer until the coffee overflows into the saucer. The cup is taken off the saucer, the saucer is lifted to the lips and one blows the hot coffee until cool enough to sip out of the saucer. Repeat or tilt the coffee cup pouring a little more coffee into the saucer again and start the process all over. Really. They did this!

Grandma Bills didn't have a toaster. She made buttered toast in a skillet.

Grandpa Bills (Louis P. Bills) was a Bull Durham man! I still have a picture of him on horseback, a string and tag hanging out of the breast pocket of his shirt. That string and tag had a canvas sack attached to it, containing Bull Durham tobacco. L.P. Bills, born in 1897, could remove the sack of Bull Durham tobacco with his right hand, loosen the string-taut bag, pour tobacco in the paper held in his left hand, roll a cigarette one-handed, pull the string to tighten up the sack of tobacco with his right hand and his teeth, put it back into the shirt pocket, take a match, swipe it across the back of his pants and light the cigarette. All on horseback, too! Man, he was cool!

Now, a little about the Meadows side, Dad's family...

My dad's parents were J.A. (Albert) Meadows, Sr., my granddad, and Lillian Garret Meadows, my grandmother. My grandmother (who we called Grandmoney) and my great aunt, her sister Lou Eva Garret Dumas, were all from Kentucky, and parts of Virginia. This heritage was a little more traditionally "Southern Genteel," free from vulgarity and rudeness, more commonly known as being "holier than thou."

Dress and mannerisms were of the utmost importance. I don't remember ever seeing my grandfather in anything other than a white shirt and tie, and a suit coat and hat when he was outdoors. I never saw the

Garrett sisters in anything other than fine dresses with lace handkerchiefs tucked into the left sleeves.

"Grandmoney"

Very, very "proper" at all times.

They all—Granddad, Grandmoney, and Aunt B.B.—lived on a beautiful tree-shaded avenue in east Dallas.

Me, my big brother Steve, my parents: Jim and Bobbie Meadows, my Granddad and "Grandmoney" at the Meadows' house, Dallas circa 1952.

Little did I know, this great old house would become mine in another 26 years.

"Grandmoney" was the name we called our grandmother, Dad's mother. This was a name given to her by my older cousins. Odd name, but kind of reminds me of Big Daddy in Tennessee Williams' *Cat on a Hot Tin Roof* (not necessarily in character, but mostly in the name only).

Our great aunt was known as B.B. I don't have a clue why that name, but I later discovered she was a Vaudeville showgirl in the 1920s with a professional show name of *Dannie Galloway* and had been married to her dance partner. I had the impression that Aunt B.B. had had a few husbands, the last a homebuilder in east Dallas, J.R. Dumas, but she had been divorced and living with my Meadows grandparents for as long as I could remember.

Granddaddy Meadows had first been a tractor salesman in South Texas, which is how my Dad was born in Houston in 1918. Granddad later became president/owner of Peerless Equipment Corp. in Dallas in the early '50s with a big showroom of industrial and farm equipment and a warehouse full of parts. It was a lot of fun to go with Granddad to his office and warehouse. There I could wander around the place and climb up on top of the tractors and bulldozers. All the people working at Peerless called my granddad "Pops," reminding me again of Big Daddy.

Dad's parents and Aunt B.B. were members of the First Baptist Church of Dallas, the largest Baptist Church in the world—and they made sure you knew it! That legalistic and "look at us" stuff, again. In fact, as I remember, there were more pictures of W. A. Criswell (pastor of the First Baptist Church in Dallas for 55 years) in my grandparents' home than there were of grandkids or any other family members.

Now, don't get me wrong. I loved both sets of grandparents very much. They both were loving, kind, and generous. They were great people of character and came from Christian upbringing, yet from very different cultural environments. One set of grandparents was more easy going, the other, well, a bit more "uppity," thinking of themselves as (maybe) just a bit more morally superior to most others. This is not said judgmentally by me, for we all have areas of weakness and, shall I say…tendencies, or we wouldn't be human.

A term long associated with the Baptist Church is *teetotalers*, which are those people who adhere to the practice and promotions of abstinence from alcoholic beverages of any kind. My parents and grandparents were not necessarily *teetotalers*. They simply chose not to drink.

I don't know the history behind the Baptist aversion to alcohol, but I must admit I think it absolutely hilarious to hear a Baptist argue that Jesus drank unfermented grape juice, or that the water Jesus turned into wine (His first miracle in the Bible, at the wedding feast) did not have enough time to go through the fermentation process. Yeah, right!

I've looked and studied and found there is much written in the Bible about wine. The first mention was that of Noah's vineyard and his drunkenness. The Bible makes no claim that wine production is evil. Israel (Old Testament) was to tithe in wine. David had extensive wine cellars. The Bible warns of excess, and even presents a code of moderation. I try to follow and imbibe in moderation, as I have a fondness for beers (especially lagers), for wines (especially the Bordeauxs), and for single malt whiskies (especially the "Islay"), all tastes obtained while globe-trotting the world of golf.

Back to the early TV era. Quiz shows started appearing on TV. *What's My Line?* was a favorite. There was *Truth or Consequences* (great name for everything, huh?) *I've Got a Secret, Password* and *The Match Game.* Most of these shows tested our knowledge right there in the living room, and "*I tell you what,*" Mom and Dad were pretty doggone smart.

TV Scandals

CHAPTER ONE

Then came the TV Quiz Show scandals, which revealed that contestants were actually given answers to the questions before or on the show. The producers of these quiz shows had rigged the outcome. One of the most popular shows was *The $64,000 Question*. Joyce Brothers became famous for being the first woman to win the $64,000 prize. Actually, the show and the network didn't want her to win, so they gave her questions they thought she couldn't possibly answer correctly. A back-fire! She stated that she was not assisted in any manner during her appearances, yet admitted others were.

Patty Duke, a child star who was a contestant on the show, testified before Congress that she had been coached.

On another show, *Twenty-One*, it was discovered that one contestant was coached to let another contestant, Charles Van Doran, win. Charles Van Doran said: "I was involved, deeply involved in a deception." The show was a complete hoax.

Intentionally letting someone else win? "That's like a prize fighter taking a fall," Dad said. *"What?"* and *"Why?"* I asked. He explained that the cheating was done, primarily for financial gain, both by the producers and contestants. "Other reasons were," he said, "for enhanced viewer interest and for TV ratings."

"For what does it profit a man... Mark 8:36." That's what Dad said. I said, "Huh?" "A question for everyone to answer. Look it up, son." So I did, and found Jesus' words:

*"For what does it profit a man to gain the whole world,
and forfeit his soul?"* (Mark 8:36 NASB)

Dad made a lesson out of it. We talked about honesty. Dad said, "Honesty is always the best policy. If you tell the truth you won't have to remember what you said. This establishes your integrity." This was just one of many of my parents' teachings.

Mom and Dad could take these kinds of things and bring them down to the basics of life. It was about how you lived your life, your conscience, how you feel about yourself, and what it meant to do things like lie and cheat. They wanted us to **THINK**.

Today, I hear and read much about golf being the teacher, Golf's lessons of Life, and golf teaching the following life lessons: Integrity, Honesty, Respect, Responsibility, etc. Later in this book I will delve into "Nudging and Fudging" and what I really believe golf teaches. I believe that golf is not the teacher of character, but the *revealer* of character.

I'm no psychologist, and I am happy I'm not. However, since the time of Freud, the foundation of theory represents that parents are the major influencers of their children and the #1 contributor to the psychological makeup that we have as adults. This is also found in the Bible, on the rearing of children.

To think that golf, which I had not yet played, is life's teacher would eliminate parents from having any lasting effect on a person's personality, intelligence, and mental health. We are born and we are totally connected in our nurturing and child raising methods. Parents first, relatives, and then teachers take us to a point of independent-mindedness, human beings capable of selecting and rejecting external influences. And we get to this point pretty rapidly, even before we enter kindergarten. Children, whose parents encourage independent thinking and learning to question rather than to blindly follow, provide vital keys to childhood development. We've all heard the phrase "the apple doesn't fall far from the tree." The fact is that we decide who we let influence, inspire, or corrupt us. Children who are taught responsibility at home are more likely to choose responsible peers.

I believe that I was taught these things (Integrity, Honesty, Respect, Responsibility, etc.) from parental nurturing and it was long before I came upon The Meridian Golf Course. Golf became a reinforcement factor of how I had been shaped in the family environment. But at this stage of development, I had not yet begun to play the game of golf.

Spankings? You betcha! A few swats on the bottom, oh yeah. Part of the training and breaking of bad behaviors, administered with love and concern, coming mostly from Mom. All Dad needed to do was unbuckle his belt and we straightened up, immediately! Respect and humility were the standards of behavior he expected.

In my analysis, children who are raised at home by parents with morals and values from godly principles will become the moral and value-based leaders of the country.

Today it seems to be all about sound bites. If you don't like yourself, don't blame your parents, blame your peers. Today, modern psychology seems to present a very opposite supposition to parental nurturing, saying that parents have no lasting effect on the personality, intelligence, or mental health of their offspring.

I find this unbelievable! If this were true, I would not have written this book and dedicated it to Jim and Bobbie Meadows.

I Didn't Know It at the Time, But I Hit the Jackpot...

when it came to parents! And it would become ever more apparent through the years. I am very proud of my beginnings. Proud of parents who raised my siblings and me in a strong work culture along with the right values and their systematic living.

I mean, I won The Super Mega Lotto of Life. (I am not talking financially.)

I know I was very fortunate to be born at this time in American history. I was born in 1946, and born to the parents God gave me, Jim and Bobbie Meadows. I understand them more today, and love them more today for their love, nurturing, and guidance.

Here's more of what I remember of being a kid in the 1950s beyond clothing, eating meals, and being driven to my baseball games, the skating rink, or church.

First of all, I didn't have a voice in making any decisions, my opinion didn't matter. What my parents said was final, the law, and I did what they told me to do or suffered the consequences. I was to follow their system.

My Mom and Dad spent more time with each other than they did with me. I was not the focus of the household. They let me know that, too! I knew I was a kid, growing up under their supervision with the goal of one day being out on my own, where, hopefully, I could provide for myself and have a better life than the one they were making for me while a kid.

My parents had a social life, as in having guests over, and if their guests brought their kids, we were to go outside and play together, unless it was raining or snowing, in which case we were expected to go to another part of the house. When it was their time to have others over to play bridge or whatever, we came out when called, said *Hello* and then off we went to do something somewhere else. When my brother and I were allowed to be around the adults, we did not speak unless spoken to.

My folks didn't buy me a lot of things, so when they did, I was very appreciative. I was supposed to take care of whatever they provided me, and if it broke I was to try and figure out how to fix it on my own, before going to Dad, who could fix anything.

I did not get help with my homework either. I had to do it on my own, which I know made me pay more attention while in school. Today, parents think that good parents help with homework.

While clothing and feeding their children (and driving them around) still goes on today, I somehow see parents treating kids as if they were the most important part and the center of the family. Parents are not acting as authority figures, but more as a petitioning agent to the little prince or princess. For example: "Sweetheart, do you think you could stop for just a few minutes and help me take out the trash?"

I am not saying that every household was a *Leave it to Beaver* or a *Father Knows Best* situation, but it was more toward that norm, otherwise, there would not have been those kinds of TV shows back then. Just compare what you see on TV today in family situations and tell me which are closer to what is real. Pretty irritating, in my opinion.

During my kid days, manners played a significant part in my life, and in everyone's life for that matter. I would never think of saying "I want." No way was that allowed! "I would like," followed by "please" and "thank you" were common words of one's vocabulary. Manners show respect and make good impressions and were part of my parents' parental system.

Go ahead and call me idealistic or guilty of nostalgic thinking, but here is what is statistically verifiable: the 1950s were a better time for kids and according to mental health statistics, we were happier, too. Also, obedient children are much happier than disobedient ones. That's me... idealizing plain common sense.

I had many shared activities with both Mom and Dad: Cub Scouts, Boy Scouts, Little League baseball, basketball, and swim teams. Dad was a true "Saturday Dad" and we had lots of activities with him including many hunting and fishing trips. Steve and I were always glad when Dad spent time with us.

There was never a question, in my mind, as to the role and responsibility of Mom or Dad as it related to my life. They clearly communicated that they were, indeed, in charge and overseer of my welfare. I did not mind putting myself under their system of authority. They were able and could teach and coach. They were leaders in control of their children.

Oh, I got upset with some of the discipline on many occasions. I remember one time, I even uttered something about how I would like to leave home, being an arrogant little kid, having an "Oh, yeah? Well, I'll show you" attitude. "I'll just run away!" I said.

Upon hearing about my intention to leave home, Dad, calmly, went and got a little suitcase out of the attic and led me into my bedroom. He opened the suitcase and my dresser drawer and said, "Mike, you'll need some underwear, tee-shirts, pants, socks," and he started packing that little suitcase. "Better take a sweater or two because it's going get cold in the winter. Here's a hat and a coat that you can carry over your arm. Do you want an umbrella?" We walked together to the front porch, he sat the suitcase down outside, and said, "You better hurry away, right now—quickly, because your Mom is going to be really upset, so don't let her see you go. We'll miss you, Mike." He left me on the porch and closed the front door. I didn't go far. I was sobbing too much. I remember Mom being very upset with Dad.

I'm just gonna leave home!

Show-n-Tell

One time in grade school, in 5th grade, when I was about nine years of age in 1955, I remember a class assignment: Go to work with Dad and report back when we had the next Show-n-Tell. We would stand up, in front of class, and explain "What does Dad do at his work?"

I was off to work with Dad. First, when we got to the base, there was a security issue in going to work with Dad, even for me, a kid. There was some kind of security clearance thing to go through to get me into where Dad worked at Tinker Air Force Base. When I finally got in there, I discovered myself in this huge and very cold room, with elevated floors and big cables running underneath them. These cables ran under the floor to a bunch of "tape drives" that looked as if they were spinning out of control. There were stacks and stacks of cards, all having holes punched in them, being loaded into other machines and those cards seemed to be eaten up, very quickly. Other machines were printing out what Dad called "data" on very large sheets of paper. I, of course, did not understand.

IBM *Punch Cards?*

What did my dad do at his work? And, what was I going to tell my class?

Dad led me out to the middle of that big cold room and said: "Did you know, son, that computers could do work in as little as a nanosecond?" I thought: *What did my dad just say? A nano-what?* What's that all about? He then defined a nanosecond. He said: "It is a unit of time equal to one billionth of a second." I thought, again, *He's talking to a 9-year-old kid about a billionth of a second.* I was confused, to say the least. And thinking: *I'm going to tell this to my class?*

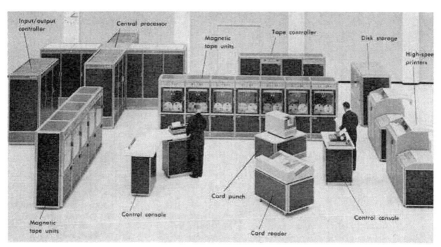

IBM *Mainframe 1955*

I was on an Air Force base, in a cold room, watching, what Dad said were tape drives spinning, and punch cards being eaten by other machines, and for what reason… I haven't a clue. But he taught me what a nanosecond is (a billionth of a second) by putting it in this perspective. He said, "Son, if I was to pay you a dollar a second, every second"—which sounded very good to me and he had my attention now—"24 hours a day, nonstop," he continued, "do you know how long it would take for you to become a millionaire?"

Of course my answer was, "No, I don't." Dad continued, "Son, you'd be a millionaire in 13 days!" Wow, I wanted those dollars to start flowing into my pockets. I had been saving change ever since I found so much of it (quarters and fifty-cent coins) between, under, and throughout my granddad's big leather chair down in Dallas. So I really liked this idea of a dollar-a-second pay out. I was going to be a millionaire in what? Thirteen days?

"OK, you got that part, son?" I replied, "Yes sir, you pay me a dollar every second and I'm gonna be a millionaire in 13 days."

"Right!" he said. "Now if I keep on paying you a dollar a second, after those 13 days and you've become a millionaire, how long do think it would take you to become a billionaire?"

Again, "Don't know, Dad." He said, "You'd be a billionaire in 32 years." What? Thirty-two years? With that said, he handed me a dollar and said, "There you go, that's what a billionth of a second is—this buck's just like a nanosecond. It's the same as one second is to 32 years, and the same as what a dollar is to a billion dollars."

There was a TV show on at the time in 1955: *The Millionaire.* Everyday, ordinary people were given $1 million by a mysterious, super-wealthy man, whom we viewers never saw. His name was John Beresford Tipton and the money was doled out (a single check in an envelope) by a guy working for Tipton, named Mike. The premise of the show was the study of the people becoming instant millionaires and how it affected their lives. I suppose everyone who watched this TV show imagined themselves on the receiving end of that million dollars. I did, but because my name is Mike, I often thought I would like to grow up and give away money like this, but to organizations with people who could really use it!

Dad said, "It's easy to be a millionaire, Mike! Do you want to know how?" I jumped on that one very quickly. "Yeah, I do!" I replied.

"Well," he said, "first you need a million dollars!" I still love that comment from Dad and I use it often with younger people. "It's easy to be a millionaire, you want to know how?"

By the way, a million dollars ain't what it used to be. Let's say you win the lottery. You better make sure you're ready to pay the taxes. Now, if you do win, don't claim it right away. You best get yourself a tax planner, financial advisor, a lawyer, and other experts to figure out your plan. It nets out to something like 40% that you'd get, maybe, of the $1 million. I would take it lump sum, pay the taxes up front, pay the experts off, and get ready to hear from family members you didn't know you had.

Now, back to Show-n-Tell and my assignment…

"But what do you *do*, Dad? I have to Show-n-Tell on what you do." He replied and not boastfully, "Well, son, they don't pay me for what I do. They pay me for what I know." I was really confused now! He tried to simplify it by saying, "*I tell you what*," he said, "I am a mechanic, a simple computer mechanic." He didn't look like any mechanic I had ever seen. Dad wore a suit, white shirt, and a tie to work and he always came home looking just as he did when he left for work. He had clean hands, too. Ricky Dugger's dad (he lived across the street) was a lawyer and always dressed like my dad, the computer mechanic, huh? And Dad had a briefcase too! I had seen Dad's leather briefcase, which had some very interesting tools in it, but that briefcase was strictly off limits for me, and for everyone else.

So, I was still a confused nine-year-old boy, not clear on what Dad did at work.

But on that day, I started seeing Dad and things, in general, a bit differently. You see, I would learn that Dad was part of the very first corporate family, ever, with a common set of beliefs and processes. Today, this is known as "corporate culture." IBM is said to be the first business organization to have a culture: the sum of attitudes, customs, and beliefs that distinguishes one business group of people from another. In Dad's office, he had a placard on his desk that simply said **THINK**. He explained that that was the motto of IBM. And this motto is ever-present with IBM as reminder of the ideas, beliefs, and practices that held the company together. Dad said that Thomas J. Watson Sr., Chairman and CEO of IBM, was speaking to a group of businessmen and told them "The trouble with every one of us is that we don't **THINK** enough…" Mr. Watson decided on the spot, that **THINK** would be the company slogan. Dad said, "You know how I'm always telling you and your brother to **THINK**? Well, *thought* is the key to success in business and in life."

THINK before you speak. **THINK** before you act. **THINK**. Dad said, "What you **THINK** is determined by what you learn. And the more you learn… then the less mysterious *things* are to you. You can only **THINK** of what you have learned and what you learn is what you apply to the circumstances of your life."

Ralph Waldo Emerson, 1803-1882, was an American essayist, lecturer, and poet who has more quotes on **THINK**ing than anyone else I've ever heard who said, "**THINK**ing is the hardest work in the world. That's why so few of us do it" and "You become what you **THINK** about all day long."

Dad taught THINKing Skills—beginning with Comprehension, Memory, Problem Solving, Decision Making, Creativity, and Awareness.

In terms of **Comprehension**, he most often concluded in making his point with the following…

"Mike, do you understand me?" Which, was usually followed by eight or nine more "comprehension questions"… some spoken in other languages, all being thrown at me, one after another… *"Lo entiendes?… Comprende?… Tu sabes?… Le capisce?"*

Then some more in English: "Do you get my drift, son?"…"Can you dig it?" And, lastly, "Have I made myself perfectly clear?"

Early in my life, with all these questions being fired at me like a Gatling gun, I took Dad to be very serious and would say, "Yes, sir" to each and every comprehension question. By junior high school, both Dad and I erupted in laughter every time that he asked me his comprehension questions. It was a riot! It was like a ritual we would go through, even though it drove Mom nuts!

I did flunk Awareness a few times with Dad, in my early years, with this one example (and one of Dad's funniest antics). He would set me or one of my brothers down in the yard and dig a couple of holes in the ground, right in front of whoever of us was the "target." He would then say, "Now listen up" as he pointed to one of the holes in the ground. "This is your butt, this one here." Then, pointing to the other hole, he said, "This other one here, is a hole in the ground." This was followed by, "You understand?" My reply was, "Yes, sir." Then the list … *"Lo entiendes?... Yo comprende?...Tu sabes?"* and so forth and so on. "Now," Dad would ask, "Which one is your butt?" and one of us would point to that first hole he had dug. Dad would then say, "See there, you don't know your butt from a hole in the ground!" We laughed like crazy! "Oh, please, Dad, do it again! Please!"

I **THINK** that you can tell, with Dad's teaching system, my memory part worked out pretty well. *Le capisce?*

Dad continued on his mission to educate me. He was explaining that IBM's Mr. Thomas J. Watson Sr. had created this strong-valued-based thought that was grounded in *Respect for the Individual, Providing the Best Service in the World,* and *Striving for Excellence* in all that they did. He said IBM was the biggest, most successful company in the world. Watson is credited with being the first to create a culture for a corporation, "the culture of **THINK.**"

Most of what I remember Dad talking about was what he said were the "important things." "Respect, Mike—that's the highest form of love."

"Why do you **THINK** all employees of IBM wear dark suits and white shirts, Mike?" he asked. I, of course, didn't know. Dad explained that it is out of respect. "You see, Mike, it is practically impossible to offend anyone by wearing a white shirt and therefore it became the standard of dress throughout the organization. "It is all about respect, excellence, and building relationships, son, Tu Sabe?" "Yes, sir!"

These were early lessons on living one's (my) life, setting standards, and understanding how my parents expected me to live—especially the parts about Dad's *Respect and all efforts directed at the goal of Excellence in everything you do.* Dad was emphatic in saying to me, "I am not going to be around when you face the problems you're going to have later in life, when you have to make some important decisions. Right now, you don't have too many problems, as I'm making most important decisions on your behalf. *Capisce?*" "Yes, sir!"

Then came the sad news. Dad told me that Mr. Thomas J. Watson, Sr. had recently died. I **THINK** this was the beginning of a new relationship between Dad and me. Life's lessons had certainly begun, and this was, again, before I played my first nine holes of golf. That day, the day I went to work with Dad, was huge. It was magical and an experience bigger than anything I had encountered, so far, in my life. I think that time with Dad was probably the first of what could be called a "heart to heart" with him that I can remember. And I shall never forget it. Dad was a great teacher and, though I didn't know it back then, he would be the best friend I would ever have. This was a moment when Dad was sharing his experiences with me and which helped build a connection and a culture within me.

My IBM *Wall*

In my office, on the wall, are Dad's **THINK** plaques, an IBM note pad, and personal letters to me, from Thomas J. Watson, Jr. written in

1969 and 1970. These are among my most cherished mementos of my father and of growing in the corporate culture of IBM.

Thoughts on THINK*ing*....
"The trouble with every one of us is that we don't **THINK** enough."
– Thomas J. Watson, Sr., Chairman/CEO of IBM

"**THINK**ing is the hardest work in the world. That's why so few of us do it."
– Ralph Waldo Emerson's quote from Harvey Penick's *Little Red Book*

"I **THINK**, therefore I don't have a lot in common with a lot of people."
– James Whistler

"You can't **Think** what you don't know."
– J.A. Meadows, Jr. (my Dad)

Well, Show-n-Tell day finally came. Still being a bit confused about dad's work, I tried to explain to my class, when it was my turn, about the "nanosecond." They all seemed to like the money part, but I didn't do a very good job of explaining what my dad did at his work.

Emily's dad was a mailman and she talked about the post office and what they did with all the letters addressed to "Santa" during the Christmas season.

The class voted my classmate C.B. Hudson as having the Best Show-n-Tell Story of all the kids telling about what our dads did. C.B.'s dad owned a movie theater, The Rodeo Theatre in the Old Historic Stockyards of Oklahoma City. C.B. brought popcorn and Milk Duds to our class and handed the goodies out during his Show-n-Tell and he talked about the cartoons and Tarzan movies and stuff like that. *Of course,* he was voted best story teller of What Dad Does at Work. The Rodeo Theater is now an Opry House and a historical landmark of Oklahoma City.

All I had was that one-dollar bill, for Show-n-Tell. However, I also had a new appreciation and more love and respect for my dad than ever. And I knew I truly loved and respected my parents and I wanted to be like them. They were shaping my life for the future and I was on board and liking the direction. What I was learning from my parents was establishing basic truths for application in the life of a young boy growing up in Oklahoma City.

By the way... *Forbes* says there are some 2,040 billionaires in the world today, and I'm not one of them. Not yet... though I think C.B. might be one of them.

My pal Phil Cornett circa 1954

I played YMCA-sponsored baseball in Oklahoma City 1954, '55, '56, and '57 on my grade school team. I played on The Kaiser Kangaroos in my grade school summers with Ricky Dugger, Phil Cornett, C.B., Buddy, Jimmy, Jack, Kenny, Johnny, Joey, and others.

We played all the other grade school teams in Oklahoma City, like the Madison Magpies, Linwood Lions, the Chipmunks, the Bull Frogs, the Bull Dogs, the Red Birds and so on. That's when I started collecting baseball cards. I still have (thanks to my mom) my collections of Topps Baseball Cards, including complete sets of 1953, '54, '55 and '56. I even have some of the star cards like Mickey Mantle, Ted Williams, Roger Maris, Hank Aaron, and Willie Mays. Today these old Star Cards, as they're called, are rare and difficult to find, which makes them more expensive, too! They are a bit rare because back then most of us kids would put the very best player cards (Star Cards) on our bikes with clothespins so they would make the cool motorcycle-like sound as they got beat-up by the spokes of our bicycle tires. We literally wore out the best and more collectible cards. The faster you rode the better the sound, and by adding more cards the more your bike sounded like a bigger motorcycle.

There was a big event in 1955 in the Meadows' household. It was the new arrival to the family in March when little brother Pat was born. Big brother Steve was 13 years old and I was nine. When I wasn't playing baseball, or looking after baby brother, I was hanging out with my big brother, Steve. He became a "paper carrier" (P.C. for a "paper boy") delivering the *Oklahoman*, a daily morning newspaper. He made about $5 a week and I would often go with him on his monthly collections trip, where customers would pay their paper bill, and give my brother some kind of tip—usually either money or cookies. Cutting through The Meridian Golf Course to get to his paper route is where I discovered golf... at "the munie (municipal) down the street." The next thing I knew I was finding and selling golf balls, and discovering and learning the game of golf. I was also seeing people of all ages playing the game. Mom and Dad thought it was good for me to be at The Meridian so they would know where I was, especially if one of my brother's paper-route bags or granddad's canvas golf bag and clubs were gone from the garage.

Growing up in the '50s and '60s was magical.

My main interests besides baseball during this time were golf and Rock 'n' Roll music.

Cars were also a very important part in my life, coming into my teenage years, even though I could not yet (legally) drive. Every year my buddies and I would anxiously await the new cars introduced to the market. My primary interest was in the new Chevrolet Impala and all those "fins." Here they are. Can you identify them by year?

Chevys... from left to right: Top row 1957 and 1956, Bottom row, 1958, 1959

It's different today. New cars look pretty much the same, as if they'd come out of the same mold and then the carmaker stuck a different grill on each one. So, I have little interest in new cars today. Oh, they're made better, safer, and more efficient, I'm sure, but in the '50s and '60s not many people cared about cars apart from their appearance. As kids, we could tell you the make, model, and year of most every car made in the '50s and '60s. I couldn't wait to be 16 years old and get my driver's license. I counted the days until September 3rd, 1962.

Of all the kids in the neighborhood, Ricky Dugger and I seemed to get into the most trouble.

But it was kid stuff, foolish stuff. Ricky lived across the street and got into lots more trouble than I did, primarily because I could run faster.

We lived in a fairly new subdivision on the NW side of Oklahoma City. Behind our house was a big pasture-like field, not yet developed in the subdivision. This field was our personal playground for activities like hunting rabbits, building forts, BB gun fights and taunting horses that were at the far end of the field. By the term "BB gun fights," I don't mean shooting those air rifles at each other—not unless you wore Levi's jeans and a leather jacket, and even then the rules were that you couldn't shoot at anyone above the neck. That said, I still can't believe we didn't shoot someone's eye out. Leather jackets were great as padding when hit by a BB, but being shot in the legs, or rump wearing only blue jeans hardly stopped a BB sting.

That leads me to the **Great Chase** and **Baptism of Ricky Dugger**, a life-long friend, God rest his soul.

One day out in the field, Ricky got tired of me shooting him in the butt (I was a pretty good shot) so we decided to go to the far end of the field, where there was a stable and corral with a couple of horses. Off we went with our BB guns. We thought it would be fun to shoot the horses in their rumps and see what kind of reaction they would have. We got close, saw the two horses, cocked our air rifles and fired. Not only did the horses react, but so did the stable owner, whom we had not seen. We both took off running with me in the lead, never looking back. Running south, back to the subdivision, there was a little Baptist Church in the southeast corner of the field that my family had started attending and where dad had become a deacon.

Being very familiar with the church building, I knew how to get into it easily. I entered through a window and quickly found my hiding place. I then heard Ricky come in through the same window and heard his footsteps followed by a tremendous bang, followed by some serious wailing... and I mean a never-ending screaming kid, like I had never heard.

Ricky's family attended the Methodist Church, so he was not familiar with the Baptist Church floor plan. Ricky had followed me into the church and had raced around, opened a door, and hurried up the stairs of the baptistery and fallen face first into the empty (no water in it) baptistery, hitting the stairs on the other side. This knocked out almost every tooth in his head. You need to picture this: Blood everywhere, teeth scattered all over that baptistery, and a hysterical Ricky lying therein. I ran to my house and returned with my mom, a quick thinker. She brought along a lot of ice. Ricky's face was swelling fast. She got Ricky to calm down, we put him under ice and even picked up his teeth and iced them, thinking a dentist might be able to replace them in Ricky's mouth. The ambulance arrived. We followed it to the hospital and waited until Ricky's parents arrived. Tough one to explain, but I told the truth. Ricky lost his teeth and I lost my BB gun to the attic.

My mother and father's attitude could be contagious. Again, "Attitude is everything." With their faith, their system of authority, and their attitude, I realized I was a lucky kid. And I think I developed and came through those times OK. However, this doesn't mean I didn't encounter personal issues, circumstances, and problems or that I haven't made some bad choices along the way. By the way, bad decisions make for good stories, but I'll leave most of those out, within these pages.

My parents were "trustful parents." They trusted me to play and explore, make decisions and suffer the consequences. I used to love the TV game show called *Truth or Consequences* as an example of learning by mistakes. I learned later, the hard way, that when it seems that everything is going against you, it's not just a cliché. Attitude is everything.

Speaking of trusting… I remember the front doors of homes were almost always unlocked and often the car keys were left in the ignition or over the visor. It was, most assuredly, a simpler time of living.

A Mother's Mental Attitude….

Later in my life, after being out on my own, I remember saying something like this to my mother: "Mom, I don't remember you ever being sick." She replied, "I tell you what, *Ma' kel*, I didn't have time to be sick. I was home with you kids, four of you. I'm 'tawkin' over 36 years with kids in the house."

"Anything is possible, *Ma' kel*." That's what Mom said, and I would say that she was a direct and positive energy for me in my early youth. We kids grew up in attitude and mental thought. "You can learn, have, and be what you want to be if you are willing to pay the price." It is pretty easy to have a good attitude when things are going well, as they were when I was a kid. I would learn paying the price and sacrifice in due time.

If your mom was anything like mine, here is a good rule of thumb. If at first you don't succeed, try doing it the way Mom told you to do it in the first place. Mom dispensed logical training this way. "*Ma' ak*, if you fall out of that tree and break your neck, you're not going to your baseball game this afternoon." And though I never did actually see an Oklahoma tornado, I was familiar with its aftermath: "This room of yours looks like a tornado went through it. Clean it up, now!"

The mid- to late-'50s were spent in grade school and playing outside—mostly baseball and trying to improve my "back yard" golf skills. I thought "real golf" was unattainable for me. Neither Dad nor Steve played golf and our economic level would not find me at any country club. But there was that "munie" course down the street that kept calling me… The Meridian.

The last season of baseball, during the spring and summer season of 1957 and just before entering Junior High School in the fall, "The Roos" (Kaiser Kangaroos) had a game against the Linwood Lions on their home field. Mom drove herself and my little brother (Pat, two years old at the time) to the game. She was seven months pregnant with baby #4. Practically all games were played during the summer months on weekday afternoons, so not many dads attended. But lots of mothers were there for our games. My Mom stayed in the car with two-year-old Pat. I played third base and was not too bad a fielder, grabbing up grounders and throwing some runners out before they crossed first base.

I have vivid memories of what happened next, in the game on the Linwood Lions field, because it only happened once in my entire little league career. It came my turn to bat and the bases were loaded. I wasn't a very good hitter and was usually placed in the #7, #8 or #9 batting position. I didn't like seeing the balls coming at me and we did not have helmets back then. We played in blue jeans, our Kaiser Kangaroo tee shirts, and ball caps. The pitches always seemed to be fast balls that were speeding directly toward my head. I was always stepping backward out of the batter's box with most pitches. As I said, the bases were loaded. And my teammates were yelling, "Just swing at it, Mike!" and "It only takes one!" Then came the next pitch, which I assumed was going to send me to the emergency room. The pitch almost hit me, as I backed away. "Ball one!" yelled the umpire. "Good eye, Mike, good eye!" Coach Hanna yelled. Another throw came from the pitcher. All I did was take a swing and the ball somehow hit my bat and took flight, flying over the shortstop, falling near the Linwood Lions left fielder, who wasn't paying much attention as the three previous batters had gotten on base with walks. Their outfielder had put his glove on his head and had been deeply involved in kicking the red clay dirt clods around him. There was no outfield fence, so the ball went bounding past him, on an endless journey to nowhere. A Grand Slam Homer! Mom came out of the car, carrying little Pat, with her seven-months-pregnant rotund body, to watch as I rounded third, heading for home. She met me at home plate with the team and coach in all the joy and excitement of the bases-loaded home run.

After all the hoopla and such had settled down, Mom said, "Anything is possible, *Ma' kel*." Yep, that's what she said.

Other highlights of the 1950s were when *American Bandstand* hit the TV airwaves, and my older brother Steve got his first car—an old Hillman Minx. (And he didn't even have a driver's license, yet.) Lucky guy! He was allowed to drive it around the gravel parking lot at our church, which was a half block east and a half block north of our house. Steve got to drive it with the understanding that he had to keep that car spotlessly clean. Steve agreed and, as usual, dad inspected what he expected. I would go with him to the church's parking lot while he drove around in circles, stopped, put it in reverse and drove backwards in circles. He let me drive some, to learn the skills of the manual transmission, using the left-foot clutch pedal. Steve was teaching me to drive... and I was 11 years old and my first Driver's Education instructor was 15. How about that? I can still hear him shouting at me: "Slower! No, that's too fast! You're letting the car jerk too much! Don't let the clutch out so slow, you're revving the engine to much... Oh no, it died!" Steve got mad and I got mad. I walked home and never got to drive Steve's car again.

I remember an incident in church when I was 12 years old, making my brother Steve 16. Well, it seems Steve had been out late, really late, on a Saturday night, missing Dad's curfew and getting home in the wee small hours of Sunday morning, which did not get past dad. Dad came into our shared bedroom, early Sunday morning, with his "Rise and shine, boys!" He added: "Ok, Steve, if you're going to act like a big man on

Saturday night, you're going to be the big man on Sunday morning. We're going to Church, so let's get a move on."

During the Utah Avenue Baptist Church 11:00 am service, we all arose from the pew for the singing of Doxology. Our whole family was lined up: Dad, Mom, Steve, and me (our brother Pat and lil' sister Lorri were in the church nursery). The piano player (pianist) began playing and we all started singing along with everyone else:

"Praise God from whom all Blessings flow,
Praise Him all creatures, here below..."

Then... CRASH! A *loud* CRASH!

Steve passed out and fell forward over the pew, right between Mr. and Mrs. Pence, forcing them apart. Song books went flying in the air, and we were looking at Steve laying face down and halfway under the second pew in front us, reeking of rum and Coke, as in Coca-Cola.

Total silence in the church!

Two ushers rushed to Steve, picked him up and helped him out of the auditorium, vertically, with his arms around two ushers' shoulders and his feet dragging, just like they were carrying a football player off the field. Mom started to follow Steve and the ushers out of the sanctuary, when she turned and quietly said to the people around us, "Steve, he gets these dizzy spells, ya know?"

Dad nodded to the piano and the choir and congregation continued:

"Praise him above ye heavenly host,
Praise Father, Son and Holy Ghost"

For that little error in behavior and bad judgment, Steve got the pleasure (the assignment... aka punishment) of building a compost pile far away from the house, way out in the back corner of the yard. He was digging a compost bed that was eight feet by eight feet and two feet deep. I was a spectator to this backyard assignment. Dad said, "Steve is digging his own grave!" How funny! Given the instructions, from Dad, on building a compost pile, Steve dug up the dirt, turned the soil and added grass clippings. He then had to go over to a neighbor's front yard, rake their leaves, bring the leaves back, and till them into the soil and grass. And to all of this, we started adding table scraps like egg shells, watermelon, cantaloupe rinds, and whatever else Dad said to mix in there. YUK!

From then on, someone (Steve or I) would get the weekly assignment of turning the compost pile and spreading the yucky stuff into the rose bushes and our tomato and okra gardens. Neither Steve nor I wanted that chore. "*I tell you what...*" Mom began as usual, "When life gives you lemons, boys, make lemonade." This proverbial phrase was used to encourage optimism and a positive can-do attitude from Mom in the face of adversity or misfortune. In this case, she meant the compost pile.

One day Steve and I found WORMS, WORMS and more WORMS in that compost pile. Dad said, "Let's go fishing!" Hooray, Yeah! Lake Hefner and Lake Overholser were the two main lakes of Oklahoma City. These lakes had water of a reddish-orange murkiness because of Oklahoma's red clay soil base—the reason the river between Oklahoma and Texas is called the Red River—but there were bass and crappie in both lakes. Our local fishing excursions would last just a couple of hours at the lake, unless Dad rented a boat, which most often he would not. A couple of young boys can get quite bored, especially if the fish aren't biting, but just getting away with Dad was always a treat.

We didn't have big super stores in the '50s, no 7-Elevens or Circle Ks, no convenience stores, like today. We had Ralph's Grocery and, since there were no credit cards back then, you would either write a check, hand over the cash, or ask the clerk to add the cost of your purchases to your account in the store billing book. Payment would be made later and not at any prescribed time.

It was in the spring of 1958 when I first heard the name Arnold Palmer—a man who changed everything about golf for me and the world of golf itself. Palmer would soon become the image of all sports heroes to multitudes of fans... and, to me, my second all-time sports hero. *He won the what?* I'd ask. "The Masters, son," Dad said. My dad knew how I was becoming hooked on golf, so he kept me pretty much up to date in the golf world. There were a few newsreels every now and then about golf on the TV, and each time I saw them it made me want to play golf more and more.

Arnold Palmer
Photo courtesy of Phoenix Country Club

In 1959, I was 12 years of age and in junior high school. Arnold Palmer came to Oklahoma City and won the Oklahoma City Open Invitational Golf Tournament at Twin Hills Country Club. The course was on the east side of town and directly across the road from Lincoln Park Municipal Golf Course, my high school golf team's home course.

At the time I did not know that that old canvas bag of granddad's with those Johnny Bulla Signature golf clubs would be the start of a life-long journey and a life dominated by chasing and beating a little white ball around the world.

Mom and Dad didn't play golf. I started taking the golf balls that I had saved from The Meridian, back to The Meridian. I started smacking golf balls around in the big field, all by myself. But it was my parents who offered the encouragement to me. They encouraged me because I was having fun. I was learning to love the game, as I obviously still do, and I loved being outdoors. Golf was a great challenge to me, and still is. Dad was always saying: "Find things you like to do that have challenge in the endeavor, have room for advancement, and incorporate competition, even if it is with yourself." In golf, I found all that, and Dad knew it. It was all there, and just six blocks down the street!

I continued spending time on The Meridian Golf Course, just fooling around trying to hit a straight ball. I would swing and miss the ball sometimes, but when I did hit it, the golf ball had a terrible tendency to veer right with an uncontrollable (and what I learned to call) slice! But, every now and then the magical happened… I would connect with the swing, the club hitting the little white orb, as Dan Jenkins would later write, Dead Solid Perfect!

What was it about bashing a golf ball and watching it fly through the air? Whatever it was, golf had me, hook, line and sinker (an old fishing term). I would later find out that golf was the best activity on earth for making friendships. Mom, later in life, said, "I wish that your father and I would have encouraged you more in playing golf." I replied with something about (paraphrasing here…) how golf had reinforced all the timeless lessons of living my life, which my parents had taught me, and I was so thankful for my Mom and Dad. I told her that every time I went on the course, I thanked God for my Mom and Dad.

I wanted to improve in all aspects of golf, so I took the lawn mower to the backyard of our house and made my own green. I lowered the blades on that old push mower and scraped the heck out of a big circle in the back lawn. Next, I took some tin cans from the garbage, washed [warshed] them out with the garden hose, then dug holes and inserted the cans in "my own new practice green." I had three or four holes on my own creation of a green, even though it was far from a smooth putting surface. Having plenty of golf balls from The Meridian, I could chip 'n' putt all over the place.

One day, thinking I was getting pretty good, I went to the front yard to hit a ball with a nine iron over the house to my green in the back yard. And, of course, that wasn't how it played out… Smash! I sent the ball flying right through the living room window. Uh oh!

Mom said, "Wait 'til your father gets home!" Uh oh, Mom was using the "your father" words—rather than saying "your dad." It was always serious when Mom used the words "your father."

When Dad did come home he took me out in the backyard where he placed some balls in circles around my cans, about four feet from each hole on my makeshift green. He handed me the putter and said, "Let's see you knock 'em into the holes." So I putted as he watched. It took a few times, hitting a ball at a can, but when I finally got one in the hole, with him watching, he said, "Mission accomplished. That is the object of the game, right, son?"

Of course, he was right. Once again. He even set up some games for me in the backyard. He created a few starting places (teeing areas), and made several par threes from four or five different little areas around the yard and numbered the holes for me. Then he set up a course, making some teeing areas and even made some little flags for the cans. Dad played with me in the backyard on my new (and very own) mini-golf course. He said, "Let's keep it in the backyard from now on, or on The Meridian, son. Pick up all these golf balls before you come inside." My reply, "Yes, sir!"

Because little sister, Lorri, was born on the 4th of July of 1957, Mom and Dad made certain that she knew (or thought) that all the celebrating was just for her! All the fireworks, black cats, and sparklers and such were all about *her*—and her birthday. So, the 4th of July was always one big birthday party for our little sister.

Steve and I were getting into the fun of fireworks. We acquired some cherry bombs and M-80s. Oh boy! These fireworks have since been banned and have been illegal to possess since 1966, by the Child Safety Protection Act of 1966. But five or six years before that, during our 4th of July Celebrations in the early 1960s, we would certainly find out why this ban came about.

The big field was still behind our house and our family's July 4th celebration—with a cook-out of steaks, hotdogs, potato salad, and all the fixin's—always happened in our backyard. Dad took a cherry bomb, lit it, and threw it out into the field. After the explosion and smoke had dissipated, we saw that the field was on fire. Mom made the phone call and the fire department trucks were dispatched (we could hear them coming) and arrived in minutes. The big trucks drove out into the field and were successful in extinguishing the inferno. However, this was not the end of this 4th of July story.

The next day, little brother Pat, age five, somehow got hold of a cherry bomb and took it into the kitchen. He (somehow!) turned on the burner of the stove and was holding the cherry bomb in his right hand, when Mom walked through the dining area into the kitchen and saw what was going to happen. Mom let out such a scream, the likes of which I had never before heard, and frightened the wits out of Pat. He fell backwards—just as the cherry bomb exploded—with his hand still ever so near the explosion. The glass coffeepot exploded, sending shards of glass all over the place and into Pat's face and body as he fell. His thumb and forefinger were severely damaged and blood was all over the walls and the kitchen appliances.

Off to the emergency room went Mom and Pat. Dad was called and he went from work to the hospital. They came back home later with Pat's right hand all bandaged in white up to his elbow. I just knew he had blown his hand off. The damage, however, was limited to his right thumb and forefinger with a lot of stitches and marks on his face from picking out the glass shards. Would he ever be able to throw a baseball? That was my main thought. And, would he ever be able to write? Everything healed just fine. Pat, today, can both throw a baseball and write… and he is a published author with a PhD from Princeton.

Back to Meridian

As a kid and novice to the game of golf, I was first simply knocking at golf balls with a wooden club that said "Driver" on it. Dad told me that was the club that was for hitting the ball the farthest distance. I thought that was what you were supposed to do, hit it as far as you could, like hitting a home run in baseball. I was putting every ounce of my being into that effort.

Dad had a great idea. He wanted us to create another project together: refinishing the driver and spoon in my set of clubs. So, in the garage at Dad's workbench we sanded, stained, and varnished those old woods. We even replaced the cords wound on the shafts where they went into the wooden club heads... the hozzles, I later learned. Those wooden clubs were beautiful. Dad was keen on us having a focus on learning and creating, rather than being distracted by "other foolish entertainment." And I did find other foolish entertainment often. Dad called it making bad decisions, and bad decisions make great stories, but that's another topic for another book.

Teachers in life...

Most of us have known people, throughout our lives, who have been very good influences. I remember a lot of mine and think often of them. First and foremost are my parents, on lessons of faith and fortitude in raising their kids. They gave me direction, messages, and discipline... Ouch!

And I am still being guided and taught today, with instruction in golf technique, in golf mental dynamics, and in Biblical Doctrine by my Pastor/Teacher. It is important to be choosy in our decisions about from whom we accept counsel.

Back in the 1950s it became very popular for boys to build model airplanes, cars, and ships. Revell was the big manufacturer of plastic models back then. I liked most all model airplanes, because you could build as many as you wanted and find a place to hang them from the ceiling in your room. I would open a new model box and all the parts were on injection-molded plastic 'trees' to keep them from getting lost. There was always something like a 4"x 4" folded instruction sheet, which unfolded to a 16"x16" two-sided page of step-by-step procedures to follow. *What the heck is all this?* I started by side-stepping a few of the instructions and went for the big pieces. The fuselage pieces had to go together, so... *Where's that tube of glue?* I had about the same amount of patience as Dad had in appreciation of Little Richard's new Rock 'n' Roll. ("That's not music," he said.)

I just wanted the finished product as quickly as possible so that I could get it glued up and hanging from the ceiling. *Oh boy, here are some decals. Let me get these on, right now!* But sure enough: Oh, no! The fuselage pieces are coming apart! *Just how long do I need to hold these two pieces together before they've dried enough?*

Dad would occasionally check in on my progress with my model building. He, no doubt, was teaching me, without really teaching me. My first few models were so very difficult. One time, Dad was checking in on me and told me that the gaps between some glued pieces were too gaping. I just wanted to get a model finished first, and then show Dad.

This was much more difficult than I ever expected. My previous airplanes were made of balsa wood. All you had to do was snap out the flat body, the flat wing and flat tail piece from a single thin sheet of balsa wood, stick the wing and tail through the body and the model would fly forever, or until a car ran over it.

I got all frustrated. I had glue seeping out of the tube half dried on my fingers and winding up on parts where glue shouldn't be. *Oh no, I got glue on the windshield of the plane.* If I touched anything, it was gonna have glue on it, and most likely, be pulled out of the place where it was just glued. What a total mess!

"OK," Dad said, finally. "Come on, we're going to go buy this model again, and we'll build it together." I felt somewhat defeated, but I knew my Dad had his plan, and I would have a new great model very soon.

The "very soon" part, however would take its time.

We opened "our" new box and the first thing Dad said to me, picking up and unfolding the instruction sheet, was, "What does this say, right here?" I read it out loud: "Read the instructions thoroughly through each step of assembly." Dad explained how this was good advice and for my benefit.

Dad explained how the model company had a proven and validated system. They had engineers and technicians who build the models to scale, created the engineering templates and schematics (*What?*) for injection molding of the parts. They also have technical writers who wrote the instructions for assembly. "Don't you **THINK** it would be helpful to follow their instructions?" I knew the drill: "Yes, sir."

First Dad set up a card table as our work station. We checked the parts list, making sure our inventory of parts was all there. "Here's the required tools and supply list," Dad said.

"Let's make sure we have everything here and available where we are working." Then, "Now, let's determine what needs to be painted first and what needs to be built before being painted."

When we took a part off the tree, we did not twist it off. We clipped it and trimmed the excess plastic on each part.

I'm getting the message. Get the right mentor to help with understanding the manual. I had a teacher and instruction guide. It took time, effort and thought, but in the end we had a beautiful, well-built model airplane... the best I could ever imagine!

Which takes me to golf...Having no formal training in golf, I was getting more and more angry and frustrated. I was becoming an arrogant, hot-headed, club-throwing kid. Oh, the frustrations of the game! Once, Dad saw me slam a club into the ground in the back yard, exposing my temper. Uh oh! The bag and clubs went back up into the attic and they wouldn't come down until Dad decided "when."

Dad didn't really teach me much about golf skills, as in "golf techniques" or instruction—but he did help me with controlling myself, my temper and anger. That is what hitting a golf ball was doing to me, getting me pretty frustrated. He could relate it all to life and simple issues, like "Take it one step at a time"... as in one shot at a time, one hole at a time. And things, such as, "The harder you work at it the luckier you'll be... huh?" I can't forget this one: "Remember to make a fun experience of it all." Dad, what a great teacher!

Yet, in my quest to get better—hit balls straighter, farther, and more in the direction I wanted the ball to go—I had developed a few anger issues. And Dad could see that.

"Anger," Dad said, "expresses nothing good. It produces bad things like irritation, exasperation, and actions that you will be sorry for. You are going to get angry, son, but it is what you do with your anger that matters." He continued, "A person is never smart when angry, which is why many stupid and embarrassing things are said and done in anger." And these zingers: "Never let the sun set on your anger" and "Nothing's ever eaten as hot as when it first comes out of the oven."

One of the important lessons from Dad at this stage of my life was, "Don't forget, golf is supposed to be fun." He said, "I think your anger is affecting your ability to improve. Maybe you should play for the enjoyment of the game, so simply let go and have fun."

Dad spent a lot of his free time with us kids. He would have to be at Tinker AFB on some weekends and sometimes on something he called "the grave yard shift," or being "on call," like a doctor. However, Dad was always encouraging me and my golf. I didn't think that I was big enough or strong enough to be good at golf.

While hitting golf balls one day at The Meridian, and working on my temper and patience and so forth, I noticed someone else out on the big field, so I moved closer. I began watching others, who were hitting balls that were flying much better than my efforts were producing, going farther, and with a lot more accuracy. I noticed that there was a style or a systematic way in hitting good golf shots.

Rather than putting all the muscular effort into the swing as I was doing with my whaling, beating, and thrashing with clubs, I saw that others could swing smoothly, seemingly rhythmically and could hit the same shot repetitively and with much less effort. They were practicing golf and not just hitting golf balls. And these guys didn't necessarily have big muscles, either. But I could see some kind of coordination in their physical effort to hit a golf ball. I thought, "I have got to learn how good golfers do this." I figured then that the movement of the body in the "right style" got the results of direction, distance, and control. Now I was on to something and it was not about being a big guy with big muscles, but how to use your muscles and coordinate them in "this system." I knew I had to learn the way to swing a golf club.

One day I met another kid my age, at The Meridian. Malcolm Haney was with his father, Mr. Tom Haney, who was giving Malcolm some golf tips. I didn't know that this would become a lifelong friendship. Nor did I know that I would make most of my friends because of golf, and that they would be a part of my life forever.

I have since read so much on golf and how golf is a microcosm of life. I kind of take the opposite view point. Golf is a game, not life. Yet, for those of us who play and understand the game, we become aware of how your integrity and character are exposed and tested in the game. But golf did not teach me honesty, respect, or integrity. Those things, certainly, came from my family upbringing. Hopefully, people don't have to start playing golf to learn these important aspects of life. As a kid, I really didn't understand that golf was helping me learn about distractions, obstacles, and difficulties to be encountered later in life.

The Annual Family Road Trip

Every year, in the summer, the family would take a trip, a Real Road Trip to Dallas to visit the grandparents. It was late summer,1958, just before we had to be back in school and off we went to Granddad's. Dad was mostly a Pontiac man. He had his 1953 Chieftain, sedan, straight eight, three on the column (today known as three on the tree), everything manual, no automatic windows or automatic door locks, no seat belts and NO AIR CONDITIONING! (Did I say a summer road trip?) We took the "53" to Dallas. The trip took about six hours, even though it was only a 215-mile drive. This was because there was no Interstate Highway at that time, just Highway 77, which meandered through every small town heading south from Oklahoma City, through towns like Nobel, Percell, Wayne, Paoli, and Pauls Valley, where we always made a stop at Fields Restaurant for some lunch and a piece of Mrs. Fields' pecan pie… my, my!

1953 Pontiac Chieftain

Then, we drove through Wynnewood to Davis, our church camp location...

Summer Church Camp

Falls Creek Assembly Church Camp was established in 1917, and in 2017 held its Centennial Celebration. Falls Creek Baptist Youth Camp, in the Arbuckle Mountains of Oklahoma, is Oklahoma's oldest church camp and also the largest youth encampment in the United States, hosting some 55,000 attendees per summer in eight two-week camps. A wonderful time of growing up a little more, "churchy-stuff," and learning (at least picking up on) life's purpose. I enjoyed the great outdoors the most.

Onward we went, in that '53 Pontiac Chieftain, with another stop to see Turner Falls, then through Springer (pronounced "Spranger") and Marietta. Upon "driving through" (and I literally mean, driving *smack dab* through) each little town, with its stop signs, stop lights, railroad crossings... everything you could imagine, at which you would have to come to a complete stop... there was *the process.* Dad, after applying the breaks to come to a full stop, would push in the clutch pedal, push the gear shift lever up and over, and pull it down into low gear. He'd then slowly release the clutch and press the gas pedal getting the car moving again... release the gas pedal, push in the clutch pedal and shift into second gear... release the clutch pedal... press the gas pedal, increasing speed and, finally, press the clutch, again, to shift the lever into high gear, as he slowly increased the speed of that old Pontiac to 45 or 50 mph after every stop. *Whew!* And this process repeated in every one of those little country towns we drove through!

"Dad, how much longer?" one of us would ask, looking up from a comic book.

There were six of us in 1958, making the long haul to Dallas. I think I mentioned that baby sister Lorri had joined the family, born on July 4, 1957. It was a car full with Mom, Dad (smoking in the front seat) and four kids, ages 2, 4, 12, and 16. Again, no seat belts, no children's car seats, and NO AIR CONDITIONING.

You know the litany: "Are we there yet?" "How much *longer?*" "Mom, I gotta pee." Pat, our four-year-old little brother was standing up in the front seat with an arm around Mom or Dad all during the trip. Mom and dad puffed on Herbert Tareyton cigarettes, and the car was filled with smoke.

No video games, no hand-held devices of any kind, nothing to stop a kid from getting bored. We made up different games of "I Spy," wherein we would have to find all the letters of the alphabet, on road signs, before the others could say, "I Spy a Z." The game caused lots of fights in the back seat, with Steve and me poking each other, almost all the time. *Ouch... Mom, Steve's hitting me!*

Dad would read out loud the Burma Shave signs along the road. Burma Shave was a shaving cream product that became famous with the Burma Shave road signs. These signs, usually four or five of them, were evenly spaced along the side of the road and each had a few words of a rhyming verse, followed by one that simply said Burma Shave.

DON'T LOSE YOUR HEAD
TO GAIN A MINUTE
YOU NEED YOUR HEAD
YOUR BRAINS ARE IN IT.
Burma Shave

We couldn't wait to see the next one...

DROVE TOO LONG
DRIVER SNOOZING
WHAT HAPPENED NEXT
IS NOT AMUSING.
Burma Shave

DON'T TAKE A CURVE
AT 60 PER
WE'D HATE TO LOOSE
A CUST-O-MER
Burma Shave

"Dad, are we there yet?"

Outside of Marietta, Oklahoma, we were close to the Red River and when we finally were crossing the Red River, the boundary line of Oklahoma and Texas, Dad would tell us all (and *every* time we crossed the Red River he instructed us, while laughing) to "Stick your head out the window, kids, and take a deep breath! Smell that sweet air, kids? That's Texas you're smellin'." It didn't smell any different to me.

We always stopped in Gainesville, Texas—right by the sign "Welcome to The Great State of Texas"—to fill up with gas. Dad would have us all get out of the car and make each of us boys reach down to the ground and pick up some dirt and rub it between our hands. "That's pure Texas soil, kids," Dad would say. Seemed to me, it was just dirt, like they had in Oklahoma. Then after washing our hands and doing our business in the filling station's fine facilities, Dad would get *the little book* out of the glove box and we were back on highway 77 headed to Dallas.

Dad's Little Book

Dad kept a *little book* (a pocket-size notebook) in the glove box of his car. Every time he filled up with gas or added (or changed) oil, he would make notation in the *little book*—date, amount of gas, cost per gallon, total cost, and gas mileage. Yes, every time. He would calculate the gas mileage and enter it into the *little book* every time gas went into the gas tank. And that was only *one* of his record-keeping systems. This all started back in the 1940s (or even earlier) when gas stations had "station attendants" who performed the following services for every car coming to the station: Check air pressure in vehicle tires, levels of fuel, motor oil, transmission, radiator, battery, and other fluids, add air, oil, water, or other fluids, as required, and wash all car windows. When not performing those services, the attendants would be cleaning the parking areas, offices, restrooms, and equipment, and removing trash. You don't see too many attendants any more, do you?

Years later, after Dad passed away in 1990, I was visiting Mom in San Antonio. We were going somewhere in her car (probably for Mexican food at La Fonda del Norte). On the way, Mom drove into a gas station. I went to the pump and filled up Mom's car. When I got back into the car, she asked me to get out *the little book* from the glove box and give it to her. She then asked me to tell her the amount of gas, cost per gallon, total cost, etc. etc. I had no idea of the details, so I went inside and got the receipt containing the pertinent information. She said, "I continue to do this in memory, honor, and respect for your dad." She turned back a few pages and said, "Look, Mike, here is where your dad made his last entry." We shared a tearful moment and we embraced right in the middle of the filling station by gas pump #3.

Back to the road trip.

Next town, Denton, the university town of North Texas State University, home of the Big Mean Green football team. Driving south we went through the city of Lake Dallas and crossed over a bridge going over Lake Lewisville until we ran into Harry Hines Blvd. and Dallas, Texas.

The Grandparents lived in East Dallas, just south of Mockingbird Lane off Greenville Avenue. On this one particular road trip to Dallas, we arrived at our grandparents' house on the tree-lined and very shady avenue. There sitting in Granddad's driveway was his brand new, 1959 Ford Fairlane 500, white on white, in white, 4-door hardtop, with power doors, power windows, automatic transmission and (yes!) AIR CONDITIONING!

We all scrambled out of the car and walked around Granddad's new car in awe and amazement. Bright and shiny new, with lots of chrome, too! Dad walked around looking at the car like all of us were doing. Then, after studying the window sticker that Granddad had left in place, in plain view, Dad said the following to my grandfather (his dad), *"Dad, for what you paid for this Ford, you could have gotten a Cadillac!"*

Without hesitation, my granddad replied, *"Son, I didn't want a Cadillac!"* Which, to this day, is one of the best comebacks I have ever heard.

Granddad's '59 Ford Fairlane 500 with all the bells and whistles.

Do you know the make, model and year of the car above? Look, I put horns on mine! It's the 1959 Cadillac Eldorado Convertible... the most flamboyant and opulently designed, extravagant automobile with more chrome than ever, bigger fins, bullet-pointed, rocket ship dual tail lights, jeweled looking front grill. What a beauty!

There was a kid down the street, in OKC, named Darrell Cain (BTW most people named Darrell are from Oklahoma, ya know), who was another neighborhood playmate. Once he came knocking on the front door. Dad opened the door and Darrell asked, "Can Mike come out and play?" Dad said, "I don't know, you'll have to ask him." Darrell replied, "He knows what he can do?" I still think that is hilarious. Dad was teaching us to be responsible in making our own decisions.

Another time, when Darrell knocked on the door and Dad answered, Darrell said "Is Mike here?" Dad told him that I wasn't there because, "Mike had to have a growth taken off his head." Darrell turned and walked away. Not long thereafter, Darrell's mom showed up on our porch with a covered dish and a fresh apple pie. She said she was so sorry to hear about my operation. Dad was confused and then suddenly realized that he had been kidding Darrell and was, now, very embarrassed. Dad explained it all by saying "It wasn't like that, Mrs. Cain. Mike's mother took him to get a haircut, that's all." I think the real "got-cha" that time was on Dad. The apple pie was sure good, though.

I remember Steve and me getting flat-top haircuts every other Saturday for .50 cents at the barber shop. You had to have a jar of Butch Wax for your flat top. It seemed like the same kind of sticky stuff you put into a grease gun to lube a car, only it came in a big jar and was only available in the color pink.

Junior high school for us kids in Oklahoma City, in our part of town, meant going to Taft Junior High School, for grades seven and eight and from ages of about 11 to 14. The school was named for William Howard Taft, the 27th President of the United States from 1909 to 1913. He was the largest President this country ever had, weighing 340 pounds. And he was the first President noted for his love of golf. Across the street from Taft Jr. High School was the local drugstore with a soda fountain and lunch counter with the best hamburgers, fries and cherry cokes a kid could buy. They used to have a big spinning wheel that you could spin and the wheel would stop on your cost for a banana split—anywhere from .09 to .39 cents. I liked taking a chance with that wheel. Next store was the Taft Shoe Repair, where you could have taps put on your shoes, even golf spikes on a pair of dress shoes. C.R. Anthony clothing store, right next to the drug store, was where we bought our Levi's jeans.

Fall in Oklahoma meant football season was here and a big deal in Oklahoma for sure! A lot of my friends went out for football in junior high school. I wanted to be part of what kids were doing and convinced Dad to let me try out for football. He said, "You're way too skinny, and you'll get the 'pee-wadlin' poo' knocked out of you!" What that meant, I soon found out, was that—once again—Dad was right. I got clobbered the first time I ran with the football. I got hit by this bigger kid, and I laid on the ground thinking I'd never be able to move. Dad bought me the helmet, pads, padded pants and cleats, and I only wore the uniform one time. Right then and there I had one thought: *"Golf!"* It seemed to be a lot better sport for me. My uniform went to another kid and I went back to Granddad's old canvas bag and golf clubs, and back to The Meridian.

I got a little weekends-and-evenings job during the summers between the 7th, 8th and 9th grades, at The Watermelon Stand. I would ride my bike from home to the stand, about three miles, where I would buy slices of watermelon and deliver to waiting customers sitting at picnic tables. The man who owned the little business had large tubs of iced down melons. At the beginning of our work shift he would start me and the other kid, Gary, off by handing us each $5, in the following denominations: two one-dollar bills and 12 quarters. With this we could usually make change easily with our customers. Gary and I worked for tips, so we got into a contest to see who would have the most tips at the close of business at 10:00 pm each night. After our duties cleaning the joint, we would pay back the $5 front money and empty our pockets to see who had the most tips. We worked hard for those tips, too. I would hand out lots of extra napkins and always had a wet towel to clean up watermelon juice on the tables and seats. I wanted to win and I knew that giving better service than Gary would be the key factor.

My folks always emphasized being truthful and teaching me that "honesty is always the best policy." I just started telling my customers the truth. I started telling them that I was working for tips, and that I'm in a contest with that other kid over there to see who can have the most tip money at the end of the evening, "so anything you can do to help me would be appreciated." Dad found out what I was doing and said, "You're hustling, son. Just give 'em the best service you can and quit that hustling business. Just give them better service and even add extra care to your customers." My response: "But, Dad, I'm just telling the truth."

By the time I ended junior high and became a teenager, I had been practicing a lot on the putting green at The Meridian and bashing balls on the big open area, where golfers of all ages would hit and "shag" their own practice balls. I still didn't have much control over my slice, though I had some help from Malcolm, his dad, and some of the other golfers. I was even making some putts and playing a couple of holes, which just happened to be on my way home.

Dad was well aware that golf was a game of honor, that it was about you out there, mostly by yourself, alone with the rules of the game and having to make your own decisions. This caused me to examine myself. Here's what Dad said, "The score is not the important thing." *OK, great* I thought. It seemed, then, OK to say I had a six when I actually had a seven. No problem, because as Dad said, "The score is not the important thing." I played a lot of mulligans too, long before I ever heard the term. His meanings about golf were a bit different than what I first thought. Dad said stuff like, "Play like it doesn't matter, because, it doesn't matter." And "You will hit bad shots, so does everyone else, so just let it go and have fun… but be true to yourself." Insistent about keeping proper score, what Dad was telling me was that if you had a seven, you had a seven. So write it down. Hitting a bad shot is part of admitting your blunders and the score is not a mirror to character—but honesty sure is!

Dad said, "*Bad shots happen!*" By the way, that would change in another 40 years and become a bumper sticker: Shit happens, or as Dad would say, "skubala" (Greek for shit happens).

Write your score down, keep track of your life. When someone, today says: "Oh, just give me an X" or "Give me a 6X" it drives me crazy. What? How can you measure improvement if you are not setting (your own) standards? I started setting standards early in life because Dad helped me do just that, in how he expected me to live my life. So, it was easy to set a standard in golf, like standard 100 strokes for 18 holes. One of my first goals, in fact, was to break 100. Then, as I was improving, I set a new standard. Like breaking 90. Dad had a major hand in helping me learn how to set goals for myself.

High School 1960s… mostly a blur of memories.

When I entered high school - way back…1961, I found my buddy Malcolm as a classmate. Remember, I had gone to Jr. High at Taft, while Malcolm had been at Classen, for grades seven and eight. Now we were both in High School at Northwest Classen High School, a brand new school, just four years old. My older brother Steve, was in the first graduating class of all four years, grades nine through twelve.

"Haney" and I (as my mother referred to Malcolm, a life-long friend, even today) both loved to play golf and became best of friends, playing golf on The Meridian, and cutting up in school. We became friends with other guys who also played on the school golf team, as well as with many others kids who played baseball, football, or ran track. These are the guys who are, today, playing golf in their senior years.

We categorized the kids, excluding ourselves, into the following categories: Cool, Cliquey, Geek or Nerds, Hot-Shot Entertainers, and Jocks. The Entertainers were into extremism to get attention or laughs. The more outrageous the better, or so they thought, but they quickly became less and less impressive over time. This labeling was not being judgmental on our part, or was it? I was and still am very visual and very observant. Knowing one's self is an important part of learning, thinking, and growing.

My parents said, "We *will* treat everyone with respect, *not* on the basis of our 'pet prejudices' regarding race, social status, ability or what a person can or cannot do for us. We *will* refrain from gossip, maligning, judging, character assassination, etc. In other words, we *will* 'live and let live.'" The principle of treating everyone with respect also means that we *will* be tolerant, thoughtful and kind toward others. We *would* hold no grudges or resentment against anyone. Now that was a big challenge, especially in high school.

High school and the highly impressionable teenage years do present the first of some big human problems: the desire for approval, fear of disapproval – both of which can influence the shaping of *who we are* and *what we do* based on praise and fear of criticism of others. We are social creatures and we want to be liked. There's nothing wrong in *that*. However, the desire for praise can often become an obsession and serious problem when it is controlled by the ever-changing judgments of other kids around us and not by something inside each of us. You want to make new and cool friends and spend time with them. Some people never grow out of this "approbation lust" and the need for approval and praise, mostly as result of a fear of rejection. Likewise, some kids never grow out of being overly judgmental.

Mom said that none of us are completely able to not be judgmental, and that we'd be better at not judging others when we'd grown into our own confidence and respect for ourselves. She said, "We don't malign, gossip, or try to straighten out everyone around us. Relax and learn to get along with others through respect." *Respect* was a constant word and concept (along with the word **THINK**) around the Meadows' household and Dad certainly demanded it (respect, that is) from us kids.

This brings up another lesson taught to me by the mistake of my older brother. Dad, Steve, and I were sitting around the kitchen table. I do not remember exactly what it was that Steve said, but I do remember exactly what Dad did and what Dad said! No doubt, Steve had said something negative and disrespectful about Mom. That's when Dad picked Steve up by the collar, held him up some two feet in the air, and pushed him against the wall. "Son, you are talking about your mother…which means you are talking about my wife, and I do not ever want to hear such disrespect come from your mouth again. Do I make myself clear?" The answer from Steve was, "Yes Sir!" Dad turned and gave me a look, too. His message was clear.

That was when I began to realize how cool it was to have a brother who was four years older, and a teenager already. I looked up to him, for he was way cool, he knew stuff. And I got to take advantage of watching my parents' way of handling a teenager, before I became one. I understood what Dad meant, when he said, "You're acting too big for your britches, son." I learned through mistakes, both mine and Steve's. There were rules and consequences. We had well-defined limits (I think they use the word *boundaries* today). There was a family system in place, and we (Steve and I) were part of that system.

In high school, the Cool category was mostly made up of the jocks; the football team, wrestlers (both big sports in Oklahoma) basketball team, baseball team, track team, golfers and swimmers. And in that order. Golfers didn't exactly rate up there very high in being "cool," as I remember. Maybe because we didn't have cheerleaders, or a stadium or gymnasium, full of people rooting us on. But we golfers weren't geeky either. Nor were we in "cliques." I thought we were the coolest, as we had lots of friends from all other groups, and golf got us out of school early!

The Geeks walked around with slide-rules on their hips and were members of the boys pep squads, there being two clubs, the Lancers and the Falcons. They sold programs at sporting events and led cheers during game breaks at football and basketball games. For a school with more than a few thousand kids, there were only some 65 Geeks, but they all knew calculus and were in the Science Club.

Formal cliques were mostly from the formalized Clubs, The Everybody-Likes-to-Belong Clubs like Boys "O" Club, Lancers, Falcons, Signets, Coronets, the Courtesy Club (I don't remember them being too courteous, they just thought they were better than the other clubs...and probably should have been called the Legalists), the Election Board (don't piss them off), Hi Y (I was in Hi Y, but don't remember *what* that was about), Red Cross, Student Council (I was in those, as well) Key Club, Round Table... and on and on. The informal cliques were made up by those with whom you hung out and with whom you drove around town. Our clique, if we had one, was golf guys, other jocks and pals, driving between the Delta Drive In, the Charcoal Oven and the Split Tee, our teenage drive ins.

In high school I remember Liz Herring. I knew who she *was*, that is. I didn't really know a lot of other students, as I was basically a very shy kid. The main reasons I didn't know Liz Herring very well were that there were some 2,500 kids attending the same school, she was a sophomore when I was a senior, and (more importantly) she was a girl. And with girls especially, I was very shy. Liz's picture appears in the 1964 yearbook of NW Classen High School four times and my picture, only three times. Feel free to draw your own conclusions here...

I knew Jim Warren a bit better, for we were both in the senior class and had some classes together. And he was a guy. Jim was an officer in the boys Pep Club, the Lancers, and (as I remember) a good guy, though a bit geeky. I found out later that Jim, by then working for IBM, and Liz married in 1968. Elizabeth Warren, now a U.S. Senator from Massachusetts, was accused of fabricating Native American heritage to gain advantage in the job market. Liz stated that she had listed herself as a minority to meet people of similar heritage and was unaware that Harvard had listed her as a "woman of color." Genealogical investigators could not find proof that Warren's ancestors were or were not Native American... and new DNA results have further fueled the fire. The Oklahoma Historical Society said that finding a definitive answer about Native American heritage can be difficult because of intermarriage and deliberate avoidance of registration. Living in Oklahoma, back then, made everyone Cherokee, I guess.

The girls in our high school had their pep clubs. Two clubs or pep squads and I think every girl was a member of one or the other: the Coronets who wore gold sweaters or the Signets who wore purple sweaters (might have been the other way around, but I'm sure you get my point.)

Most every high school activity was centered around sports and the trophy case. We were State and/or District Champions in baseball, football, track, wrestling, and swimming. In fact, more than 20% of my 1964 yearbook, 57 pages, pertains to sports and sport pep clubs.

There was absolutely nothing about the golf team in the annual, until the Summer Supplement came out after graduation, where the golf team got three tiny paragraphs and a single 4"x 3" photo of four guys on the team as well as a 2 ¾"picture of my buddy, Malcolm Haney. We played a lot of golf together, and still do. I'm pretty sure that all those other sports stars (football, basketball, etc.) are no longer playing those sports and I would wager that they have been playing *golf* in their adult years.

I recently read a book by Dr. Ben Carson, MD and retired director of pediatric neurosurgery at Johns Hopkins Hospital after a groundbreaking medical career of more than 35 years. He was a *Washington Times* columnist, author of more than 5 books, (several of them *New York Times* bestsellers), and (with his wife Candy Carson) the recipient of our nation's highest civilian honor—The Presidential Medal of Freedom. Together they funded the Carson Scholars Fund, dedicated to recognizing academic achievements of deserving young people. As a past Presidential Candidate and now secretary of HUD, Dr. Carson has been widely outspoken on the subject of education in this country. "What about the intellectual superstar?" he asked during his speech at the National Prayer Breakfast.

He continued: "I don't like to bring up problems without coming up with solutions." Boy does that remind me of my dad! Carson continued, "My wife and I started the Carson Scholars Fund after we heard about an international survey looking at the ability of eighth graders in 22 countries to solve math and science problems, and saw that we [the United States] came out number 21 out of 22. We only barely beat out number 22... very concerning."

Carson said, "We go to these schools and we see all these [sports] trophies. The quarterback was the big man on campus. What about the intellectual superstars? What did they get? a National Honor Society pin? A pat on the head, 'There, there little nerd (Geek).' Nobody cared about them. And is it any wonder the smart kids try to hide? They don't want anybody to know that they are smart. This is not helping us as a nation. So we started giving out scholarships from all backgrounds for superior academic performance and demonstration of humanitarian qualities. Unless you care about other people it doesn't matter how smart you are. We've got plenty of people like that. We don't need those. We need smart people who care about other people."[1]

One of the most obvious signs of peer pressure had to do with image. Our dress and the clothing brands we wanted to wear were very important, and, so too, the looks we wanted to copy. Elvis, for some (the "hoods"), James Dean for others, and then the Beatles. Boys started growing their hair longer and brushing it down into bangs. I couldn't get away with that! Not good with my Dad, no way!

Behavioral changes in high school kids are definitely something to look out for, especially around certain groups of friends. This could be a sign that they feel like they don't fit in, yet want to very badly. I don't know who was at fault in the massive behavior change at my high school, but a lot of kids started doing the "Twist" in the hallways between classes and at lunch time. We were molded by the music of Chubby Checker and the Beatles.

Ya got trouble, my friend; I say trouble, right there in Oklahoma City.
Trouble with a capital "T" that stands for Twist, which starts with "T," and
that stands for Trouble at NWC! (Northwest Classen High) Trouble, trouble...

Our high school fashion: Boys wore shirts, preferably a Gant button down collar, with slacks or jeans and Bass Weejun penny loafers. That is if you wanted to be really cool.

Peer pressure often gets kids to try new things, which may be negative, even hazardous and un-healthy. I wanted to fit in and not feel isolated. I tried a cigarette when I was out with the smokers. Fortunately, I didn't like it nor did I understand why someone would purposefully take smoke into their lungs. I am, today, nicotine free. "I don't smoke and I don't chew…"

September 3, 1962… 16 years old (oh boy!) and a driver's license

A home builder, Mr. Harry Reeder, was building new homes on the scraped out lots in the field behind us. He hired me (gave me a real job) when I turned 16 and had my driver's license. First, we had a meeting at our house with Mom, Dad, Mr. Reeder and me. Mr. Reeder talked about what my responsibilities would be on the job. He said the job was to drive one of his pick-up trucks (*yeah! oh, boy!*) around and clean up-as in sweep up the saw dust and pick up the scrap lumber and any trash from the houses being built. I had the keys to a pick up truck, *wow!* I would walk to the subdivision, get the truck out of one of the garages, do my work, and leave the truck back in the garage of one of the newly built houses.

Dad had a talk with me about my responsibility in this new job and what it meant to be using someone else's tools, especially the truck. He talked to me about respecting someone else's property, having the use of this man's truck, what that meant and the amount of trust Mr. Reeder was giving me. Trust and Respect stuff, again. We talked about working for him with respect, working as if it were my own business, or like it was my dad's business (even "as unto the Lord" Dad said) and providing him with the very best of me while working for him. It was that Excellence thing again. Dad always emphasized doing more than what was expected or required, consistently, and thereby adding a mark of quality to your work.

Once a week, I also had to drive over to my boss's house and mow his huge lawn. The mower was in the garage and so was a refrigerator filled with ice cold, Miller Highlife Beer, "The Champagne of Bottled Beer." Uh Oh! This would be my first time I'd drink an entire beer, and on the sly – get my drift? I was lucky that my folks didn't figure out that *I was suffering from the effects of peer pressure, to drink!* I simply thought about cooling off from sweating and working hard in the sun and, well, having a simple, self rewarding cool refreshment. Of course, no one else was around.

Kids, what's the matter with kids today?

Kids today seem to be under a lot of pressure to fit in. They feel they have to try things (often goaded by others) and if left to their own devices (and didn't feel the intense need to 'fit in') they would have no interest in. It's a big deal today. If not checked, these peer-pressure-induced actions could lead to unhealthy habits, even a downward spiral in life. And, number #1 thing today seems to be drugs. Kids are making comparisons between themselves and others, wanting to be thinner, taller, tanner, have different color hair, or tattoos (the coolest thing today). Add to that fear of failure, fear of looking weak, fear of missing out on something. Let's not forget the addiction, today, to technology. OMG!

We are being bombarded with so much information and influences on our TVs, computers, iPhones, tablets, and with whatever is next, we can be sure we'll continue to be controlled by these things. Unfortunately, you can Google anything. Yes, anything… and see it instantaneously right in front of you. That cannot be good.

We see it at the gas station when we go to fill up: a screen with images and information selling, selling, selling-right in front of us on the pump itself. *"I'm fed up with my fill up."* Seems everyone is walking around with a phone in their ear, everywhere you go. There are continuous amounts of advertising on TV, while I get bombarded with emails proclaiming that I will have a better lifestyle if I would simply buy their crap. (Order today! Now!) Ads are telling people that they are not who they should be, and won't be until they have this gizmo or that one to make them the latest and greatest… the best.

We witness less interaction with peers (in favor of time spent watching TV or looking at a phone) which stops engaging and interaction with others, which definitely affects knowledge and behavior. There may be some good in TV, but I can't often find it, as TV exposes kids to vices early in their lives. No doubt, TV distorts a kid's view of the world. Just, how many advertisements does a kid see today? What I see on TV is the encouragement and promotion of kids to consume, and consume more, mostly unhealthy food and drink. Then the parents become the victims as kids insist on having more stuff. It is simply unbelievable what is viewed on TV today! Just thinking about marketers creating strategies, based on children as such strong influencers of household consumption, has me shaking my head.

As kids, we would rush back to school after summer vacation (even walked back) to catch-up on what our classmates did over the summer months. I remember the song, *See you in September*, ("…when the summer's through") by Frankie Valli and the Four Seasons. Today, social media allows you to check in with friends daily, no matter where they have gone. And you instantly know what's been going on and what others have been up to.

I grew up without anything having to do with the cyber world: electronic, digital, wired, virtual, Internet, online. These things had not yet been invented. I learned to type on a manual typewriter in high school and when you wanted to make a phone call, you needed a payphone, not an iPhone. All our relationships were face-to-face.

The day that Albert Einstein feared has arrived

It's been said that Albert Einstein shared this thought decades ago:

"I fear the day that technology will surpass our human interaction. The world will have a generation of idiots."

I figure that the failure of morality and ethics in keeping pace with all the new technology and population explosion is the most significant crisis of our time.

Don't get me wrong, I use most all of today's technology. My concern is that most kids have lost the skills of interacting with each other, looking at each other, eye to eye, and having the simple social action of conversation without a screen in front of them.

Today, some students are being forced into "Techno Detox" (a good thing) by handing in their mobile phones and other devices, before class. Because of today's "addiction to technology," Brighton College in the UK (a $50,000/year coed boarding school) for grades 7, 8 and 9 has kids handing in these devices at the beginning of the school day, to be put in lock-up and are returned to them after 4:00 pm. The Techno Detox bans the devices for all grades, in classes and public places, including the cafeteria. *Now get this:* The school's strategy is to wean kids off of their addiction while they are young, and to provide time and space for youngsters to learn the simple art of conversation and to look up and take notice of the wonderful (and not so wonderful) world around them. Additionally, it is hoped that the kids will discover the pleasures of physical activity.

What? All I can say to that is… *unbelievable!*

Today your GPS gives you directions, keeps you from getting lost, and even tells you if you've made a wrong turn. Kids may also get messages on the phone from their parents like, *"Dear Andy, How have you been? Your mother and I are fine. We miss you. Please sign off your computer and come downstairs for dinner. Love, Dad"*

There seems to be so much addiction today, especially with kids. It's become a part of our daily lives. News, Movies, TV—even a TV show titled *Intervention*, where we learn of yet another 17-year-old high school kid…rich, educated, and who loves to party and snort some cocaine. Why? "Emotions and personal Issues," they say. The indulgence gradually leads to daily use and then to an all-consuming compulsion. It's soon over. Under the weight of the addiction, the family eventually collapses.

Today there are very smart scientists and psychiatrics who are working hard to capture the multitudes of people who will ruin their lives through obsessive game playing, known as Addiction to the Grip of Gaming. But there are even smarter people building new e-stadiums and massive electronic game parlors (penny arcades, in my time) all for the purpose of keeping the addiction alive. All so very serious and dangerous. I keep hearing about "youth temptations" today and addictions of kids, because of their loss of emotional control.

And this is all in junior high and high school…and due to loss of emotional control?

There is extensive science today analyzing the brain and the subliminal triggers therein that excite the brain's reward system and thus the creation of addictions. Research is trying to find ways to keep people from the evils of these unseen triggers. It has touched every one of us in some way and will continue to be a major disaster in America and elsewhere.

There seems to be overwhelming concern and frustration with traditional addiction treatments. So now there are drugs that one can take to overcome the drug addiction on which they are hooked. Medications can help people quit drinking. While on this medication, if one takes a drink, the drug will make you throw up and feel like you're having the worst hang-over of your life (Let me think that one through…? Isn't that the same outcome of overindulging in alcohol in the first place?)

There are medications, today, that help people quit smoking, or help people quit using heroin. However, relapse is the most common, "you-can-bank-on-it" result. And there's still no known effective medical remedy for addiction to stimulants like cocaine and meth.

What's the answer? What power do others have in the way of control, and isn't this power available to everyone? Isn't there the power to take control of one's emotions and apply life's problem solving devices? Is that possible? Can everyone have these problem solving devices? The answer, of course, is… *YES*.

1960's High School Golf

I was on the high school golf team, basically by accident, at Northwest Classen High School. (The Knights, purple and gold, "Always Brave, Always Bold.") What I mean by 'accident' is that I had golf as a PE class. Mr. Smelser was head of PE and our golf coach was Mr. Hanes in our senior year. This was not a class on golf, per se, and I cannot remember any instruction. No fundamentals on the grip, the stance, none of that. And therefore, being on the golf team meant that during the last period of school we were off (out of school at 2:30) and either on The Meridian Golf Course or Lincoln Park Golf Course. As I remember, every now and then, Mr. Hanes would give us each a golf ball and say, "Have fun, boys." We would pile into cars and head out. We had days when we would play, trying to qualify for competitions with other high schools. I can't remember ever qualifying to play in any other school match, but I loved to play golf, just the same... and my golf-related anger was getting under control. Sometimes, instead of the golf course, we could be found at the Highlander. The Highlander Bowling Alley had a pool, snooker and billiard room where some of us "on the golf team" played golf on a snooker table. Each player had a numbered ball and the objective, like golf, was to play the course, in this case the six holes of the snooker table—in as few strokes as possible.

A great movie came out in 1961: *The Hustler*. It was a black and white drama about a small town pool hustler, Fast Eddie Felson played by Paul Newman, who thought he could make it in the world of big-time gambling. It also starred Jackie Gleason who grew up, in real life, as a pool hustler. Gleason did his own pool shots in the movie, while the great Willie Mosconi, advisor to the movie, did pool shots for Newman when Newman wasn't making his own. All three were very good pool players! The movie took place in a lot of dingy pool halls, full of unsavory persons, and actually sparked and legitimized a new pool craze, making it a mainstream sport in America. Thus making us, a bunch of "arrogant, snot-nosed, high school know-it-alls" and "wannabe hustlers" in the pool halls of Oklahoma City.

Malcolm has helped me recount some of our experiences during high school, as we then had our golf clubs, skate boards, and pool cues in the trunks of our cars. One of the great things about getting older, if you have friends from earlier days in your life, is that they can help you remember times, events, and things you can't pull up out of your own memory banks.

Ya got trouble, my friend; I say trouble, right there in Oklahoma City. Trouble with a capital "T," that rhymes with "P" and that stands for Pool. Trouble, trouble…

Malcolm filled in details on those times—as follows:

We had ourselves a couple of "little dingy" joints, for sure. The Empire Pool Room was on the 2nd floor, upstairs, above the Criterion Theater in downtown Oklahoma City. It had full sized English snooker tables. The place we frequented the most was the Ace Pool Room on 10th street. You didn't rack your own balls, as that was done by a one-armed attendant named Abdul. He did the racking of pool balls for you, when you shouted "Rack 'em" and then paid him 15 cents.

I remember watching Curly Hicks, a professional gambler and bookie, play one pocket (all pool shots had to hit each object ball into one specific pocket of the pool table) against Don "Fats" McLaughlin for $1 a ball. That was big, big money to us… back then!

Fats had performed something one might see only once in a lifetime. On a cold windy day five players had started a game of "golf," on the snooker table at the Ace (11' 8.5" x 5' 10") next to the front door, when Fats blew in and expressed his desire to get in the game. All the players had already taken their first shot at the "# 1 hole" and so there were 5 balls strewn about the table. The players could have been hospitable and cleared the table to restart the game for Fats. However, that meant everyone would have to draw a pill again. There was a strange looking little black bottle that contained red marbles (pills, the slang word) with a number on each pill. Each player would shake the bottle and draw a pill and the number on the pill would determine the order in which the players would shoot and the number of their object ball. Fats was by far the most skilled of all the players and the others knew that having him shooting sixth would put him at a disadvantage. Their only offer was to allow Fats into the game that had already started, but he would have to shoot in the sixth position. Without any argument Fats placed the #6 ball on the spot, positioned the cue ball behind the line and made a full table shot banking the #6 ball off the far rail and back into the #1 hole. He then proceeded to make all the shots, running the table, making his ball into holes #2 through 6 without a miss. This meant he placed his object ball on the spot after he banked it into the #1 hole, and each time thereafter. He then would play his next shot from where the cue ball came to rest, after his last shot. He had to play perfect leave of the cue ball every time while avoiding being "snookered" by the other five balls already on the table. I am pretty sure that this was the first and only time Fats or any of the other players had witnessed a player run all six pockets in a game of golf on a snooker table. This feat could be likened to a score of 59 in golf, a perfect game in baseball or rolling back to back 300 games in bowling. It was... well, I can't come up with any words to describe it.

The hustling gene must have been strong in the McLaughlin family as Fats had a brother named Booger Red. The legend was that Booger Red didn't even have a social security number. His main hustle was the card game of bridge. He hustled rich folks all over the country in high stakes card games.

In addition to all those great memories that Malcolm Haney wrote and sent to me, he reminded me, "Fats was also an accomplished golfer, but not good enough to beat my brother, Tom Haney, and Wayne Kime in the quarter finals of the Oklahoma City Four Ball Championship." Fats and his partner, Curly Hicks, lost to Tommy and Wayne 1-up at the Lincoln Park Golf Course. Years later, Fats won the national Gin Rummy championship in Las Vegas and wrote a book on how to play gin.

You literally don't see characters today like those we saw growing up. They were guys who didn't have jobs, nor health insurance or families or pension plans. When I try to describe the aura of Meridian Golf Course, I say it is best described as an outdoor pool hall that had Stormy Williams as our Minnesota Fats.

Stormy Williams at that time was a living legend to me, and a close family friend with the Haney family. Stormy Williams was born in Tuttle, Oklahoma in 1922, part Choctaw Indian. He graduated from Oklahoma University and thus was an avid OU Sooners fan and a New York Yankees fan, as most "Okies" were during the '40s and '50s. He liked to say that he and his wife Pat had 50 years of marital bliss, but Pat's version differed slightly. Stormy retired as a Claims Adjuster for the Ford Motor Credit company, where he was the world's foremost expert on finishing work early, so he could head to the golf course, and that most often would be The Meridian Golf Course. He won the Oklahoma City Amateur Championship twice, the Oklahoma Senior Amateur twice, and three times, teaming with partners, he won the Championship Flight of the Oklahoma City Four Ball. Stormy held the course record of 62 at his favorite OKC golf course...The Meridian. He also had a lifetime six hole-in-ones. He won countless other golf tournaments throughout the state of Oklahoma and was politely urged not to return to at least one golf course after fleecing the locals.

A character unlike any other, and a truly unique individual, Stormy was a legend of immense proportion. Many people said, "You haven't played golf until you have played with Stormy." I had not met or played golf with Stormy until Malcolm made that happen in the 1980s, just after Stormy's third OKC Four Ball Championship at 58 years of age. Malcolm and I were 34- year-olds at the time.

Through my work at Xerox, during those years, Oklahoma City was part of my Southern Region responsibilities. I was there a lot, especially after my first invite to play golf with Malcolm, Roy Clyde Walker and the legendary Stormy Williams.

Wearing a pith helmet, long sleeve work shirt, tennis shoes, and with a long towel hanging out of the back pocket of his shorts, Stormy, after our first three holes of golf at Kicking Bird Golf Course in Edmond, Oklahoma, started calling me Slats. He was referring to my legs, I guess, as in the long, thin wooden slats of a fence or bed. He never called me anything but Slats, from then on.

He talked out of the side of his mouth in a very gruff manner. When he talked, he was loud and the language he used was very colorful. He was the best of anyone I ever saw when it came to gamesmanship. A round of golf with Stormy Williams was a thing to behold. I had never laughed so hard, for so long, as I did in the time spent with Stormy on and off the golf course.

Stormy talked about the good ole days at The Meridian, where he played with a cast of characters like "Long Thumb" Kelly, "Whiskey Nose" Wilson, Al "The Indian" Cornell, Sam "Sausage" Wimbish, Fred "The Fat Man," Schindler, Lloyd "Pinky" Custer, and enough other reprobates of whom Dan Jenkins could write a couple more novels about.

Dan Jenkins has to be one of the best sports novel writers who ever sat down at a typewriter. (By the way, you can see Dan's letter to me from his fabric-ribbon, manual typewriter of 1980 vintage, later in this book.)

In 1974, I was given a copy of Dan Jenkins' 1970 novel, *The Dogged Victims of Inexorable Fate*. It contains the funniest golf story, *The Glory Game*, as an entire chapter of the book. Jenkins' characters in this book were Cecil *The Parachute* (because he fell down a lot), *Tiny, Easy, Magoo, Grease Repellent, Moron Tom,* and others—all characters Dan knew playing golf at Worth Hills, or Goat Hills as the locals called it. This was recognized as one of the *Sports Illustrated* Best Golf Stories ever run in the magazine.

Dan autographed my personal copy of the book as follows:

Go with God and your 1-iron! Dan Jenkins

Stormy Williams was, indeed, a Dan Jenkins kind of character, and was truly the real King of The Meridian Golf Course, for he was the perpetual club champion. The Meridian had a meager facility of a cinder block building as the clubhouse and was located down a gravel road, which almost every afternoon would billow with dust as the chiselers sped down the entrance to The Meridian, to get in the game.

When I got to play with Stormy, Malcolm Haney and Roy Clyde Walker, "ole Stormy" would verbally abuse Haney and me to no end.

Stormy said Malcolm had 'rabbit ears" and could pick up on all sounds in the vicinity while trying to hit or putt a golf ball. (Back in the '50s with advent of TVs, nearly every box had a "rabbit ears" antenna system consisting of two rods forming a V-shape connected to the set, used to pick up "over the air" TV broadcasts).

Just about everyone knows some golf etiquette, especially as golf is played with and in a moderate kind of behavior. Unlike baseball, football and basketball, there are no air horns blasted or heckling of golfers. Being quiet while others play their golf shots is normally understood – with no jingle-jangle of change in one's pocket, no talking, no messing with the golf cart or your golf bag, etc., etc. There are many players who are very sensitive to sounds around them when they play. Malcolm was one of those who was very easily distracted by sounds as he was preparing to hit a shot or putt.

Stormy, out of the side of his mouth would say: "Gawdam, Slats, you know a mouse can't piss on cotton, anywhere near ole Malc!"

Malcolm and I, plus many others sure do miss "ole Stormy," who was laid to rest, back in Tuttle, OK in 2012.

More high school days in the 1960s

As kids, "ole Malc's" and my interests were in golf (playing The Meridian, Lincoln Park and Lake Hefner golf courses) shooting pool and snooker, skateboarding, music and in cars. Malcolm and I liked going to The Meridian best of all because it was where we both began our golf experiences and it was just down the street from my home, less than 5 blocks away, and only one mile from Malcolm's house.

While playing high school golf I realized my golf skills were nominal at best, and I therefore could be very inconsistent with my drives –not long off the tee and not very straight. I never had any formal training… but the challenge was there for me and golf had me hook, line and sinker (an old fishing term, as I may have mentioned earlier in the book).

In the 10th grade a few of our buddies started calling ourselves names made by SPELLING our names backwards. I was Ekim Swodaem,

Malcolm was Mloclam Yenah and there was Evets Snommis – who even signed my year book that way. Others were Y'ddor Y'ddag, Mij B'boc, H'tiek Nitram, and K'caj Samoht.) Do you know any of these guys?

Another kid named Ronnie Winkler (Einnor Relkniw) had moved from Southern California to OKC in my junior year at NWC. He lived in the newest part of my subdivision (the big field with the horses was being developed) and we became friends. He certainly must have been in *transcontinental shock,* having moved from the ultimate thrill and excitement of surfing in Malibu to a place almost dead-center of America on the plains of Oklahoma. I walked over to watch his family move in, mainly because I was fascinated by a car they had. It was a 1957 customized Ford Station Wagon for drag racing and toting surfboards. I thought, *Surfboards in Oklahoma City? Hmmm?*

Ronnie's souped-up '57 Ford Wagon

And a station wagon at that? A station wagon was the car you never wanted your folks to get. However, this Ford Station Wagon was really *souped-up*, with the engine and air intake rising out of the hood. This machine had been modified for high performance, increased horse power and it could beat anything on the road. Ronnie became a hit with the custom car guys and drag racers. We didn't hang out together that much, as he didn't play golf, but I went to some drag races with him and that station wagon could fly if he just put some wings on it. My interests weren't in the drag racing so much, but I was interested in the surfing culture. The surfers in the movies seemed to have the best chicks, like Annette Funicello (the really cute girl and former member of the Mickey Mouse Club on TV). I was getting interested in girls and Surfer music, like *Wipe Out* and the groups such as the Beach Boys and the Ventures, which happened to be the greatest surf band ever. This had my attention. Their recordings of *Walk Don't Run* and *Pipeline* were the best. Ronnie's surf boards were hanging from the garage ceiling, and I knew for sure that they would never be on another wave. Not in Oklahoma, anyway.

I had quickly picked up on surfer tee shirts and longer hair. Not much longer though. Dad certainly wouldn't allow that. I discovered that lemon juice could highlight my hair with some blond streaks, but it was so sticky. Then I found *Light 'n' Bright* from the drugstore and I was now looking like a surfer dude: a tan dude with blond highlights. *Yes!*

That's when we discovered "the skate board." It was the summer of 1962. Malcolm and I made our own skateboards. We had to, there were no commercial made skateboards in Oklahoma City. Our skateboards were made with street roller skates attached to a board. As surfing became more and more popular because of the music and movies, skate boarding became the way for us to have our "surfing" fun, in a place where there were no waves. I didn't know of any waves in Oklahoma. We were sidewalk and middle-of-the-street surfers, no surf and certainly no sand beaches. It started in my garage. All we needed was a pair of skates, the kind you tightened on your shoes. We could find street skates, no problem. We would separate the front two wheels on the skates from the rear wheels, get a board of some kind and attach the skates to the front and rear of the board. We painted the boards with surfer stripes running down the middle of the board. Malcolm customized his skateboard, painting it gold with a black stripe. Mine was red with a white stripe!

How we made our skate boards

We didn't have Ronnie's souped up Ford Station Wagon to drive around in. The best vehicle that Malcolm and I had, which looked like anything close to a surfer's car in California, was Malcolm's parents' little Chevy II station wagon. Malcolm got his license four long months before me, in May 1962. We drove around surfing (looking) for paved hills in Oklahoma City, with his dog named Jigs sliding around in the back deck of the Chevy II along with sets of golf clubs and a shag bag of golf balls. "Get them cats, Jigs!" Just whispering those words would make Jigs go absolutely bonkers—barking and jumping around in that car like crazy. When we found the right kind of surf (paved incline of streets and sidewalks) we would park and go "skate boarding" down our concrete waves.

As a teenager, my free time (when not in school, in church activity, or working off my demerits by picking weeds out of Dad's okra or tomato patch and tilling Dad's compost pile given in punishment in my dad's system of punishment) was spent as follows:

Daylight – Golf on The Meridian, Lincoln Park or Lake Hefner golf courses, or skate boarding. Skate boarding proved more dangerous than golf, what with traffic on the streets, or worse—the likelihood of skating into a crevice in the pavement or even a skate wheel coming in contact with a small pebble. Any of those would send us over the top of the board. Scrapes and bruises were commonplace. It's hard to believe we never broke any bones.

Weekend Evenings – Cruising our favorite triangle, between the Delta, The Split Tee (named for the famous OU football formation) and The Charcoal Oven drive-ins or shootin' pool at the Highlander.

The Drive-in Theater

As the evening wore on and before the curfew hour, we would do a late-night stop at Bob's Big Boy restaurant for a coke float or milkshake—if we still had a quarter left after the Caesar Burger, fries, and coke from the Charcoal Oven. Or we might be sharing a quart bottle of 3.2 Coors beer that someone had been able to acquire from the Milk Bottle, a drive-through market on Classen Blvd. which is still there today.

The Milk Bottle on Route 66

The Milk Bottle market, a triangular building located on historical old Route 66 and on the National Register of Historic Places, was a likely place to obtain some 3.2 Coors beer. Coors beer back then could only be purchased in Colorado or Oklahoma because the beer had to be transported refrigerated because the beer was non-pasteurized, unlike today's Coors beer. Only 11 states could obtain the product which gave a mystique to the beer and a national cult following. Back then if the beer wasn't transported in refrigerated transport, it easily went flat.

The 1977 comedy-action flick *Smokey and the Bandit*, (starring Burt Reynolds as a trucker hired to illegally transport cases of Coors from Texas to Georgia) may have increased the mystique. Coors wasn't available in all 50 states until 1991.

Whenever I was out on a weekend night, Dad had this rule, "You'll be home by 11:45. And, son, if you're not early, you're late." His reason for the curfew was: "Nothing much good ever happens after midnight." I almost always remember Dad ending such comments with, "Do I make myself clear?" "Yes, sir!" was always my reply. As I've mentioned, I learned more about Dad and his resolve to establish absolute policies for us through the blunders of my older brother Steve. I learned from Steve's mistakes and Dad's authority in enforcing the house rules. And I had a lot of laughs with both my dad and Steve about the rules and regulations while living together as family. I was a slow learner at times, but I was learning "the system."

My dad was not a mean man, at all. He was tough, yet fair. I was learning that his system of discipline for me was for my own good and, most every time, he'd make a lesson when imparting the discipline. If some discipline was warranted for my failure to abide by some understanding on which we had agreed, he'd often ask me what I thought my punishment should be. Most often he would agree with what I came up with as the punishment task. I think of him now as unpretentious, kind, and gracious. He, in my opinion, was a very good LIFE teacher.

Oftentimes, when Dad was working on something around the house (he was very good with his hands and could fix or build most anything) he would say, "Hang around, you might learn something." I did. And I learned. I learned to listen and I learned that Dad often wanted to spend time with me. And those were always the greatest times, he and I being together.

Mom and Dad loved the music of the '30s, '40s and early '50s. Dad had a fabulous collection of LPs (long-playing albums) by such greats as Nat King Cole, Dean Martin, Patsy Cline, The Ink Spots, Ella Fitzgerald, Tony Bennett, Frank Sinatra, Bing Crosby, and anybody else who made an impact in that era.

Most everyone had a record console, not us.

While almost every household had some sort of record player-console cabinet (mostly in mahogany wood with a flip-top lid and record changer that played stacks of records), not Dad. That wasn't for him. Dad, being such an electronics enthusiast in home electronics, built it all himself. He had all the magazines and eagerly waited for the next issues of Popular Mechanics and Radio Electronics. He bought, by mail order, from Heath Kit Publications. I had never seen "component high-fidelity" systems in any of my friends' homes, so at first I thought all Dad's stuff was kind of nerdy—until I heard the results of his ongoing efforts to achieve the finest listening possible.

Dad's speaker cabinets were 3 x 3 feet, length and width, and stood some 4 feet in height, very big rectangular boxes. No one had anything like these that I had ever seen. Dad built and did all the hand finishing of the cabinets by himself. He sanded and applied the stain to the wood until he had just the surface finish he wanted. Then, came the application of a beeswax coating, for just the right luster. The inside of his cabinets were lined with a spongy, waffle like material before placing the drivers, bafflers, and 24-inch-diameter speakers inside. These monstrosities of boxes took up the corners of the living room with cables and wires connecting them. On the top of one speaker, Dad had a turntable, which could hold only one record at a time. (No record changer for him!) On the other speaker was an amplifier, whatever that was.

Dad said he built his own system so that he could sit down in the living room, close his eyes, and be right in front of the orchestra and vocalists. "Balanced and in phase," were his words. "Like your life should be, '*Tu sabes?*" Followed by my, "Yes, sir." When our friends heard the unbelievable sound quality of Dad's high-fidelity system, our house became more popular.

With the birth of Rock 'n' Roll music in the early- and mid-'50s, Little Richard, Elvis, Bill Haley and His Comets were recording on 45 rpms with one song per side. I liked the record changers that my friends had and asked Dad to get one. But Dad said "no way" because changers would easily damage the surface of the records by stacking them, and then the handling of these records by kids would scratch them for sure. Scratched records played with popping noises and the badly scratched records would move the needle. Plus, he believed that the Stylus of these crappy record players would ruin the records. (Dad had diamond tipped needles.) Damaged records would cause the record to become stuck, jumping back a record groove, and… replay, replay and replay. Hence the term "you sound like a broken record" referring to someone being annoyingly repetitive. Anyway, Dad's system was off limits to us kids and our 45s. But not for long.

With Mom's persuasion, Dad begrudgingly got us a 45 rpm changer, hooked it up to his Heath Kit custom sound system, and played those scratchy 45s of rock 'n' roll records. I think Dad became the first-ever dedicated DJ at a party. I remember a pretty good party that my brother Steve had at our house. Dad was lording over the equipment, taking requests. His face was in a grimacing expression of distaste and pain as the rock 'n' roll music with all the scratching and popping sounds of beat up vinyl discs filled the room with what he deemed to be "such annoying noise."

"…and it goes like this…Let's twist again, like we did last summer…
"Come on, baby… let's do the twist
"Come on, little miss… and do the twist!"

We would put a nickel on the top of the needle cartridge to keep it in the groves (literally) when our records were scratched and damaged.

A Corvette Story

I think everyone has a favorite car story or two… *ya know*, like a Corvette story, Mustang story, Chevy convertible, or a truck story.

Here is my Corvette story. Well not *my* Corvette, but a "Corvette story which is my story." Just to be clear…

Malcolm's older brother (Tommy) had an appointment to the Naval Academy at Annapolis, Maryland where he was the Captain of the Academy's Golf Team. Roger Staubach had an appointment at the same time and he was Captain of the Academy Football Team and Heisman Trophy Winner.

Mid-shipmen, that's what they call the undergraduates at the Academy, were not allowed to have automobiles at the Academy until the last six weeks of their senior year. This was in late 1962, which was when the new model of the '63 Chevrolet Corvette Stingray, the Split-Window Coupe, was introduced. And Tommy ordered one.

Malcolm went to the Naval Academy and drove the Stingray back to OKC. And, when it was back in "The City," I got to ride in the "Vette"— "The Midnight Blue," as we called it—a few times with Malcolm, even on a Friday Night "cruising" the drive-ins and looking so cool!

By the way, the "Vette" cost some $3,300, which was about half an ensign's yearly pay at that time. Tommy wound up selling the '63 Stingray Split-Window Coupe not long thereafter. But, for a little while, we were two 16-year-old kids driving the newest, latest, and coolest car ever!

On the TV program, *Counting Cars*, on June 25, 2018, the star of the show, Danny Koker, owner of the Las Vegas auto shop, who buys collectable cars and restores them before reselling, showed a '63 Split-window Corvette Coup, that he had acquired after a long search. It's quite something just to *see* one of those iconic original 1963 Split-Window Corvette Stingrays. This one was identical to Tommy Haney's. On the program Danny told viewers "Less than 11,000 of the model were produced" and that was some 56 years ago. Koker bought the "as is" '63 Corvette for $45,000. After restoring it to show room condition, it sold for $115,000.

My dad's 1960 Nash Rambler

Malcolm's mom's '62 Chevy II station wagon

Tommy's 1963 Corvette Stingray Split-Window Coupe
"The Midnight Blue"
Now valued at a minimum $115,000

So, you're 16 years old in 1962, just recently got your driver's license, and you have the choice: You can drive any one of these three autos for a weekend evening. How long to make your decision?

Our insurance agent, Mr. Kent, lived down the street and also dealt in used cars. He and Dad were good friends and we hung out with the Kent kids. Dad bought his cars from Mr. Kent, including the Rambler, a small Datsun, and Mom's Pontiac. It was Dad and Mr. Kent who, together, came to the scene of my first car accident.

This was an incident that I didn't want to fully explain, not in exact detail, anyway. Three of us (Malcolm, Bill Rankin and I) were out on a weekend night, in my dad's Rambler. The back of the front seat in Dad's car, could lay down flat and make a complete bed with the back seat. So, I was driving on the bed from the back seat, down 39th Ave., old Route 66, sitting so far back that I was steering the car with my long legs and my feet on the steering wheel. There was absolutely no way my feet could hit the clutch, accelerator, or brake pedals. I was showing off, driving from the back seat, cruising in high gear, when all of a sudden I needed to hit the brakes—but couldn't. I rear-ended the car in front, which threw all three of us forward. No one was seriously hurt, thank goodness.

Back in the '60s the drivers involved in a car accident, if not serious, would exchange license and insurance information and go on down the road. I decided to call home. When we found a pay phone I had my two buddies do the clean up on the inside of the car (beer bottles, cigarettes etc.) and move the seat back to its forward, normal and upright driving position and waited for Dad. My friends were going to help me with this one!

Dad and Mr. Kent arrived, and gave inspection to the vehicle. I said, "Just not paying attention, I guess, and ran into the back of the car belonging to this person." I handed the information on the other driver to Mr. Kent. "He drove on, as there wasn't enough damage for him to care about," I told them… but the front of the Rambler had a good dent in it. "My fault, Dad," I said. My dad and Mr. Kent stood there for a moment, looking quizzically at the three of us. "Mike just didn't see the car in time to brake, Mr. Meadows," said Malcolm. Since there was no major injury or damage, that could have been how it happened. But Dad seemed to know there was more to the story.

The Summer of '63

We were kids, each with our own driver's license, and in just a couple of months we would be seniors walking the halls of school—snazzy, cocky seniors! All other students would soon be looking up to us, for sure!

Playing golf along with cruising and shooting pool and snooker at the Highlander were our main activities. Cruising is that social activity of driving a car and was certainly our major summer evening's thing to do at the time.

It's best described as slowly driving one's car (or parent's car) to show off that car or to admire other cars. Oh yes… and to cruise chicks. "Don't look, but I think those chicks are checking us out."

Car radios were blaring KOMA or WKY radio stations, setting the mood. Our primary cruising vehicle was Maxine Haney's (Malcolm's mom) Chevy II station wagon. Not too impressive, as I wrote earlier… but we didn't have that many options.

The top songs were still the surfing songs: *Surfin' USA* by The Beach Boys, *Wipe Out* by The Surfaris, *Pipeline* by The Chantays, *Surfer Girl* by The Beach Boys and *Surf City* by Jan and Dean. "Come on, crank up the music, Malc!"

The girls liked the softer sounds of *He's So Fine* by The Chiffons, *Blue Velvet* by Bobby Vinton, *Hey Paula* by Paul and Paula, and everybody liked *It's All Right*… by The Impressions. *Say, It's All Right, It's All Right… It's All Right, Have a good time…'Cause It's All Right, Whoa, It's All Right.*

We heard about a new English rock group and their first hit Love Me Do in late '62, yet little did we know what that would mean to music and to American culture.

It was the best of times when we were out in Tommy Haney's midnight blue '63 Corvette, split-window-coupe Stingray. We would slowly drive through the drive-ins, as we got all the attention. Sometimes we would pull in and park next to other kids sitting in and on the convertibles or next to some cool kids sitting in a much desired two door hardtop.

This was long before the drive-thrus of McDonald's, Burger King, or Wendy's and the drive-ins allowed us to simply keep on circling the place, until you found a parking spot, if you even wanted to park. If you had "the car" you just kept circling.

One of my favorite movies of all time is *American Graffiti*, the George Lucas film, which came out 10 years later in 1973. For me this was a nostalgic look back to these times of being a teenager, accurately portraying the emotions we experienced as teens. I definitely connected to this distinctive American classic film and soundtrack.

I will, forever, remember one time while cruising with Malcolm, that was similar to what the film *American Graffiti* portrayed. We were parked at the Delta when a stunning, dazzling beauty of a girl (unlike any girl I had seen before) came driving by in some mother's station wagon. She was sitting in the front-seat passenger side and the wagon was slowly moving past when our eyes met. In that momentary glance she sent me her special, spiritual, romantic message… while slowly moving by.

"Malcolm, that's her! She wants me, Malc!" Malcolm was talking to kids on the other side of the car. "Yeah, right," he said. "No really, please, let's go… follow that Ford station wagon, please… Now!" I continued to rant: "She's the most amazing girl, ever! This is my chance Malcolm, please follow her! Come on, let's go!" But we didn't go, and my heart sank. *Oh, no,* I thought, *I will never see her again.*

I was mad at Malcolm for the rest of the night. Our last stop was at Bob's Big Boy, where the guys would meet up and talk about girls and whatever else teenage boys talk about. After finishing off some fries and a Coke, we drove to my house just before midnight. I hardly spoke to Malcolm on the way home. I was still mad at him.

Pulling into my driveway and as I opened the car door, Malcolm said, "Hey, Ekim Swodaem, I think the girl was looking at The Midnight Blue, don't you?" I would never know.

Senior Year: 1963 - 1964

We were, indeed, walking the hallways of high school, now the big shots. Talk of college, football, golf, and our "new music" were the most important subjects in school.

November 1963: Beatlemania and the shocking Kennedy Assassination

The Beatles seemed to come out of nowhere to conquer America in 1964, but in fact, we knew they were coming. We had already heard of The Beatles' extraordinary success in England. This was a big story in the months leading up to their arrival here, and some of America's top news outlets took notice. The biggest among them was NBC's Huntley-Brinkley Report, the leading network evening newscast of its time, and the forerunner to NBC Nightly News.

The hit *Love Me Do* had reached the top of record charts in the United States, and soon five of the top 10 songs of '63 would be by the Beatles.

The Beatles

Roy Orbison, the rockabilly star from Vernon, Texas with his soft hits *Falling, Blue Bayou,* and *Only the Lonely,* had just toured Europe with the Beatles and they became the top draw over Orbison.

In just a few years' time in the early '60s, the Beatles had grown from being a hot local band in Liverpool to the headlining act on tour across Great Britain. Yet only a few new little spots appeared on TV about the new rock group. I was interested in "Why Liverpool?" Why would this place have so many British groups birthed there? Probably because it was a major seaport of England, and the English sailors were bringing back Rock 'n' Roll, Rock-a-Billy and Blues from various U.S. ports like New Orleans.

But 1963 was the year the Beatles really caught fire in the United Kingdom. Their debut album, *Please Please Me*, was released that January, followed by two successive number one singles, *From Me to You* (in May) and *She Loves You* (in September).

On October 13, the frenzy surrounding the Beatles was given the name Beatlemania, with the group's landmark appearance on *Sunday Night at the London Palladium*. It was Britain's top-rated entertainment program, the equivalent of the Ed Sullivan show in the United States.

The Beatles were on tour in Sweden, Germany, and elsewhere overseas with lots of radio, television, and concert appearances. Returning to London on October 31, the Beatles were greeted by more than a thousand screaming fans. In the crowd at Heathrow, the day the Beatles returned from a tour, was Ed Sullivan, who soon booked the band for his New York show.

In America, the news media took notice. *Time* magazine described Beatlemania in an article headlined "The New Madness." That same week, NBC and CBS sent crews to cover the Beatles performing on Saturday, November 16 at the Winter Gardens Theater in Bournemouth. NBC was the first on the air the following Monday with its report by Edwin Newman. CBS aired a similar story on its morning show later that week.

American news coverage, including NBC's, took a bemused, patronizing approach, dismissing the Beatles as a passing fad perpetuated by throngs of hyperactive teenage girls. The focus was on haircuts and all the frenzy, while little attention was paid to the music itself. It wasn't until later that most people were able to see this moment clearly as the beginning of a huge generational shift and an unbelievable change in popular culture.

That same year, there would be another monumental change, brought on with the assassination of President Kennedy, that would change our nation forever.

I would guess that anyone over the age of 10 at that time, remembers where he or she were on Friday, Nov. 22, 1963 when they heard of the assassination of President John F. Kennedy. I had been out to lunch with high school buddies.

Upon returning to the school at about 1:00, someone said, "Did you hear President Kennedy was shot in Dallas?" The next thing one of us said was probably something like, "Yeah, right, what's the punch line?" As we all know, it wasn't a joke. We found our way into a classroom where there were TVs.

Nothing close to this had ever been "live" on any broadcast, ever. "Live from Dallas," they were transmitting from the Parkland Hospital where the President had been taken.

As we watched and listened, the story unfolded about the President arriving at Dallas Love Field, after a short flight from Ft. Worth, then the motorcade through downtown Dallas, driving by the Texas School Book Depository Building. We listened to reporting about shots fired that hit both the President and Texas governor, John Connally. Everything was so surreal, and so very quiet, except for some students and faculty in tears.

I knew downtown Dallas very well, including the location of the Texas School Book Depository. Our family drove by it every time we were in Dallas on our way to the First Baptist Church… so very close to where the assassination took place. This was all very eerie for me.

The major news stories forever changed our culture and especially how the public would receive news coverage. The assassination led the way into the all new "live TV coverage" and the media would now have to be ready to cover anything. Then it would be "live in front of us," just a few days later, when Jack Ruby murdered Lee Harvey Oswald—in front of our eyes—in the basement of the police building. That was the first murder broadcast nationally on TV. These were major turning points in broadcasting.

In the classroom, on school TVs, Walter Cronkite then made the announcement at 1:38pm that President Kennedy had died at 1:00pm Central Standard Time.

The country was in mourning; all Americans felt a tremendous sense of loss and for four days—from the time the motorcade passed the Depository Building and ending with the funeral procession in Washington—all major TV networks went live with suspended commercials.

We became "TV America" and all of a sudden it was the worst of times and the best of times.

The spark of Beatlemania jumped the Atlantic and set fire to a huge American audience. *I Want to Hold Your Hand*—the next great Beatles song—was promised for American release in January, but demand was so great that it was pushed up to December. The song exploded onto U.S. airwaves, topping the charts for 15 straight weeks, including a phenomenal seven weeks at Number One. On February 7, 1964, when John, Paul, George, and Ringo landed at New York's newly renamed John F. Kennedy Airport, the Beatles were at the top of the charts, even the world—just where they said they would be—and began the redesign of a worldwide culture.

Graduation

There were 600 students in my Senior Class, in the spring of 1964, and I was 17 years old. In cap and gown, the entire graduating class filed into Taft Stadium, climbed the concrete steps, and sat in alphabetical order. During the ceremonies, sitting on one side of me was the very cute Carolyn Meek (cheerleader, Princess of Friendship, Top Teen, All-Sports Princess, that Courtesy Club thing again, and every other membership that could be listed in the space by your name in the yearbook). On the other side of me sat Charlie Meadows (no relation), a Lancer (Geek), Chess Club (Geek) and Golf, which made him OK in my book! Charlie and I played a lot of golf together, primarily because our rankings were pretty equal on the golf team, that being mostly last, which seemed to always have us teeing off last. He had an incredible snap-hook and I had the big banana-ball slice. Charlie and I met up on the tees and greens, but didn't see much of each other during the times in between.

We filed down the steps, ceremoniously in order, walked over the cinder track (used for stock car racing and the Demolition Derbies on Friday nights) and up on to the stage in the middle of the football field.

The name "James Meadows" was announced on the loud speaker, right after Charles Meadows and before Carolyn Meek. I walked by and the principal, J. Frank Malone, handed me my diploma and shook my hand. That's when I said, "Hey, J. Frank Malone, my name is J. Michael Meadows, Graduate." I flipped the tassel to the other side of my cap and left the platform and podium and headed for the parties.

A few historically significant Baby Boomer events in a boy's life: 1946-1964

1948 – My igloo

1950 – Television

1952 – Mickey Mantle, World Series

1953 – Cub Scouts

1954 – I am a Polio Pioneer, at age 8… first group of kids to get the Polio vaccination

1955 – Little Richard and the beginning the Rock 'n' Roll phenomenon

1956 – Elvis Presley on the Ed Sullivan Show… and Boy Scouts

1958 – Arnold Palmer wins the Masters, Tommy Bolt wins the U.S. Open at Southern Hills in Tulsa, and Nikita Khrushchev is Soviet Premier

1957 – Ford Edsel car and Elvis is drafted into the Army

1959 – Arnold Palmer wins the Oklahoma City Open and NASA's first astronauts selected

1960 – Arnold Palmer wins the Texas Open, the Masters and the U.S. Open. Civil Rights, Elvis' two-year enlistment is over, The Twist is the rage, JFK elected as the first Catholic President. The introduction of the birth control pill

1961 – Arnold Palmer wins Phoenix Open, Texas Open, The Open at Birkdale with Tip Anderson (caddie). Alan Shepard in space, The Supremes, the Berlin Wall. I'm a freshman in high school

1962 – Arnold Palmer wins Phoenix Open, the Masters, Texas Open, The Open at Royal Troon with Tip Anderson (caddie), John

Glenn in orbit, The Beach Boys, Peter, Paul and Mary, Marilyn Monroe found dead at age 42… and I get my driver's license!

1963 – Arnold Palmer wins Phoenix Open and JFK assassination November 22, 1963

1964 – Arnold Palmer wins the Masters, OKC Open, The Beatles on the Ed Sullivan Show and mark a pivotal moment in American cultural history. High School Graduation at 17 years (and eight months) of age. Registering for the Draft on Sept. 3, 1964 at age 18

Parental Guidance 101

While growing up in Oklahoma with Texans as parents and grandparents I learned many things in interesting ways, with some lessons in life that have stuck with me through the years.

"One must understand that those you associate with and look up to are human beings, just like you." And, a personal favorite: "There is only one thing wrong with the human race," Dad would say, "People."

Mom, regarding people: "If you don't have something nice to say…" and you know the rest of that. The key was always respect. That "respect" thing, again.

Have respect for all individuals, especially family… and watch your mouth.

CHAPTER TWO

THE OLD COW COLLEGE

"You've got four years... that's it, son!"

That's what Dad said...
That's the amount of time given me to graduate from college.

It wasn't a goal, as in something you might possibly achieve. No, it was mandatory, and for more than a couple of reasons. So, I had been given the responsibility to make certain that "it" happened... *Le capisce? ... Tu sabes?... Lo entiendes?*

I knew during my high school years that I wanted to go to college at Oklahoma State University, the Old Cow College. The two state universities were my only choices, and it was OSU for me. This was because some good guys in high school and my brother Steve had gone to OSU. I was hoping to get a bid from Kappa Sigma (aka: "Tappa Keg Bumma Sig") fraternity during rush week. Some of these older friends were Kappa Sigs and when I did get their bid during rush week, the week before classes began, I pledged. I wanted to be in a different fraternity than my brother Steve (who was a Kappa Alpha) and make my own mark, so to speak.

This would be the first time that I was out of my parents' sight for more than just a few nights, like when I was camping out or at a friend's house. I was moving away, going to "live on campus" and (practically) "on my own" for the first time ever. I knew I was never going to live at home again. From now on I would be a son visiting his parents.

In the Fall of '64, I hugged Mom, reminded her that I'd only be 72 miles away, and left for university life. Dad drove me to Stillwater to the OSU campus and I moved in to the fraternity house where I would be living. I knew the college experience was going to be a lot more than just classes and homework.

On September 3, 1964 I turned 18 years of age. All male citizens of the United States, by law, had to register with the Selective Service within 30 days of turning 18. This meant registering for the draft into the Armed Forces of the United States. There has not been a military draft since the Vietnam era and the last Draft ended January 27, 1973.

Driving to Stillwater, Dad had another serious talk with me. He did most of the talking on the way, basically about how I had just four years to graduate, period, exclamation point! He said that he would be paying for my room and board, tuition, and books. "Your objective," he continued "is to graduate." He reminded me that by staying in school and making good grades, I would stay out of the "Vietnam thing," for a while anyway. I, of course, was thinking about chicks and all the fraternity parties. He then informed me that if I was going to be a party boy in this "fraternity thing", he strongly suggested I should get some sort of a part-time job when not in class, to make my extra money. True to form, he followed that suggestion with his standard question: "Do I make myself clear?" One of those talks again… followed by my dutiful "Yes, sir." Dad explained how he would be paying the $85 per month fraternity house bill, broken down, as follows: Room: $31, Board: $39, Social Fee: $15 and an annual building fund fee of $85. Dad also instructed me to keep my pants zipped. "You clear on that?" he asked. "Yes, sir," again, was my reply.

I would, therefore, be looking for a job—to acquire my FAM and WAM. That's Fooling Around Money and Walking Around Money.

KAPPA SIGMA
FRATERNITY

aka: Tappa Keg Bumma Sig

A few of the fraternity brothers and other students were "working their way through college" with part time jobs. I quickly got a job right where I lived. I was a kitchen boy at the Kappa Sigma house for my first year which eliminated my board payment of $39 per month. That gave me $39 more FAM and WAM, which meant I could drive around in my own car (a car Mom bought me for $220 of her own money, that I didn't think Dad knew about). Dating chicks, oh boy! I could buy a $1 worth of gas and a .25¢ can of Conoco oil on a weekly basis, and still have some $34 per month for dates, pizza, and beer. In those days, a pizza was $1.25 and a mug of beer was .50¢—and even a late night sandwich delivered to the house from the Sandwich Man was only $1.50. I was doing all right! "All…right?" I had it made! I was focused on girls, parties, pizza, beer, the fraternity and—oh yes… can't forget this—staying in school. Absolutely no flunking out, period. I clearly understood the main priority, as Dad said, "NO IFs, ANDs, or BUTs."

The best part of being a Kappa Sig pledge was the discipline instilled in the pledge class. Without that, I don't think I would have made it through my freshman year. The fraternity had a requirement of a 2.25 grade point average, minimum, for initiation. That is an equivalent C+ GPA. Dad, however, had the talk with me about what kind of grades he expected of me, saying that a C was not acceptable. He told me, "The grade of C is either the worst of the best, or best of the worst," and no matter how I looked at it, "C" he said, "was not acceptable. Period" Followed by (you guessed it…) "Do I make myself perfectly clear?" Followed by the mandatory "Yes, sir!"

I had a Big Brother assigned to me from the fraternity for guidance. There were rules, regulations, and protocols to be followed. In some ways it was somewhat like living at home with Mom and Dad, but with a lot more freedoms. There was a definite "pledge system" to follow. Rudolf Irving Greer (aka Rudy) was one of two high school pals who also pledged Kappa Sig. The fraternity had mandatory study halls for pledges in the dining room on Sunday through Thursday nights, most every week of the school year. Dad liked this part of the KΣ pledge system for my freshman year, and first year away from home. They had upper classmen as tutors in most every field of study. And my pledge class had the strict duties in the Pledge System as stated in the Pledge Manual, in regard to:

1. House Cleaning – every Saturday night, beginning at midnight and we all had to be sober and present.

2. Cleaning of the room you occupied, which was checked, literally, by a member wearing white gloves. (Fortunately, I had already been somewhat molded into the concept of having my work tasks inspected by my dad.)

3. The watch-care of the House Mom, Mrs. Sparling, was the pledges' responsibility. Escorting her to dinner every night, to and from her apartment in the frat house. We escorted her to church every Sunday morning and to any other functions on her schedule. We had to stand every time she entered any room of the house. I already had these things drilled into me from Mom and Dad, so they were no-brainers. Mom Sparling had all pledges attend her etiquette class—mandatory! I had already had much of this training from Grandmoney and aunt BB so I sailed through.

4. After Initiation and becoming a member of the fraternity there was a required "jacket and tie" dress code for the monthly fraternity chapter meetings and the same for the Sunday meal in the dining hall. No exceptions.

5. Each semester we had one formal dance in the house, requiring formal attire, as in "rent a tux."

6. House parties had dress codes, many informal (aka "grubby"). There was always a live band at our house parties.

7. We had a no-girls-in-your-room policy (strictly monitored) and a no-alcohol-in-the-house rule (yeah, right!) House parties had the proverbial punch bowl, which got me very familiar with the Singapore Sling, a delightful sweet concoction of gin, cherry-flavored brandy, more gin, triple sec, a little more gin, pineapple and lime juices, more gin, and grenadine. The trick was making sure there was enough gin in the concoction. We drank so much of that shit toward the end of the dance (and before the band played

"Don't it make you want to Shout... A little bit softer now... a little bit louder now, a little bit louder now..."). Someone yelled "Gator," and most all of the brothers were on the dance floor groveling to the music.

Fraternities and sororities were large and dominant institutions on campus in the '60s. The main activities were studying, playing bridge, poker, watching too much TV, and waiting for the late night arrival of Sandwich Man coming through the front door of Tappa Keg Bumma Sig.

The main campus hangout was the Coachman Inn for a great burger and a beer. Stillwater back then was a small college town with nearly everyone living there associated somehow with the school. The only time it was difficult for an under-aged student to buy a beer was during an election year, when someone wanted to tighten up the availability of beer, as a campaign tactic. How foolish that was! There were private "Bottle Clubs" in Oklahoma for those who preferred spirits over beer, which was not a lot of students. Those drinking establishments required that you have a paid membership and your own bottle stored there with your name on it and you paid for just the "set-ups," the mixers.

Oh yes, there was one other little thing before the start of my '64-'65 freshman college year. There was the beginning of a steady escalation by President Lyndon Johnson in an attempt to explain the need for increased military intervention in Asia. He explained that America had no choice, because North Vietnam and Communist China sought to "conquer the South, to defeat American power, and to extend the Asiatic dominion of communism." Johnson stated, "An Asia so threatened by Communist domination would certainly imperil the security of the United States itself." Johnson's administration was called "The Great Society," the goal of which was to eliminate poverty by instituting federally sponsored welfare programs. We had fun with that one! Our Freshman Pledge Class had the responsibility of decorating the outside of the fraternity house each Homecoming. My pledge class acquired an old beat-up car, raggedy furniture, trash, and a barrel with a fire in it and placed all those items in the front yard of the frat house as we stood around as hobos with a big sign that read THE GREAT SOCIETY.

KΣ '64-65 Homecoming Theme: The Great Society

I had a student deferment, II-S classification, like all male college students, but that was only good if you made passing grades and advanced to the "next level" — for me, getting to my sophomore year. Flunking out of school was an automatic and immediate ticket to being inducted into military service: six weeks basic training and then off to Asia. We (Dad and I) knew this conflict was not going to end during my four years of study and that "the draft" would continue.

Dad had been part of my enrollment process, helping me to select the classes I would be taking my freshman year. He put me in Physics, of all subjects. Oh, no! Knowing also, that I had a military obligation ahead of me and the certainty of "the draft" in the Vietnam conflict, Dad and I came to the conclusion that the best preparation for military service would be to enter the service as an Officer, rather than being drafted. Therefore, I enrolled in the Air Force ROTC program at OSU. That year, my freshman year in 1964-65, more men and boys were drafted into military service than in any other year. This conflict in Asia was not going away.

The conflict in Asia pretty much kept all male students wanting to stay in school and focused on "making grades." College kids were, of course, presented with the moral temptations of the times, and I was no saint.

100

We were not exactly uncompromisingly moral. Many undergraduates, good kids from good families, spent too much time getting drunk and throwing up on each other, but that eventually resulted in poor grades and flunking out. And flunking out back then meant that one had lived a college life with disregard of the intellectual work entrusted to them by their parents. What a waste, for then it was... Good Morning Vietnam!

The Reserve Officers' Training Corps (ROTC) has a proud legacy within the U.S. military and on college campuses, where hundreds of thousands of cadets have trained since the program began in 1916.

ROTC classes were military classes and actual military drills on campus as part of college credit. After four years and my completion of the training, I would enter the Air Force branch of the U.S. military service as an officer, Second Lieutenant, and that would be much better than being an army "grunt." This was preeminent in my college plan, preparing me for post-grad military service. I signed up knowing, for sure, that I was going to have to serve my country.

So, there were four major factors (incentives) for making better than a C average in GPA:

1. Initiation into the Kappa Sigma fraternity

2. Avoidance of being drafted into the Vietnam Conflict during the next four years by staying in school and ROTC—period, exclamation mark!

3. Meeting Dad's criteria, and fulfilling my commitment to him, which was second in importance, only to...

4. To Go With God, live faithfully, even do more than survive in college...to enjoy it, even bask in the opportunity and privilege made possible by my parents and my own resources to learn, grow, and mix in a little partying, too!

The mandate was to stay in school and graduate within four years. There were no other options. No one could take time off from school. There was no such thing as a "gap year." Taking time out from school was called "dropping out" and that meant being drafted into military service.

After getting me settled in the fraternity house, Dad said "Come on, I want to take you to the bank." The bank? I didn't get it. But, we drove to the Stillwater National Bank, met with a bank officer and we (Dad and I) cosigned on a 90-day note for $200. We opened an account with the $200 and put the money in a savings account in my name. We then opened a checking account for me.

We left the bank, had a burger, and talked about what had just happened. He said, "Don't touch that money." He explained how he wanted me to go back to the bank in 60 days or so, before the note was due, and pay the note off, including interest. *Why?* I was wondering. Dad said he'd be back, maybe for a football game, and that we would go and do the same thing all over again. Dad continued, saying it would cost me a little interest, but we were building a relationship with the bank and the banking officer, and getting me some financial references and building my credit history. Dad said, "It's time for you to manage not only your time, but your money, too." Into my checking account, I was to deposit Dad's monthly check. He expected me to pay my tuition, house bill, books, and other expenses from my own account. This was the first of many other business transactions that Dad and I entered into with each other. There would be loans and purchase agreements between us and he would always say, "Let's write down what we are agreeing to and both sign it, because I might forget what we have agreed on."

College life was an interesting mix of experiences. For example: The attire for all football games at Lewis Field (OSU Stadium) back then was jacket and tie. What is it today? Body Paint!

Oklahoma University's longest football winning streak against Oklahoma State was from 1946, my birth year through 1964. In other words, OSU never beat OU until I arrived on the campus at Stillwater! The Oklahoma State Cowboy football team finally beat the Oklahoma Sooners in both my freshman and sophomore years in 1965 and 1966. The first time ever in my life! Go Pokes! So, *Boomer Sooner that*, to *all y'all* OU "Buttholes!"

Dad did come back to Stillwater, but not for a football game. There was a little hazing accident at the Kappa Sig house that happened not long after classes had begun. During one of the "white glove" inspections of my room, a couple of upper Kappa Sig classmen thought the room windows needed cleaning on the outside. My room was on the second floor and outside of the window was a ledge about 24 inches in width. I was sent out on the ledge with soap and water. I slipped and fell to the concrete basketball court below sustaining a concussion and a broken wrist.

Dad, in his standard IBM dark suit, white shirt and tie returned to Stillwater, and after visiting me in the hospital, went straight to the fraternity house. I was glad I wasn't there for his meeting with the officers. As anyone might imagine, pledging Tappa Keg Bumma Sig became quite a bit easier, for me, during the rest of my freshman year.

I made my grades, made it through Hell Week and was initiated into the secret bonds and brotherhood of Kappa Sigma. My first year at OSU was just great. I had older friends from high school who were members of KΣ. My pledge class was made up of "still-wet-behind-the-ears tenderfoots," who were away from home for the first time in their lives. We lived together, studied together, worked together, and even serenaded the sorority houses together. And the strictness imposed on me as a pledge was not much different than that imparted on me in my youth at home with Mom and Dad. The pledge system was a necessary part of my freshman year, and I believe it greatly helped with the transition from living at home to college life.

In late 1965 my parents moved to San Antonio, Texas. It was a result of Dad's request of IBM and was more than 500 miles away from what I knew as 'home.' He wanted to get back to Texas and work until he was 55 years of age, take early retirement, and live out the rest of his years in his beloved state of Texas. He requested and was assigned to Kelly Air Force Base and the newly announced IBM O/S (Operating System) with 360 installations there. His plan had, definitely unfolded. No real surprise there.

After my freshman year I returned to my parents' home in San Antonio for the summer, where I had a summer job with IBM, as an IBM Installer in the Office Products Division of IBM. I was primarily installing—of all things—the new "golf ball" typewriters, the IBM Selectric Typewriter, in business offices all over town. The Selectric Typewriter was unbelievably popular and I lost count of how many times I heard people say "Hey, looks like some kind of golf ball in there…"

First, however, I had to attend a week-long class on Customer Care before IBM would allow me to set foot in any of its customers' places of business. This entailed lessons in IBM culture of Respect for the Individual, Providing the Best Service in the World, and Excellence. I mean "déjà vu." My training came with a Systems Manual, too.

Customer Courtesy was of primary importance. I was also trained in how to unpack the Selectric Typewriter (and other equipment), how to plug it in, how to go through the installation test, how to give perfect instructions to the operator, and (finally) the proper repacking of the packing material and disposal of the same. There was a process for everything at IBM. I worked in proper IBM attire, too! Just like Dad: dark suit, white shirt, tie… and no loafers.

This is when Dad made the strong suggestion that I should take an evening class at San Antonio College and continue my college studies during summers. *"What?"* He said, "You should enroll in a class where the course credit would transfer to Oklahoma State, thus reducing my study load the coming year. I enrolled in Civics class where I met another Kappa Sig, from North Texas University (The Mean Green), in Denton, Texas and he also played golf. He introduced me to Breckenridge Park Golf Course in the middle of the beautiful Breckenridge Park, in the center of downtown San Antonio where in 1955 PGA professional Mike Souchak scored a 60 and a 257 total in the oldest Texas PGA Tour event, The Texas Open. With that 60, Souchak set and held the single-round scoring record for 22 years, until Al Geiberger shot a 59 in 1977.

I got to know all the IBM Office Product Division salesmen and customer engineers in the San Antonio office. I was in all of their customers' offices, and there was nothing more important than an IBM Customer.

I was invited to play golf many times with the IBM salesmen and was even invited to play in the IBM office tournaments. We played at Breckenridge Park, Oak Hills, and Pecan Valley Golf Clubs.

After returning to Stillwater for my sophomore year at OSU in 1965 and '66, I got a part-time job (and a highly desirable job, it was) at Harold's Men's Apparel, as a clothing salesman, selling men's very fine, traditional clothing. It was there, at Harold's, that I met Mike Hyatt whom I have known and called my friend since 1966. Our salary was 75¢ per hour plus 1% sales commission. Gant shirts sold for $5, as did all neckties and belts. Cole Hahn shoes sold from $29.95 to $85 (for the alligator saddle oxfords) and suits, slacks, and accoutrements were in the inventory to sell.

Mike was a Finance major and Economics was my major. Mike was a member of another fraternity, Phi Gamma Delta. We had six salesmen, each from a different fraternity, working different shifts, and as finely dressed as we could be. One of our other salesmen was Burns Hargis, Sigma Nu, who is now president of Oklahoma State University.

Mike Hyatt and I established our sales fraternity of the clothing store and named it Eta Mu Alpha in the Greek letters for HMA, Harold's Men's Apparel. The purpose of the clothing store fraternity was to organize our own group of guys, who were all friends and clothing salesmen at Harold's... and for fun and giggles, of course.

"Hey Mike, the next guy coming into the store... you have to sell him a pair of socks." And "The next person that comes in, Rudy, you have to sell him an umbrella," and stuff like that. Located on the corner of University and Knoblock Street, Harold's was the glue that bonded us as good friends and we had fun selling clothes to the students and faculty of OSU. Without a doubt we were the best dressed students on campus, real B.M.O.Cs.

During my four years at the Old Cow College, 1965 – 1968, OSU was not a hotbed of unrest. I saw no student protests. I cannot remember seeing any peace or freedom marches, love beads, draft card burnings, or use of marijuana or LSD. There was, as I remember, a Panty Raid outside of one of the girls' dorms where girls would throw down some panties to the screaming guys gathered outside. That was the most likely way any of us would get to see panties, as girls back then wore girdles, which I must say, was one of the best methods of birth control ever. There is no easy way to get a girdle off! This was long before panty hose. Panty Raids never became part of the sorority culture, however. There were no co-ed dorms. There were curfews for all women. OSU fraternities and sororities were a big part of social stability and educational influence on campus.

A fraternity brother, Chad Alexander, who grew up in Stillwater and whose parents still lived there, moved into the fraternity house. That proved again that few kids want to go to college while living at home. Chad had recently won the State Left-Handed Amateur Golf Championship. We quickly became friends. He helped me with my golf game and I made the Kappa Sig Intramural Golf Team, ranked #8 man… out of the team of eight. We became fraternity house roommates and removed everything from our room, including desks. We only had our bunk beds and our stereo record player-radio. We listened to either the Four Tops, or Buck Owens and the Buckaroos. I spent my leisure time selling clothes at Harold's, working as Kitchen Boy at the frat house, and playing a little golf. I had no time for student protest. In fact, I never was aware of any protests on the campus.

As I remember college days, we wore jackets and ties to most frat house dinners, monthly chapter meetings, and most football games. Our house parties were in the dining room (no alcohol allowed in the house) with a live band. Studies were important, even after initiation, because "flunking out" would mean the end to a student deferment and, quite possibly, an involuntary trip to Vietnam.

Oklahoma State University has had quite a record in college sports. As of 2018, Oklahoma State has 52 NCAA team national titles, which ranks fourth in terms of most NCAA team national championships. These national titles have come in wrestling (34), golf (11), basketball (2), baseball (1), and cross country (4). There are, currently, 14 OSU golfers on the PGA Tour and five on the Champions Tour.

CHAPTER TWO

I had known that I would never get a college scholarship, academic or for any sport. I also knew that there was never even the remote possibility that I would be a professional sports figure of any kind. Yet, I was continually seeing just how important the game of golf was going to be to me throughout my entire life. By the way, an amazing golfer from OSU, Bob Dixon, in 1967, won both the U.S. Amateur Championship and the British Amateur Championship.

It wasn't until later, after graduation and when I was out of school, that I noticed our nation's students turning to more political issues. The fraternities and sororities seemed to redefine themselves on social issues with seemingly less emphasis on scholastics, parties, and appearance.

Appearance? At Oklahoma State University? Certainly, we did have Preppies— to whom, we (at Harold's) sold clothing. We had our Aggies, as well. Before becoming OSU in 1958 the school was known as Oklahoma A & M (Agriculture & Mechanical). I had some fraternity brothers who didn't own a pair of shoes, just boots. A couple of them, two brothers, were from just outside of Pawhuska, Oklahoma, and the Van Edwards Ranch empire. Which reminds me of Edna Ferber's book *Giant*, and James Dean as Jett Rink. There was even a fraternity on campus, named Farm House, made up of guys from the ranching and farming communities, not to be confused with National Lampoon's *Animal House*. There was a good cross-section of students at OSU—rich, poor, Aggies, Preppies and everything in between. Back then, we didn't think much about all that.

My college experience was actually (despite the Vietnam "conflict" pressures and Dad's pressures on me) a great experience and lots of fun. In hindsight, I've realized that I owe it all to Systematic Parental Guidance.

At college we all talked about Vietnam. One could not avoid seeing the fighting, casualties, and political posturing in the media, almost daily, and most everyone felt strongly about stopping the threat of Communism. Few people, it seemed, thought of doing anything drastic to avoid the draft. It was all about being well prepared for military service, should the conflict continue. I think everyone thought, in 1965, that it wouldn't last more than a couple more years. Yet in 1967 alone, some 228,000 more eligible young men were drafted.

107

One out of every 10 Americans who served in Vietnam was a casualty. Of the 2.7 million who served, 58,148 were killed and 304,000 wounded. Although the percent of brave men who died was on a par with other wars, amputations and crippling wounds were 300 percent higher than in World War II.

It was March 1968, my senior year, when I was summoned by the Selective Service System, through my local (OKC) draft board, to take the pre-induction physical. This was a sober reminder of the fact that graduation was fast approaching. After which I, too, would be entering into military service. But at least I would have an officer's commission as "2nd Lieutenant Meadows," which of course, was the best way to enter active duty, as an officer and not a grunt.

Of course, the Selective Service Administration was more anxious about my college graduation than I was. It was certainly OK by me to have my pre-induction physical completed before graduation. I would have my Second Lieutenant "ticket" upon graduation. Not only that, but I had, through summer work with IBM, made acquaintance with high-level military personnel at Fort Sam Houston including Colonel Hume who said something to the effect of, "Let us know when you get any notifications on entering the service, and we'll find a place for you upon your graduation." Seemed like I was a shoe-in back in San Antonio, Texas.

Air Force ROTC and pre-induction physical exam

The Selective Service's goal was to have the induction physical out of the way and the country's "Greetings Letter" from Uncle Sam in the hands of graduating college students so that the military drafting proceedings could begin immediately following graduation. Graduating male students were being grabbed up fast, sometimes even on the day they were getting their diplomas.

I went to Oklahoma City for the pre-induction physical. I found myself there with a lot of other college students from OSU, some I knew from classes we'd had together, others I recognized from campus. I even saw some old high school friends who had elected to go to *that other* university in Norman, the University of Oklahoma.

In a big room, we were processed with assembly line-like precision. Undressed down to our skivvies, doctors gave each of us a quick "medical exam." We were told, "Just stay in line and follow the guy in front of you." That guy happened to be some guy in his underwear, following another guy in his underwear. It was a slow line and finally someone took a look at me. I was being checked out mostly with those tiny flashlight things, with the doctor looking into eyes, ears, listening to heart and lungs, a quick rectal exam and then the "turn your head and cough instructions."

On that day, I had two recent letters with me, both from otolaryngologists (ear, nose and throat doctors)—one from the Oklahoma City Clinic and one from a doctor at a clinic in Stillwater. The letters included the records of my most recent otitis media (chronic, middle-ear infections). I had received written instructions from my draft board to "BRING PHYSICIAN'S CERTIFICATE DESCRIBING ANY CONDITION WHICH, IN YOUR OPINION, MAY DISQUALIFY YOU" when reporting for the physical exam. Well, the OKC Clinic had been seeing me and treating me for 19 years, regularly since 1949, and that was all documented in one letter. The other letter referenced my two visits, in 1968, at the OSU Clinic.

One of the doctors looked at the letters and gave me a little bit more attention with his flashlight. Looking into my ears again, he said, "I can't see into your ear canals." That, I knew. I was told to get back into line and go through the last examinations. When I had my clothes back on I was told, "You'll be getting notification in the mail from your draft board."

There were many men (men-boys) who went to all kinds of lengths to resist the draft during the Vietnam conflict. Some of the ways used to evade the draft were quite ingenious. Many took the Conscientious Objector route and some even defected to Canada. The tidal wave of resistors and objectors was larger than experienced in all other wars in U.S. history and more than 20,000 men were indicted for non-cooperation with the Selective Service System.

WWII was considered a "just" war, a justifiable response to the aggression of Germany and Japan. During the time of that induction process, a few young men would fail the physical exam, due to poor vision or shortness of stature. Those who were refused induction were most often embarrassed and felt ashamed at being classified as "unfit to fight."

However, during Vietnam, there were many ways that men went about misleading the Selective Service System and obtaining some kind of "not qualified for military service" classification. One's notification to appear for pre-induction physical allowed some 30 to 60 days to prepare for the examination. Some moved (defected) and changed citizenship. Many went on extreme diets and came to the physical underweight and malnourished. Some got drunk the night before their physical or took drugs to throw off the doctor's findings. Faking a stutter, another trick, most often didn't work. You could always commit a felony, because felony convictions keep you out of the service. But a felony record could have life-long ramifications... so that was low on the list of tactics. Another method was that of total non-cooperation, which would get you a sentence of four years in jail.

Young men were going to crazy extremes to convince their draft board that they were unfit for service, seeking the IV-F classification. Sometimes it worked; sometimes it didn't. There was one guy who soaked a pack of cigarettes in black ink, let them dry out and then smoked them before going for his physical. The exam's chest X-ray showed enormous amounts of black spots on the kid's lungs. He got his IV-F. Soon, thereafter, those who were giving medical exams learned of that particular "cheating method" and when black spots appeared on a chest X-ray they would hold the young man in a military hospital for a few days only to find that, miraculously, the "TB" was gone in the next X-ray.

Evaders even went as far as entering a seminary in order to get the IV-D draft evasion classification, as ministers of religion or divinity students. Atheists, agnostics—all sorts of non-believers enrolled in Divinity and were showing up in classes on Theology, all to evade military service. No doubt some of these "wackos" are standing at pulpits today.

You may wonder what my stance on military service was in the '60s and where I stand today. I have always believed that, in principle, war was good. It is a nation's duty to guard its sovereignty, maintain its freedom, and protect its citizens from the horrors of conquest by a foreign power.

I believe we, Americans, are free today because of military victories. A strong military averts conflict and deters aggression.

Preparedness is the key, and when I entered college in 1964, during the Vietnam conflict and having a military obligation to fulfill, my best plan for "preparedness" was to train through ROTC at OSU.

After my pre-induction physical, I drove the 72 miles back to Stillwater and the Kappa Sig house. Later that day, I found a note on the message bulletin board—a telephone message for me from Howard Kochwelp, the branch manager of IBM in San Antonio. The note said to call him back.

When I returned the call, Mr. Kochwelp said, "Meadows, the reason I called you was to tell you that I want you to join the sales team here in San Antonio, and be with us as soon as you can." My reply was something like, "But Mr. Kochwelp, I haven't even graduated yet and, besides that, I just had my pre-induction physical. Upon graduation I will have a two-year obligation in the Air Force." "But," I told him, "I would have absolutely loved to work for IBM and for you."

He replied, "Well, if you have to go, you have to go. But rest assured that when you come back, I will have a place for you on this team."

I was not uncomfortable with the uncertainty ahead, because (I think) I was prepared for either of the two outcomes: becoming an IBM salesman or serving in the U.S. Air Force as an officer, USAF 2nd Lieutenant Meadows. I was fully expecting the latter. The Air Force song— "Off we go into the wild blue yonder... flying high into the sky..." played in my head again and again. I was prepared for military service and ready to serve, as I had paid the price (Air Force ROTC classroom training, drills, and wearing an Air Force Blue uniform) at least once a week during my four college years.

All senior male students at OSU as well as young men across the country at other colleges and universities were all in the same sort of dilemmas— not knowing their fate, yet expecting to serve in the military for at least two years. Many, soon-to-be-graduating males began interviewing for jobs with the uncertainty of their fate. Everyone was pondering the same question: *Am I going to be drafted?* Companies who wanted to hire new graduates were in the same fix of simply not knowing.

As to my personal beliefs regarding war and this Vietnam conflict: The enemies to American freedom are other nations that are power oriented and function under some system of tyranny. The United States has come to be the greatest nation in the world because of our military power. The military preserves our freedoms, keeping us safe from external enemies, just as the police protect us internally.

During that period of uncertainty, I never had any questions in my mind about how the concept of war aligned with my religious beliefs. I asked myself: *Can a believer in Jesus Christ, a Christian, serve his country as a soldier, kill the enemy, and at the same time still be a good Christian?* ABSOLUTELY! Yes, was my answer!

Did God contradict Himself in the commandments, "You shall not murder." Absolutely Not! If you know The Bible you know the answers.

God established a principle by which a nation may guard its sovereignty, and an alert and stalwart military force averts armed conflict and deters wanton aggression. When an enemy aggressor will not be deterred, then the military must defend and protect those who cannot defend themselves.

Six weeks after my pre-induction physical I received word from the Selective Service Administration notifying me of my classification: **"FOUND NOT ACCEPTABLE FOR INDUCTION UNDER CURRENT STANDARDS."** This was a medical deferment of 1-Y in my qualification for service in the U.S. Armed Forces that stated: "draftable only in time of war or national emergency." Vietnam had not been, nor ever would be, classified as a war; it was referred to, merely, as "a conflict." The date of my notice was May 2, 1968 and stated on my classification card in a small notation, "Re-exam six months," which would have been Nov. 2, 1968. What was I to make of that?

Little did I know that this was going to be an unbelievable roller coaster ride and one long nightmare of unimaginable proportions for a young man's future.

I immediately called my parents in San Antonio and talked to Mom and Dad. I explained the Selective Service pre-induction physical, my classification, and told them that I was going to call Mr. Kochwelp at IBM and discuss the situation. I made that call and Mr. Kochwelp said he had a place for me right away, as soon as I graduated. I accepted and he congratulated me on my decision to join IBM. He told me that he would have me in the first available sales training class at IBM following my graduation in May.

In regard to the "re-examine six months" issue, I was sure that if I couldn't pass the pre-induction physical examination the first time, I wouldn't have any problems if and when I was called again.

May 1968—age 21 years and eight months—Mission Accomplished

Graduation ceremonies took place at Lewis Field, Oklahoma State University.

The whole shebang: cap and gown, diploma, *Pomp and Circumstance...* and an undergraduate degree **Bachelor of Science in Economics**.

Important worldly stuff which happened during College years 1965 – 1968

1964 – KΣ Pledge JMM becomes Kitchen Boy at Kappa Sigma fraternity

1965 – Students for a Democratic Society (SDS) anti-war marches in Washington, DC, Draft Card burnings
Oklahoma State Cowboys beat OU Sooners in Football at Louis Field, Stillwater, and first win over OU in 20 years! Go Pokes!
JMM initiated into Kappa Sigma
Mom buys me a 1955 Chevy sedan without Dad knowing about it
Malcolm X, an African-American Muslim activist, assassinated in Harlem
The riots in the Watts area of Los Angeles for six days, and the first of several major urban riots

1966 – Department of Housing and Urban Development (HUD) is established
Clothing Salesperson of the Year at Harold's Men's Apparel

JMM with Mike Hyatt founded the Eta Mu Alpha social
    fraternity

JMM is elected first semester Social Chairman of Tappa Keg

Oklahoma State Cowboys beat the OU Sooners in football
    (again) at Norman, OK!

JMM is forced to be second semester Social Chairman (a matter
    of the budget and amount of moneys spent on parties the
    first semester)

Department of Transportation created

JMM buys 1966 Chevy sedan on return to Stillwater for $95

Miranda v. Arizona establishes Miranda Rights for suspects

JMM becomes 8th man on the Kappa Sig intramural golf team,
    with teammate, Chad Alexander the former Oklahoma State
    Left-Handed Amateur Champion

Feminist group National Organization for Women (NOW)
    formed

Heavyweight boxing champion Muhammad Ali (Cassius Clay)
    declares himself to be a Conscientious Objector, refusing
    induction into military service

1967 – The first Super Bowl: Green Bay Packers defeat the Kansas City
    Chiefs 35–10

Detroit race riot precipitates race riots in 159 other cities

The "Summer of Love" counter culture… and Hippies

Dad buys Mike 1957 Chevy convertible

My pin-mate from Okmulgee, OK becomes Tappa Keg Dream
    Girl at the Rose Formal

1968 – Dr. Martin Luther King Jr. is assassinated

The Civil Rights Act is passed

J. Michael Meadows graduated OSU at age 21, joins IBM

New York Senator Robert F. Kennedy is assassinated

Police clash with anti-war protesters in Chicago, outside the
    DNC

United States presidential election with Richard Nixon elected
    president

CHAPTER THREE

LIFE IN THE REAL WORLD

The IBM Corporate Man
June 1968

In June of 1968, shortly after OSU graduation, I was sent to White Plains, New York to attend the IBM Office Products Basic Sales Training for six weeks.

Back when Dad went to work for IBM, aka Big Blue, in Data Processing around 1938 - 39, IBM was already thirteen years old and had just acquired the Electromatic Typewriter Company of Rochester, New York. That company had been manufacturing a big, black noisy frightening monster in the early years of the Depression. Their product neither looked nor operated like the machines that IBM was going to produce.

IBM put its engineering, production, and marketing savvy into perfecting and manufacturing the electric typewriter and started a revolution.

The first successful electric typewriter

In 1934, more than $1 million was invested by IBM in the new typewriter, which was designed to be completely free of the operating deficiencies inherent in the Electromatic design.

IBM realized that sales techniques had to overcome a multitude of groundless objections to the application of electricity to the typewriter.

People had to be convinced that this electric machine was safe, reliable, and efficient. Only after this pioneering stage was completed could IBM sell the need for greater efficiency in business communications through the use of IBM electric typewriters.

IBM management saw the need for an effective service organization to work with production and sales. A customer engineering operation was established to ensure all typewriter customers that their machines would be kept in top running condition at all times.

Most important, however, was the IBM determination to keep up-to-date with business needs as they developed. This determination engendered a policy of continued product research and development. With this program supporting it, the IBM Electric Typewriter was introduced in 1935 and became the first commercially successful electric typewriter marketed in the United States. The product line was rapidly expanded in the late '30s which greatly increased the application of the electric typewriter to office procedures.

A new expanded division

In October of 1955, the Electric Typewriter Division was established as an autonomous segment of IBM's corporate structure. The division was completely integrated—developing, manufacturing, marketing, and servicing its entire product line.

In 1957, the division began the manufacture of typewriter supplies to ensure customers that rigid quality controls would be maintained in the production of typewriter ribbons and carbon paper bearing the IBM trademark.

The division moved its manufacturing and engineering operations to a new plant in Lexington, Kentucky. The new facility contained the world's most modern typewriter assembly operation as well as the only engineering laboratory in the world devoted solely to electric typewriter development. It soon became a showplace for advanced manufacturing and engineering techniques.

All I knew about typewriters I gleaned from Ms. Evelyn Findlay's typing class during one semester in high school. We learned to type on Royal Manual typewriters, and I could pound out "Now is the time for all good men to come to the aid of their country" with the best of 'em.

In 1958, the division produced its one-millionth typewriter, a fitting climax to its silver anniversary year. Next came the Introduction of many new electric typewriters and new dictation equipment.

The Selectric® Typewriter Revolution

The Selectric Typewriter
Many called it the "golf ball typewriter"– fancy that!

In the 1960s the division announced a technological breakthrough which revolutionized the typewriter industry: the IBM Selectric Type-writer. It printed by means of a single, interchangeable sphere-shaped typing element. It had no type-bars and no movable carriage. The printing element was mounted on a small carrier which ran along a cylindrical metal bar while typing. Because the writing element moves, and not the paper-carrying unit, the carriage had been eliminated. For this reason, the Selectric typewriter required less space and vibration was practically eliminated, as there was no longer a jolt from the carriage return. Another important feature of the new machine was the ability to change type styles in seconds through the single-element typing principle.

First Magnetic Media Typewriter... Word Processing is Born

In 1964, the division introduced the IBM Magnetic Tape Selectric Typewriter which was capable of automatically producing error-free typing at a speed of 150 words per minute. These machines used a magnetic tape which stored typed information in coded form.

A change of name and I walked right into the business of The Office Revolution

To indicate more accurately the scope of the product line, The Electric Typewriter Division changed its name to IBM Office Products Division (OPD) in August of 1964. That same year continued growth was reflected in a move to expanded headquarters facilities to 590 Madison Avenue in New York City.

I found that I had a head-start in IBM Sales Training, with my experiences of:

- IBM Culture: a lifetime of being in the IBM Family

- Product Knowledge from being an IBM Office Products Installer in the summer months

- My relationships with IBM Sale and Service teams (OP Customer Engineers), both on and off the golf course

At the beginning of each day, bright and early at 8:30am, IBM Basic Sales Training began. All of us in the class—in dark suits, white shirts, and neckties—would stand, and our *crescendo* began. The gradual, steady increase in the volume of our voices kept escalating until the door to the classroom would open and Mr. Bob LaDue, head of IBM Office products sales training, would run into the classroom and jump up on a desktop. The yells and applause were almost deafening. Sales Class always began on a very high adrenaline rush!

Basic IBM Sales Training became known as the best sales training in the world. We had Systems and Sales Training Manuals that supported the high bar set by the company on both sales and service. Systems, I learned, were a critical component of IBM's success and led to the consistency of experience that was its hallmark.

I remember one time, while in New York, a small group of IBM trainees went to a Chinese restaurant. I wasn't too excited about that, as I had never eaten any Chinese food before. I thought it was all Chop Suey or Chow Mein. But this was another first for me, and I found that I liked the Chinese food.

Then, the real, outside-the-classroom excitement came for me in New York City.

Another group of IBM Sales Training trainees became aware that the N.Y. Yankees were in town, so one of the guys in our class made all the arrangements for the next Saturday's games. Games, as in plural, because on...

June 29, 1968

There was a doubleheader... meaning two games, another game between the same two teams would be played right after the first! *Are you kidding me?* I thought I had died and gone to heaven. Mickey Mantle and Yankee Stadium, the Yankees against the Oakland Athletics in a doubleheader! We took a train to Grand Central Station, then connected to the "Train to the Game" that took us directly to Yankee Stadium at 161st Street and River Ave. in the Bronx. I got off the train and was looking at the original Yankee Stadium. I knew all the names it was known as: *The House That Ruth Built, The Big Ballpark, The Stadium, The Cathedral of Baseball.* This was the most famous venue in baseball, just like St. Andrews is the most famous venue in golf. And there I was: Yankee Stadium.

Its history includes numerous World Series games, including no-hitters, the perfect World Series Game (1956, Yankees against the Brooklyn Dodgers, Don Larsen pitching, throwing only 97 pitches), historic home runs (including The Mick's) and on and on. And, I am there! Yankee Stadium was showing off its new 1967 paint job—white exterior, blue interior—and I could hardly believe I was there and going to see Mickey Mantle.

We got to our seats as they were starting the National Anthem, and The Mick (#7) was on first base. Only about 25,000 fans were in attendance that day, so it was easy for me to sneak down and sit for a while on the first base line. When I was sitting there, a couple of rows behind the Oakland A's dugout and when the inning ended, *I swear* that as The Mick went jogging back to the Yankees dugout, he looked left into the crowd and saw me and acknowledged me. Yes, he did! Mickey Mantle looked right at me!

Mickey had two hits and two RBIs in the first game, but the Yankees lost.

Mickey had one homer and 2 RBIs in the second game, and the Yankees won!

Yankee Stadium 1968

With completion and graduation from six weeks of IBM Basic Sales Training, I returned to San Antonio and learned from my Branch Manager that I had two new assignments.

HemisFair '68

The 1968 HemisFair was the official World's Fair of 1968, held in San Antonio and that meant considerable city development in the heart of downtown, just south of that famous Texas shrine, The Alamo. Among the Corporate Pavilions at HemisFair were Kodak, Ford, GE, RCA, SW Bell (now AT&T), Humble Oil (now Exxon Mobil), Frito-Lay, American Express, and, of course, IBM.

My Assignment: OPD products demonstrator, IBM Pavilion, HemisFair '68 in San Antonio. Now, *I tell you what.* I think everyone who attended the HemisFair wanted to sit down and use, operate, and play with the Selectric Typewriter. The Selectric came in a variety of colors: emerald green, topaz bronze, garnet rose, sapphire blue, raven black, and sandstone beige. It just might have been the most revolutionary office product ever! And today, I still have my garnet rose Selectric Typewriter in my office, on display.

Original postcards from IBM pavilions HemisFair 1968

Also in July of 1968: the PGA Championship and Arnold Palmer

After only a week's break from HemisFair, something else—something very big—came to San Antonio: The 50th PGA Championship at Pecan Valley Golf Club.

Arnold Palmer
Photo Courtesy of Phoenix Country Club

My Assignment: Carry a walkie-talkie on course at the PGA Championship, inside the ropes, to relay pertinent information (as in, hole-by-hole scores and such) to the huge IBM trailer scoreboard situated near the 18th green. Scores, when received, were key- punched on IBM data cards and loaded into the data processing machine which would light up the scoreboards with current player information.

On Monday and Tuesday, July 15 and 16, I attended IBM orientation on walking inside the ropes, taking notes, and learning the correct operating procedures for radio relay back to the IBM trailer. It was sweltering—it was July in Texas, after all. Each day we would be assigned a group to follow, for whom we would relay the stats.

On Thursday, the first day of the Championship, I was walking along the edge of the second hole, a par five, in the fairway and checking out my radio with the HQ trailer, back to #18 (you know, as in "Testing... Testing...1, 2, 3, 4").. I heard a voice yelling, "Hey, hey... you!" Looking up, I saw (in the middle of the #2 fairway) PGA Golf Professional Gardner Dickinson staring right at me. He continued yelling at me, "Do you mind? We're trying to play some golf out here!" *Ooops!* I then learned to do my radio check prior to getting out on the course, and to speak a little softer into my radio.

On the last day of tournament play, I was assigned to Arnold Palmer's group and walked inside the ropes with the Palmer foursome. Pecan Valley Golf Course, just like The Meridian, isn't there any more. But back then, in July of 1968, a sweltering-hot PGA Championship would also give us another late, last-round charge for the PGA Championship, a prestigious event that Palmer had never won. And I would be right there in the middle of it—Arnie's Army and me—walking with one of my all-time sports heroes.

Photo Courtesy of Phoenix Country Club

As I've mentioned, the tournament was held at the same time as another great event for San Antonio: the 1968 HemisFair World's Fair. I doubt that San Antonio had ever enjoyed such a national, even world, presence with all the press in town.

Dan Jenkins had the lead paragraph in *Sports Illustrated*, with this quip about the land and the golf club: "A few miles southeast of The Alamo, in a sunken oven of pecan trees and thick, baked Bermuda grass, on land so unpicturesque it makes you wonder why Mexico ever wanted to keep it or why Texas wanted it even for shopping centers..." He also wrote, "It looked pretty much like a place where you pull in, drop off your cleaning, and pick up hamburgers for the kids..." And "...despite the look of Pecan Valley, it proved to be a course that provided the best PGA tournament in years, an old-fashioned kind of tournament, in fact, that forced players to think and plan and finesse their shots reaching for the wedge or putter."

Jack Nicklaus had missed the cut and as was written in the San Antonio newspaper: "(Nicklaus) reportedly said the course was too hard and compared it to a hay field. Legend has it that a group of Pecan Valley members responded by sending Nicklaus a bale of hay."

On that Sunday, July 21, I could hear through the radios and see the scoreboards, positioned all around the course, to know what was happening. On the backside Palmer was playing in front of Julius Boros, and they were both making a run. And I was inside the ropes watching Palmer! He wanted to win the PGA Championship trophy to complete the career Grand Slam, already having won the Masters, as well as the U.S. and British Open Championships.

Arnold Palmer and I shook hands on the first tee. (Check that one off the Bucket List.)

He hitched up his pants; his shirttail was loose, like it was most always. He hit the shots and twisted and turned his head in typical Palmer fashion. His forearms were gigantic, very fit and solid, though he stood only some 5'10" tall.

Fans were lined up along the fairways, sensing something was happening with Arnie. Mr. Palmer made sure he was paying attention to the fans, even talking with them from time to time, seemingly almost overboard in reaching out to "his Army."

Palmer started the last round just two shots off the lead and with a birdie on #18 he would win, or at least get into a playoff. His tee shot was a big wild hook into the pecan trees, but he got a drop from TV cables.

He was 230 yards out with a second uphill shot to a two-tiered, elevated green. Palmer slashed his three wood, in his inevitable style, and the ball took off like a jet. He later called it "one of the best shots I ever hit, and the best three wood I ever hit." This was later confirmed in an interview with Doc Giffin, Arnold Palmer's life-long assistant and right-hand man. Mr. Palmer would confirm this with me at our next meeting, some 23 years later.

They placed a plaque there, where Arnold Palmer and I stood on July 21, 1968, which reads:

ARNOLD PALMER...
FROM THIS SPOT, ON SUNDAY JULY 21, 1968, ARNOLD PALMER HIT ONE OF THE MOST REMARKABLE SHOTS IN PGA HISTORY ON THE FINAL HOLE OF THE 50TH NATIONAL P.G.A. CHAMPIONSHIP.

PALMER NEEDED A BIRDIE THREE ON NO.18 WHICH MEASURED 488 YARDS THAT DAY, TO BE SURE OF TYING JULIUS BOROS FOR FIRST PLACE AND TO COMPLETE HIS CAREER GRAND SLAM OF WINNING ALL FOUR MAJOR CHAMPIONSHIPS.

PALMER HOOKED HIS TEE SHOT INTO THESE TREES, RECEIVED A FREE DROP FROM TELEVISION CABLES, AND THEN STROKED A THREE WOOD 230 YARDS ONTO THE 18TH GREEN COMING TO REST ONLY 12 FEET FROM THE HOLE.

HE MISSED THE PUTT, HOWEVER, AND FINISHED WITH A PAR 70 AND A 282 TOTAL TO TIE BOB CHARLES FOR SECOND PLACE. BOROS LATER PARRED THE HOLE FOLLOWING A SPECTACULAR PRESSURE PACKED WEDGE SHOT TO THE HOLE AND FINISHED WITH A 281 TO WIN THE CHAMPIONSHIP.

LIFE IN THE REAL WORLD

Somehow they omitted from that plaque the following: "THIS IS ALSO WHERE J. MICHAEL MEADOWS (age 21 years, nine months and 18 days) WAS STANDING ALONGSIDE MR. PALMER." (For the record: This was also the first time, ever, that a zealous young golf fan (me) was recorded and broadcasted yelling: "*YOU DA MAN!*" after a golf shot.

Julius Boros won the 50th PGA and, at age 48, was the oldest to do so. It's a record that still stands today for oldest PGA Tour professional to win a Major.

Another fantastic experience, never to be forgotten!

Following the PGA Championship I went back and finished my HemisFair assignment, until I was called back to IBM OPD Advanced Sales Training—six more weeks in White Plains, New York.

IBM Advanced Training was in new Product Training that was being introduced to the market, more product demonstrations, cold-calling techniques, sales presentations for office systems by IBM (for the new integrated products line), Closing Skills, etc. etc. etc.

IBM trained its sales representatives in the system of selling known as: **Feature-Function-Benefit**

Example: FEATURE: the Selectric Typewriter "typing element" (that golf ball-looking mechanism)

FUNCTION: interchangeable type fonts

BENEFIT: ability to create many different documents, either 10 or 12 pitch, and styles: Gothic, Script, OCR for scanning documents to computer format, or any of many different styles for any purpose, to customize a document.

I had thus far, in my own thinking, been advancing pretty well in "the fairways of life." I had successfully made the two big graduations from high school and college, and had completed IBM advanced training. I was working for, and being trained by, one of the largest most respected corporations in the world. I was now wearing a charcoal grey or pin-striped suit, white shirt, and tie every day, except for the PGA Championship assignment.

CHAPTER THREE

So, what about getting married?

After all, I was an "executive" now, and marriage was the norm in my work environment. Thinking that I was well established (as most 20-year-olds often think), having "the career of a lifetime" in hand, and secure and with all my peers at IBM (all older than me), I knew that they were all married and secure with their long careers at IBM. So, marriage was what I thought I needed. Hey, my mom and dad had married early. They eloped in 1940 when Mom was 19 and Dad was 21. Therefore, marriage seemed perfectly logical.

I had been dating a very nice, pretty girl, from Tulsa, OK, for almost all of the last year at OSU. We had dated for nearly a whole… 2 semesters at OSU. Of course, experts today say that if you haven't dated for at least 2 years (not semesters), it is too early to think of marriage. But, I really thought I was ready.

Becky was a very lovely young lady and a Pi Phi at OSU. You didn't get a bid (invitation to join) from that sorority if you weren't an exceptional young lady, and everyone knew Pi Phis were very exceptional, even very cool.

Dating back in the 1960s, as I remember, went something like this: boy opens door for girl, boy buys the movie tickets, which allows boy to put arm around girl at the movies (maybe even hold hands, a very intimate gesture), boy pays for pizza, and maybe gets a kiss good-night when returning girl to her sorority house.

I had met Becky's mom and dad when they came, from Tulsa, to OSU Homecoming or some other football game during our senior year. I do remember the mums! I liked her parents very much.

There were my prerequisites for marriage and I'm sure Becky had hers. Sociability, a pleasing disposition, stability, and a Christian. If I were to place an order, everything would have had a check mark on the checklist of desired qualities. She was beautiful and had all the fine attributes of character, so I asked her to marry me.

We were married on November 2, 1968, and moved into our rented apartment in San Antonio, Texas. Thanksgiving was 25 days thereafter and my parents, little brother and sister, celebrated with us there in our apartment.

At age 22, I had just spent the last 6 months in two IBM sales schools, working the PGA Golf Championship with IBM Sports Network, working at the IBM HemisFair Pavilion, and gotten married, too. I felt very blessed.

I would start 1969 with my own sales territory—and my own sales quota. A quota is the yearly amount of each product line I was assigned to sell, in the Office Products Division of IBM. I was extremely excited about having the responsibility of my own Sales Territory.

In January 1969, both my father and I received letters from Thomas J. Watson, Jr., then President of IBM and the man who built IBM into a computer giant. This was a letter of congratulations for becoming members of the IBM Second Generation Club along with a gift of gold cufflinks, with my dad's and my initials inscribed: **JAM/JMM**.

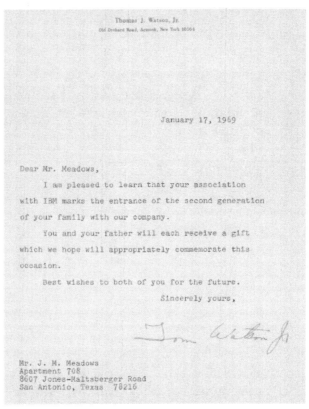

Watson's Letter – IBM's Second Generation Club

I bought some more white shirts that would accommodate those beautiful cufflinks and I still occasionally wear them... you know, weddings and funerals (funerals, now however, outnumber the weddings). I have officiated at both of these types of services.

Assignment: My Sales Territory was a geographical territory in Texas from San Antonio to Laredo to Eagle Pass, but not including San Antonio or Laredo. I had most everything in between, which was five counties: Dimmit, LaSalle, Zavalla, Frio, and Maverick counties. I also was assigned a few commercial accounts scattered within a small geographic area, primarily on the south side of San Antonio (and if you know anything about city geography, then you know south sides are not too desirable).

I must have had the largest geographical sales territory in the history of IBM. It was 7,551 square miles of Texas, just to the north of Mexico, north of the Rio Grande River. I even had to drive through two other, very large, counties to get to my sales territory. It didn't matter because I was so excited and proud, and saw nothing negative, only vast skies of Texas smiling down on me!

Dimmit County, all 1,335 square miles of it, had only two viable prospective towns for typewriters, dictation equipment, and/or word processing. They were Carrizo Springs, the largest town and county seat, and Asherton. Both were very small towns.

My other counties were:

LaSalle County, Texas –1,487 square miles
Zavalla County, Texas – 1,302 square miles
Frio County, Texas – 1,134 square miles
Maverick County, Texas – 1,292 square miles

I am sure you're getting the picture. I was on the road a lot, but I did make my sales quota in all product lines in my first year as an IBM Salesman.

The IBM Hundred Percent Club

IBM salesmen celebrate their membership in IBM's Hundred Percent Club in 1925. The club was developed exclusively for those salesmen who met 100 percent of their annual sales quota. Members were rewarded with attendance at the annual Hundred Percent Club convention, which featured dinners, speeches and entertainment, as well as public recognition and often, promotions.

My first Hundred Percent Club convention was in San Francisco, California and (not surprisingly) it's the golf courses I remember most vividly: Olympic Club, San Francisco Country Club, Pebble Beach, and Spyglass.

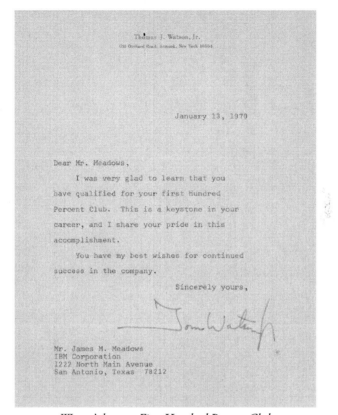

Watson's letter – First Hundred Percent Club

It was impossible to work for IBM and not have a profound sense of respect for Thomas Watson and all that he had accomplished. One of his more noteworthy thoughts:

"There is only one way to gain knowledge and that is through study...."

Thomas Watson, Sr.
IBM CEO

Life was good! No, life was GREAT!! I was on top of the world!! And I was going to get a larger sales territory beginning 1970.

Most of us remember the TV show *Hee Haw*
with Buck Owens and Roy Clark, in which they always had a scene
with them, two ole boys laying about the shack,
and claiming Gloom, Despair and Agony coming down on 'em,
and if it weren't for bad luck, they'd have no luck at all…

Well, that stuff was fixin' to come down on me—and hard!

Uncle Sam

Wednesday April 1, 1970
Age 23 years and seven months...

What is this, an April Fool's Day prank letter?

No, it is not.
And I'M HIT WITH A TON OF BRICKS!

This can't be happening to me! *Are you kidding me?*
A startling blow! I am not talking about a bad lie in a bunker....
The world I am living in is about to be ripped out from under me!

I received a letter from my local Selective Service draft board, in OKC, with notification of a reclassification of my Selective Service status to that of 1-A. Meaning (*can you believe this?*) Available for Military Service.

This little "conflict" thing called Vietnam had continued to escalate, even into the 1970s, and so, too, had the Selective Service Administration's drafting of young men into military service. It would continue into 1973.

Does this mean what I think it means?
Oh, Lord, NO! Please God, not me!

My mind went haywire, then blank, then numb… as shock set in. Then a feeling of sickness… nausea. I was shaking. *Why me, Lord?* Please no, not at this time in my life.

I needed information, and fast. With great trepidation I made a phone call to my draft board in Oklahoma City, and asked questions about the letter, the new classification, and well, just, what was next. I needed answers and asked "What can I expect?"

Point of information: Local draft boards were made up of members of the local community who volunteered to administer and execute the main provisions of the Selective Service Draft Laws. Their functions included the registration as well as rejection or selection of men of military age to induct into military service.

In that phone conversation with my draft board, I was told that all temporary Medical Deferment Classifications of 1-Y, which was what I had, were being abolished by Administrative Action… whatever that meant. As I learned, it simply meant that local draft boards had been instructed to reclassify all 1-Y deferments to 1-A, Available for Military Service.

So, naturally I asked, "Just what, then, does this mean for me?" I was told that the military draft continues, and that all previous 1-Ys were being called up to go through another pre-induction physical and I would soon receive notice of where to report for my pre-induction physical.

OK, I got that. "Am I going to be drafted?" was my next question. "That depends upon your lottery number and your new pre-induction physical results" was the reply from the other end of the phone.

Oh yes… just then I remembered. *The Selective Service had gone to a lottery system wherein 366 blue plastic capsules containing all dates of the year, "birthdays," were drawn (from a big glass jar sitting on a simple three legged stool) in the first Vietnam draft lottery drawing on December 1, 1969.* By that time, I had already been working for IBM for more than a year and a half. The Selective Service System went to this *Lottery System* as a means of drafting men into the Armed Forces of the United States based upon one's birth date. Those 366 dates (including February 29 for leap-year babies) were placed in blue capsules and then drawn, one at a time. The first date drawn was September 14 and it was assigned draft #001.

Selective Service Lottery Draft Drawing

Up to that point I hadn't paid much attention to this new lottery system, because 1) it was put in place after I had received my 1-Y classification, and 2) I was well into my IBM career and certainly not thinking about military service.

On December 1, 1969, if you were registered for the draft as the law required, had a 1-A classification, and were born on September 14… you could pack your toothbrush because you were on your way to six weeks of

Boot Camp and then on to some place with a name like DaNang, Pleiku, Tonkin, or Van Tuong for some guerrilla warfare, in the rice paddies—or maybe even to Hamburger Hill, a location we watched daily on TV in 1969.

"So, let's see what your birth date is, Mr. Meadows…" Pause.

"Uh, let's see, Mr. Meadows, your birth date is September 3rd…" *Another* long pause.

My heart is palpitating and I'm sweating during this pause on the other end of the phone. The report came back and was delivered to me, again like the proverbial "ton of bricks"…

"So, your lottery number is 49, Mr. Meadows." I thought, "**Holy crap! Are you kidding me?**" "**Why me, God?**" I then asked, "So, what can I expect, next?" The response: "After your pre-induction physical, YOU CAN EXPECT TO RECEIVE, VERY SOON THEREAFTER, YOUR NOTICE OF THE INDUCTION CENTER TO WHICH YOU ARE ORDERED TO REPORT FOR ACTIVE DUTY."

Oh, no. I thought: *I am almost 24 years old, have been working for two years, married, house, cars, in the acquisition stage of life with a life that's been so great, thus far. Then, I thought about being in debt and how I would be put into such financial hardship if drafted! Holy shit!*

"Wait a minute… Wait a minute!" I said, "The original 1-Y classification was a medical deferment and it says on the card, right here: Re-exam six months. What happened with that?" I heard the following explanation: "Well, Mr. Meadows, I suppose with the readily available, able-bodied men in the 1-A classification, it was not necessary to call in the earlier 1-Ys for their re-examination physical." Then I heard: "That was then, this is now." My mind is racing: *But I'm almost 24 years old!* **You gotta be kidding me… This just can't be happening.**

After regaining my breath and senses, I thought: *OK, if I couldn't pass the physical back in '68, I won't be able pass it this time either, as nothing has changed in my medical condition.* In fact, I was under regular care with ear aspirations (a medical procedure for removal of skin and wax from the ear canal) with a local San Antonio ear specialist.

Six weeks later I received a letter from the draft board requesting me to appear in Oklahoma City for my second pre-induction physical.

I reported to OKC with letters in hand from ear specialists from Oklahoma City, Stillwater, San Antonio, and New York City—all of whom had seen me for the same reoccurring ear condition. One of the letters detailed records of seeing me regularly since 1949 (beginning at age three and for the past 20 years) with record of having 11 surgical operations for my medical condition in the left ear alone. I went through the routine of another insignificant physical examination in Oklahoma City.

Six weeks after that I received another notice from the OKC draft board and a 1-A classification.

I was now struggling with this new reality, and grappling with disorientation like I had never experienced before. *What is going on here?*

I, now in fast-action research mode, learned that I could request an appearance with my draft board. This had to be in written form and sent to my draft board in OKC. That request was sent that very day.

I also wrote letters of appeal to the Selective Service State Director and National Director of the Selective Service. I included my medical records and letters from my doctors (those ear specialists who had been treating me since I was a child) along with a copy of published Army Standards, listing the causes for rejection for appointment, enlistment, and induction into the Armed Forces of the United States. The specific U.S. Armed Forces policy is in Section V. 2-6 – Ears and Hearing, paragraph (a) 3. Severe external or internal otitis, acute or chronic, and paragraph (f) 1. Any perforation of the tympanic membrane (hole in the eardrum), and Section V. 2-7– Hearing loss of certain measured levels.

Six weeks later I received mail from the draft board with a date and time for my personal appearance before the board. I appeared, in full IBM attire (suit, white shirt and tie) and stated my case with full documentation.

Another six weeks later I received notice of the draft board's decision and another 1-A Classification Card.

I did further research and I pursued all legal ways and means to stop this madness—to find further legal possibilities and to employ anything and everything possible in my process. Therefore, I immediately requested, via mail, a transfer of draft boards due to the fact that I was now residing and employed in San Antonio, some 500 miles away from my Oklahoma City draft board.

I had my "bases covered," my "ducks in a row," however you wanted to say it. I could emphatically show all causes for rejection into military service, according to published Army Standards, of which I had copies. I believe that in any courtroom I would easily win my case. In every letter I wrote and in each personal appearance I made (to two different draft boards: OKC and San Antonio) I presented myself in this manner:

1. Now 24 years old, I was established in my career, married, having personal indebtedness, etc. I cited examples of the financial hardship that would be caused by being drafted.

2. As a college student I had prepared for military service through the ROTC (Reserve Officer Training Corp.) whereby I would have entered my military service, as planned in 1968, as an Air Force 2nd Lieutenant. This was now lost, not available, and gone forever. I had followed a planned college program in Officer Training, and yet I would have to enter into military service at the lowest grade level (a grunt vs. the 2nd Lieutenant commission I had earned). How is that happening? This can't be real! I would have been an officer in 1968, would have served two years ALREADY! So, now they, the Selective Service System, would be taking that commission away from me?

3. I had been prepared for a physical re-examination after six months of the 1-Y classification, spring 1968, but I was not prepared for being "called up" two years and nine months later!

4. I presented all above records and requested a re-classification of not qualified for military service. Here was their reply: "Thank you, Mr. Meadows. We'll be in touch."

Six weeks later I received another letter. *This has to be the good news I've been waiting for. Think positive!* It was the notification of transfer of draft board and a new 1-A classification, same as before.

Hello, God, are you up there? Why me? If God is LOVE, why is this shit happening to me, now? I am losing control as I am at a loss for any way to handle in this situation. And more than a half a year had gone by now, with me dealing with draft boards, with the issues of having lost my officer commission into military service, and now my pending direct induction—all with no regard for my documented medical issues. I am unable to make any head-way.

With every piece of mail I received, I was going through serious anxiety. I was so off balance in coping with life, marriage, work… every aspect of my being. I am now so angry with everything in life… and especially angry with God. God had turned his back on me, not paying attention to what was going on with my life. I'm being punished, but for what?

Hey, God, how could you allow this to happen to me? I have to tell you that God was not looking all that good to me at the time.

As a man of action, I immediately requested, via mail, an appearance before the San Antonio draft board.

Six weeks later I receive approval to meet with my new board, date and time. I appeared early, in IBM attire (looking very professional, I must say). I was very prepared, having copies in hand of the actual Armed Forces Medical Standards and all my medical records, which in my opinion, conclusively showed (and which I, to this day, emphatically believe) that I was not qualified for service. Here was another opportunity, with a different draft board… and I thought: *I am a damn good salesman. Yeah, I'll make another presentation this time, even better than the last one.*

I stated my case, yet again, and presented all the pertinent documentation, again, and *I gave one hell of "a bang-up, knock-'em-dead, stand-up-in-front-of-the-jury, best-defense-attorney-presentation ever!"*

All the board said was, "Thank you, Mr. Meadows. We'll be in touch."

Six weeks later I received mail from the San Antonio draft board, including my new, but unchanged, 1-A classification.

What? *Say, God, are you looking at the newspapers?* Thousands are getting killed in this "conflict" (aka: war) and yet no one seems to understand what the hell we were doing over there, somewhere in Asia. Most every day we were seeing this all play out in the media, including daily TV spots and coverage that showed a lot of innocent people, even children, being killed. Many of our young boys sent over there are being returned in body bags. *Just how many people, God, are you going to let die in this stupid war, excuse me, conflict? It's just not fair.*

I felt like an innocent prisoner facing the parole board every few weeks, where my case fell on deaf ears each time, and after each board meeting, I went back to my cell.

Soldiers returning from World War I were said to be *"shell shocked,"* a phrase coined to describe the type of post-traumatic stress disorder many soldiers experienced back then.

I think it was WWII when they came up with Battle Fatigue, a military term for an acute reaction to the stress of war.

Later, all this became know as PTSD, Post Traumatic Stress Disorder.

I certainly had my share of PTSD in my life, *Pre*-Traumatic Stress Disorder where, yes, I was scared and having feelings of helplessness, hopelessness, and panic, with the inability to reason, sleep, or function very well. All the while I was doing everything within the established rules of reason and military rules of conduct, as published. And I had a job, being a professional IBM representative.

Both my dad and my wife's father wrote letters to the Draft Boards in October of 1970 in regard to each of them being placed in financial hardship if having to take on any further financial obligations of mine. My father was retired, supporting not only two children at home, but had taken on the additional responsibility of providing for my mother's mother, grandmother Roxie, whose only son was in the Navy and on his third tour in Vietnam.

I had done everything in my power and was totally exhausted. I had run through every known legal method, except trying the Conscientious Objector route, which I could not do within my belief system.

I was exhausted and had exhausted any and all legal means to avoid being drafted into military service. In 1971, three years after expecting to enter the Air Force with a commission of 2nd Lieutenant and getting a Medical Deferment that stopped that process, I was being drafted into military service. My present life was being put on hold, for two years, while I went to Boot Camp en route to Southeast Asia!

The Draft continued, by the way, until Jan. 27, 1973 when the Selective Service announced that there would be no further draft calls. I was just nine months shy of my 25th birthday, after which one cannot be drafted for military service unless in time of war or national emergency, and neither had been declared.

I could not, *did* not, understand any rhyme or reason for what was happening… and I was one pissed-off guy! Both my parents and in-laws told me that they were praying for me, while I was in total self-absorption and having my own pity-party on a daily basis. Thoughts came out of nowhere: *I had to have done something to deserve all this.*

My dad had started coaching me in my mental attitude to become the best soldier possible. He suggested that I commit to being just that—or be miserable—while in military service for the next two years. This was a difficult task, for both Dad and me.

Dad asked me if I had I prayed. And I had, as in, *Listen, God… you get me out of this one and I'll get out of the next one by myself.* I was trying to make a deal with the Big Guy in the Sky. So, I prayed, *Is there anything you can do for me, God? I'll never cuss again, I'll be more kind to people, and I'll give a lot of stuff to poor people… anything you ask.*

I had developed a mindset of a young and arrogant, highly productive, greedy, professional. Yuppie was the new term for those attempting to climb out of the middle class. I was blinded by achievement and materialism. I knew that I had a head-start in my journey in professional life, somehow circumventing the Vietnam conflict… until now.

Dad continued talking about my anger, and what I was going to do with it. I had never been so angry in my 24-plus years of life. My life had already been severely disrupted during the past year, fighting this, and would continue to be disrupted for another two years—if I made it through military service alive. It was a very dark time and my attitude was rotten.

I turned 24 years old, had a wife and now a baby on the way, due in seven months. A baby I will not see, in all likelihood, until the child was almost two years old. I won't see the baby take his or her first steps. Then fear rushed over me: I might not ever see this baby.

The rug had been pulled out from under me… I am in a humanly hopeless situation, and I haven't a clue why.

I had already prayed in every which way I could think of. So, I prayed for forgiveness of my rotten attitude and then the prayer that most every Christian, as well as others, have repeated many, many times, and probably without even thinking of the words…

Our Father, who art in heaven,
hallowed be thy Name,
thy kingdom come,
thy will be done,
on earth as it is in heaven…

Message on Anger
revisited with Dad 15 years later…

"Anger," Dad said, "expresses nothing good. It produces bad things like irritation, exasperation, hatred, and actions that you will be sorry for. You are going to be angry son, but it is what you do with your anger that matters." He continued: "A person is never smart when angry, which is why many stupid and embarrassing things are said and done in anger. I think your anger is going to be affecting your next two years unless you change your mental attitude. Otherwise, the quality of your life will be miserable."

Anger was certainly exacerbating some mental attitude problems in me… worry, anxiety, bitterness, self-pity, self-righteousness, and irritability—just for starters. *It is so easy to have a good attitude when everything is going great.*

I had nothing to sustain me through this dark period, this trial in life.

Hold it, time out, let's stop right here!

All of a sudden, it came to me. I was hit by the reality of what I was thinking (or wasn't thinking) when I prayed "thy will be done on earth…" I had an epiphany on that part of the prayer… a prayer I had said for as long as I could remember. That line had always seemed to me to be a prayer of resignation, or defeatism, in that God had willed this for me, therefore, well... so be it, accept it, it is done. It had allowed me to sink even deeper into my own pity party.

I then realized that I had a wrong interpretation of "Thy will be done on earth..." I had seen it as, yes, resigning to what was happening to me and "Oh, well, woe is me, there is nothing I can do about it."

But, all of a sudden, with this situation that I was in, I found myself really wanting to understand God's will as fully as possible. Standing in the way of my understanding of God's will was my mental attitude of personal selfishness, worry, bitterness, irritability, self-righteousness, self-pity, and ignorance of knowing (or not knowing)... just what was God's will for my life anyway?

Major Attitude Adjustment: **RESOLVE**

It became clear to me, that as a Christian believer—in this situation, with this struggle—that it was not about enduring the struggle and suffering, but it was about **serving God in it and through it!**

I was hearing my dad all over again, back from my boyhood days, and his guiding me when I had my first jobs in my life. Dad's advice was work, when employed, as if it were my own business, or even like I was working for Dad, like it was my dad's business. He encouraged me to give honor to the work at hand and work as though **I was working for the Lord** and providing him with the very best of me.

It was that Excellence thing, all over again... applied to yet another of life's opportunities.

I recalled a Vince Lombardi statement: "The quality of a person's life is in direct proportion to their commitment to excellence, whatever their chosen field of endeavor." Though I had not chosen this field of endeavor, I was waking up to what I needed to do... or risk being miserable for the next two years. *Had God chosen me for this?*

Here was an important revelation to me, at this time. **I knew *about* God**, as I had made the decision to Go with God (placing my faith in his plan of salvation early in my life). However**, I realized that *I did not know* God or His plan for my life.**

I began to get my affairs in order. There were certain benefits I would continue to receive by IBM, my employer, such as health insurance for my wife, but a lot more details needed to be worked out for her…like the financials and the arrival of a new baby while I would be away for the next two years. Where would they live? We had been in the acquisition stages of life and we hadn't saved a lot of money. There were many details that needed to be addressed. I definitely needed to get myself, my life, and my mental attitude in order for what was about to happen to me.

Finally, as expected, after some 50 weeks of gloom, despair and agony for a lot of people, I received a letter from Uncle Sam on March 10: The "Greetings" letter, including the date that I was ordered to report to the Induction Center, San Antonio, Texas for a two-year stint of active service in the Army.

The Selective Service gave me just two weeks and two days notice before my induction date, which was Friday, March 26, 1971, at 7:30am PROMPTLY. And, as the orders stated, I was told what to bring along with me: Bring a list of all medical documents concerning any medical conditions. Bring enough clothes for three days. Bring: enough money to last one month for personal purchases. Written in bold was: **"Willful failure to report at the place and hour of the day named in this Order subjects the violator to fine and imprisonment."** The document also stated: Bring this Order with you when you report to the Induction Center.

The Induction Notice with orders gave me just 16 days before I had to report for military service. Sixteen days! The Greetings letter also had an ending statement: **"Mr. Meadows, you are advised that no further call for a physical examination or meeting with your draft board will be issued to you. It is suggested that you comply with any instructions received from your Local Boards of Oklahoma City, OK and/or San Antonio, TX."**

Here's what I did. I prayed, again, for forgiveness of all my mental attitude thoughts and thanked God for his grace in my life, his love, and watch-care over me and my family. I prayed for all those who had been in support of me, and asked God to take away my negative thoughts and give me strength to serve Him in whatever His will for me, to glorify the Lord Jesus Christ, in whose name I prayed. Amen.

On Wednesday, March 24, my IBM branch office had a farewell party for me. There were a few banners on the wall. One said, "From White Shirts and Pin Stripe Suits to Army Khakis." Another banner said, "Farewell, God Bless – See you back in two years." and "You'll Never Get Rich you S.O.B. You're In the Army Now!" Another said, "We'll Never Forget Ole What's His Name."

On that Friday morning, Dad and I drove to downtown San Antonio, to the Army Induction Center. I had already said my good-byes to my wife and mother, leaving from Mom and Dad's house. At the induction center, I would be taking the oath "to defend the Constitution against all foreign and domestic enemies."

While Dad was driving me downtown, it was pretty silent in the car until he asked how I felt. "Truthfully, Dad, I am very queasy. I feel like I could up-chuck at any moment. But I have prepared for this, the best I could mentally, and come to my resolve. I am going into the Army and I'm going be the best damn soldier possible and serve my country!" Dad said, "You'll probably wind up getting a desk job." To which I responded, "Shit, I hope not!" and we both started laughing… as we both knew I was never cut out for a desk job, anywhere!

I had Dad pull to the curb and drop me off. We prayed together for strength and for me being prepared to fulfill my military responsibility. We shook hands, hugged, and said our good-byes. I got out and walked into the induction center, where no one was very cordial in greeting me or dealing with me… or the hundreds of 18-year-old, pimply-faced kids in there with me.

There was a rush of activity everywhere. First, I was put in a group that simply sat waiting. Eventually they came for us and we became part of the hurry-up-and-wait process.

Following the orders now being yelled at me, I undressed, down to my skivvies, put on my paper socks and placed my clothes, wallet, and all sundries into my little duffle bag. Then, I was told to get in line. The pushing and prodding began, all over again, in the military style which I was growing accustomed to. I had my orders and medical papers in hand, as I had been ordered to bring them with me, and continued through, seemingly, the same old process. But this time, it struck me squarely in the face: this was the real deal. It was hard to believe anything else when I heard comments like "as soon as we finished here we are headed for Fort Polk, Louisiana for six weeks of basic training."

And, that's when "the sign" appeared before me, hanging over a desk with a lone uniformed Army personnel sitting at desk number 10. The sign read:

"The Purpose of the Induction Physical
Is to Determine, as Fairly and Accurately as Possible,
Your Qualification for Service in the Armed Forces
of the United States of America
If You Feel You Have Been Overlooked in Any Way
Report to Desk Number 10"

The Uniformed Army Personnel at Desk Number 10

Well, I just shuffled right over to Desk Number 10, in my paper socks and skivvies, where *the uniformed Army personnel at Desk Number 10* just stared at me, with a look of *Well, what is it?*

I presented in a most calm and tranquil manner, void of any excitement whatsoever, speaking at a slow and confident pace (as slow and confident as any 24-year-old has ever spoken, I'm sure), while hundreds of 18-year-olds were being yelled at and while the induction process continued all around me.

With the deliberation of a confident orator, without rushing to speak, I said to *the uniformed Army personnel at Desk Number 10* something to the effect (paraphrasing here…): "I have my orders in hand, and medical records from five different Otolaryngologists, from New York to San Antonio. One is of the first medical record of me being seen in 1949, and of having a total of 11 operations on my left eardrum, with the latest report from just last year being treated for my disorder by a specialist, here in San Antonio, last December. All of which state that according to *your* current Army Standards, a copy of which is here also, clearly indicating in Section V. a-f, reasons (plural) for rejection for appointment, enlistment, and induction into the Armed Forces of the United States… Those being Section V. Ears and Hearing: a. (3) Severe external otitis, acute or chronic, e. (1) Acute or chronic otitis media, (3) adhesive otitis media, f. (1) any perforation of the tympanic membrane, (2) Severe scaring of the tympanic membrane with hearing loss. Any one of these conditions is cause enough for rejection, and all these conditions are now observable in any relevant examination of me as noted by the professional signatures on these medical documents."

I continued and all the while *the uniformed Army personnel at Desk Number 10* gave me his attention. I said: "I have already lost a 2nd Lieutenant's Commission into the Air Force, just three years ago because of the same noted disqualifications."

My final comment, "Therefore, I would think that the Army might want to look inside my ears, just as the United States Air Force did, using something a bit more diagnostic than a hand-held flashlight. I believe it would be beneficial for the Army to do just that, and that seems a reasonable request on my part as I feel, as the sign says, OVERLOOKED"—and pointed to the sign above his desk… desk Number 10.

The uniformed Army personnel at Desk Number 10 took considerable time, in what seemed a careful and thorough examining the documentation. Then he said, "I am sending you over to Ft. Sam Houston in a van with a driver. Go get dressed and bring everything you have back to me." I moved faster than anything with two feet.

Upon my return, with duffel bag et al, *the uniformed Army personnel at Desk Number 10,* handed me a file folder with a form on the outside, my paperwork inside, then handed another slip of paper to a soldier that I guessed was the driver. He said to me, "You should be back here within a couple of hours, so report back to me, right here."

I was a single passenger in an Army-drab green van with a uniformed driver, headed to Ft. Sam Houston, just north of downtown San Antonio. I was familiar with Ft. Sam. It had been an Army Post established in the mid 1800s, back when it was "The Republic of Texas" and named after the President of the Republic, Sam Houston. I knew Ft. Sam had a huge IBM computer installation. I knew it was also the Home of Army Medicine and learned that day that Ft. Sam Houston was the Command of U.S. Military Entrance Processing (MEPS), because that's precisely where I was delivered: MEPS.

There was quite a remarkable difference in the reception I received at MEPS at Ft. Sam compared to the treatment at the Induction Center earlier that morning. Everyone was very pleasant and courteous.

After waiting for some time, I was escorted into a large examination room where there were four or five Majors and Captains dressed in white, each of whom introduced themselves to me. I assumed them all to be medical doctors. They were peering over my paperwork, when one said, "Well, you must have stood out like a sore thumb down at the Induction Center." Everyone was smiling.

"Tell us about yourself," one of the officers said. As I began my story, I was, again, comfortable and calm. I talked about my medical history beginning at infancy and the 11 surgical procedures of "lancing the ear drum and draining of the middle ear" along with the other ear situations as documented over the past 24 years. I told them of my planned training in ROTC, the expectation of an earned Air Force Commission out of college, and now being given a 1-Y classification by the draft board.

I talked about my career at IBM, about the surprise and dismay of now being drafted, all of my efforts of the past 12 months with two different draft boards, being married with a baby on the way. I even told them of the party that was given me by my branch office, about saying my good-byes and having Dad drop me off at the Induction Center that morning. I told them of seeing the sign and *the uniformed personnel at Desk Number 10*, and my comment about the Air Force and how I had quoted Army Standards, its Section V and reasons for disqualifications that pertained to me.

They all were smiling, some shaking their heads, as in having a real sense of understanding, or maybe it was their disbelief of my plight. "You said the past 24 years so your age is…. let's see…" one said. "You are… uh… 24 years, uh… and some 7 months. So, you'll be 25 in just five months, September 3rd, right?" My reply, "That is correct, sir."

"Well, first of all…" an officer began, "about doctors' letters: They are considered inadequate by the draft boards, as all too many doctors are unaware of current directives, have no concept of military training or what military duty is like, and their letters are always strongly biased in favor of the draftee. Draft-age men could often find a sympathetic doctor to write a false letter about mental or physical conditions. Draft boards simply take the position that letters to draft boards are most often produced by individuals who are anti-draft and anti-American action in Vietnam."

"So," he said, "let's get you over here on the table and take a look." I was laid out on a huge examining table equipped with some kind of imaging technology (CT or MRI, I assumed) used to study the external, medial and inner ear, the ear drum, and the related issues.

After a thorough examination a doctor commented with a big smile, "Well, I'm glad you reported to *the uniformed Army personnel at Desk Number 10*." They advised me that I had a significantly narrowed ear canal which will continue to cause conductive hearing loss, that the eardrum was significantly scarred, no doubt due to the 11 lance and drain operations. They said I would certainly have continued ear problems and loss of hearing. All that was the bad news, but the good news was that the Armed Forces of the United States was most certainly not going to need me.

I was stunned!

They, the medical doctors at MEPS, Ft. Sam Houston, signed some papers and sent me back to the Induction Center where *the uniformed Army personnel at Desk Number 10*, said, upon receiving my file: "You are released."

I remember very clearly having two distinct feelings: one of complete shock and, at the same time, a feeling of total euphoria.

Call it as you see it. Fate, Luck, God's Will, Providence, whatever. *The uniformed Army personnel at Desk Number 10* had certainly changed my life in a huge way! That is undeniable!

I literally ran all the way up North Main Ave. to the offices of IBM, 1222 N. Main, San Antonio, and hurried into the Branch Manager's office and said, "Mr. Kochwelp, you haven't hired anyone to fill my spot, yet, have you?" As you might imagine, he and everyone was like *"Huh?"* What had happened? The office was in total disbelief! Jaws were dropping, as people saw me and heard the news…*WHAT?* "You can't be serious!" There was total disbelief and everyone was stunned! Including me.

I then called my parents' house, knowing my parents and wife were there together dealing, each in their own way, with the fact that I had just left for a two-year stint in the Army, as a grunt and was most likely destined for combat in Southeast Asia.

I recall that I could not find words to describe the deafening silence on the other end of the phone. Dad had answered my call. "What?" he asked. Then, "What are you talking about?"

I said, "Dad, they released me from military service…. Hello, Dad? Hello?"

I heard him saying, in the background, "They released Mike." Silence again, and I heard him say, "He's back at the IBM office and they released him from military service." It was so surreal, I mean really strange and I don't know how to explain the feelings of others as they first heard the news, except as a stunning stillness, total silence, at first, for they were all overcome, struck in amazement, as I was. Then, again I heard, "What? You can't be serious."

My branch sales manager, Howard Kochwelp, was in awe—stupefied and dumbfounded. He stared at me and said, "Meadows, take the rest of the month off, come back after the first of the month and we'll re-organize and reformulate our plan."

So, Thursday April 1, 1971, one year to the day from my April 1, 1970 Induction letter, was a new start for me. No April Fool's prank here. But I didn't know how to re-start. I was very dazed, still confused, and felt that I did not have a clear understanding of what the last year of my life had been all about.

Maybe I should not have taken those five days off, as I was slow in getting back into the swing of being an IBM sales representative, questioning many things and looking more closely at what the future opportunities could be for me. Describing myself as somewhat "screwed up" would have been an understatement, and I still remember walking around in a daze and shaking my head. Some kind of PTSD from the past year, I guessed.

In my meeting with my Branch Manager, I picked up more geographical territory, as one of our other San Antonio representatives, Ray Croft, had accepted a sales position with Xerox in Houston. So, I got some of the rural territory he had serviced:.

Comal County, Texas – 575 square miles
Hays County, Texas – 680 square miles
Guadalupe County, Texas – 715 square miles

For sure, I must have had the largest IBM sales territory ever: 9,521 square miles, and lots of driving, and then more driving in the country.

Reality was setting in. Here I was, living in San Antonio and working out of the local IBM branch office, and it appeared to me that I was going to be limited in opportunity and advancement with the corporation.

San Antonio had a huge military presence with Kelly, Brooks, Lackland, Randolf, and Fort Sam Houston bases. It also had a great market presence with various medical centers, state, local, and federal government agencies, colleges and universities, insurance companies, and plenty of community industries and businesses. All were being covered by our Senior Sales Representatives who had their own "gold mines" to work and weren't going anywhere any time soon. They were not concerned with upward movement in the ranks of corporate Big Blue, aka IBM. They were right where they wanted to be. The same could not be said for me.

Satisfaction and fulfillment from my work and my position at IBM was deteriorating. I wasn't going to be content or remain in a situation where I could not see the opportunity to move up at a steady pace. I asked my self: *Should I do something else?*

On September 30, 1970, the beautiful Kristin Kaye Meadows was born.

During that time I met and developed a friendship with Mike Johnson through the San Antonio Chamber of Commerce. He was a commercial real estate agent with the D.B. Harrell Company of San Antonio. Mike and I were both members of the San Antonio Chamber's Round Up Club, the sales club of the Chamber. We were outside sales reps, who "rounded up" new members, encouraging new businesses to join the Chamber. It was lots of fun, with sales incentives, and fraternal bounding. There was an annual recognition meeting, a golf tournament, and a trip down to Port Aransas, Texas where we went fishing in the Gulf of Mexico.

Commercial Real Estate

It was on a Chamber expedition that Mike and I came up with the great idea to join forces in our own real estate company, Johnson & Meadows. Our first deal was landing a building management contract with an office building in downtown San Antonio, the Travis Park West, a seven-story building and parking complex. This was early in 1973. Inside the office complex, located on the beautiful Travis Park in central downtown, was a bank on the first floor and a legal firm on one of the higher floors... offices of one Herb Kelleher. Herb had just started a little airline company called Southwest Airlines.

"So, these two guys walk into a bar..." (Sounds like a joke, but it ain't.) They ordered drinks, and one of them grabs up a napkin and draws a triangle on it. At the top of the triangle he writes Dallas, at the lower left corner he writes San Antonio, and lower right corner of the triangle he writes Houston. "There you go," he said. "There's the business plan." Rollin King was a pilot and a businessman, Herb was a lawyer. "Let's start an airline," one of them said. The other's response: "You're crazy! Yeah, let's do it."

One of the great stories of Southwest Airlines is the fare war fought with Braniff in 1972. Braniff launched an effort to "drown" SWA by offering a fare between Houston and Dallas of just $13. Southwest responded with an offer to fly between any three of their cities for $13 or (now get this) your choice—the matching $13 fare or $26 per flight and get a bottle of Crown Royal, Smirnoff, or Chivas Regal. Yes, a bottle of booze. And no, not one of those little bitty one-shot bottles. These were full bottles of booze! Surprise… Southwest was Texas's biggest premium liquor distributor during that promotion! Braniff waved a white flag!

So, these two guys walked into a bar, in San Antonio, and made aviation history!

They adopted the name Southwest Airlines, and flew the first flights between Dallas, San Antonio, and Houston on November 14, 1971. The airline saw operating losses in 1971 and '72. Just like… guess who? Johnson & Meadows.

Soon I was asking myself: "What am I doing in the commercial real estate business? I knew nothing about it. I was sitting in an office building, at a desk, making sure there were enough light bulbs, inspecting the janitorial services, building maintenance, and resolving tenant issues and complaints.

Johnson already had his commercial real estate broker's license, so I spent my time in study, preparing to take the Real Estate test and get my license. The idea was to help clients buy, sell, or lease properties that would be used for business purposes. I quickly found that real estate is a very competitive field that required long work days for career success, and the sales cycle was so very long.

Getting back to what I knew

It was 1974, when I got a call from Ray Croft, formerly with IBM in San Antonio, who was now in Houston with Xerox, and their newly establish national Office Systems Division. They were very active in hiring trained IBMers from the IBM Office Products Division. I flew Southwest Airlines over to Houston, to hear their pitch.

They rolled out the red carpet and presented their plan to have me join the Xerox sales force, which was a top-notch group of professionals from IBM, Lexitron, DataPoint, and Wang. They wanted the best, and no one from the Xerox Copiers or TeleCopiers side was being brought in, because they would need to be trained in the word-processing market place. Xerox simply wanted to hire individuals who already had experience with the major competition.

The compensation plan was in line with IBM's, even better in some regards. "OK," I asked, "what would be my territory?" Get this: a big chunk of downtown Houston and the Post Oak area. Oh my gosh! It was hard to contain my excitement, but I tried my best to do just that! Xerox was a great company, with great benefits, and no slouch when it came to business machines. And I was thinking, *This is quite an opportunity and some kind of step up and over the status I had at* IBM. I asked, "What about my move?" Their answer: "Lock, stock and barrel, we'll cover everything in your move to Houston." And then the close, "We need you to give us a decision, as we would like you to be in Leesburg, Virginia ASAP at our Training Center."

The decision was an easy one, as my position in life was so very uncomfortable. Scary is a more accurate description. I had been asking myself, *What have you done?* Switching to commercial Real Estate was way off base for me with my personal situation, my emotional state—remember I had left the security of IBM to *zero* security. It had been a crazy move, and now we had another beautiful baby girl, Courtney Ann Meadows, born February 7, 1974.

The Xerox Campus in Leesburg, Virginia

A few weeks later, I arrived at The Xerox Center for training. It was originally situated on 2,265 acres of land in beautiful Leesburg, Virginia. Among its 265,000 square feet of meeting space was a 16,500 square foot ballroom, a 5,000 square foot athletic facility, and 250 conference rooms. The remainder of the nearly 1,200,000 square feet of the facility included 917 guest rooms and common areas. There was also a bar, which we appropriately named the Concrete Bar, as the whole place was a modern design built of concrete. Don't get me wrong, it was an amazing and beautiful place for the training of Xerox personnel, and a structure the likes of which I have never seen, even in today's world.

Xerox International Center for Training and Management Development was designed to be a wholly new and self-contained education community designated exclusively for the training of Xerox employees in sales, service, and management growth. The campus stretched as far as one could see.

Upon my arrival in Leesburg, I met another new hire for the Houston sales office, Dick Taylor, formerly a salesman with Lexitron Corporation. Dick and I hit it off immediately, as we discovered that we both played golf and we both liked to hunt and fish.

Our classroom training was being conducted by two former IBM employees, Joe Puleo and Joseph F. Wyzkoski, Jr. one Italian and other Polish. How fun was this going to be? The first thing Dick and I did, on our second day, was to find Joe Puleo's office cubical in a large open area of the center's Offices for Instructors. We disassembled his office, moved it all, and re-set his office, even pictures, into an elevator. Yes, we re-hung his pictures on the wall in the elevator. We were two cut-ups for certain. At least *we* thought so.

The two Joes—Puleo and Wyzkoski—kept a running battle of "gotchas" going while we were in Leesburg. We were able to play golf and even go bird hunting in Virginia, during our training sessions.

Xerox Sales Training at the time was based upon the system: **Professional Sales Skills.**

This system of selling would have the representative ***Probe*** (ask the right questions) for responses that could be supported with product benefits, and then close for the order: ***Probe, Support, then Close.*** Later the Selling System was changed and called ***Need Satisfaction Selling.*** Yes, we had manuals for the Xerox Learning Systems, too.

After two six-week sessions of classes in Leesburg, Dick and I returned to Houston and our respective sales territories.

In my first year, I ranked 16th among the top salesman in the nation with the Office Systems Division of Xerox, which landed me a Region Sales Specialist position in the Division.

In 1976, I received a promotion with Xerox that put me in the position of National Sales Training Specialist. My new position meant a move to Dallas. I called my new job "Airplanes, Wrinkled Suits, and Hotel Rooms," as it was primarily a rah-rah position that entailed presenting programs to the country's sales forces as well as riding with and making sales calls with Xerox sales people.

I remember one meeting in particular, flying into Ft. Lauderdale, Florida for what had been billed as an important sales meeting on how to convert Xerox clients from leasing their equipment to purchasing it. The sales managers and sales forces were gathered and sitting in a hotel conference room when I walked into the meeting wearing only a swimsuit. I said, "This isn't going to take long, because I'm going to the beach and then to the golf course."

I had their attention and when the laughter subsided, I simply presented them with the ways I had used to convert so many Xerox leasing customers into purchasers. I even had a name for the process: the MEU program. It was based on sending a letter, with a stamped return envelope, to leasing customers. In the letter, I asked the client to simply answer one question by checking the appropriate box and then return their response in the envelope provided. The question was stated like this: In an effort to be of better service to you, please indicate the Minimum Expected Use of the Xerox, model # 27-20-671 (or whatever was appropriate for that customer). There were three options and I was asking them to check the 'box' that reflected their needs and send me that answer.

Option one: **BOX** 12 - 24 months
Option two: **BOX** 24 - 36 months
Option three: **BOX** Longer

When they were returned, via USPS mail (no email at that time), and we had their response, the sales rep could make a presentation of how it was less expensive to purchase the equipment—"… what with depreciation… etc."—than to continue leasing. This program "went national" and lots of cash came into the corporation. Xerox, for the most part, was an equipment leasing company. This is just one of the tactics I developed and why I became National Sales Training Specialist. As a result of that promotion, in 1976, I moved my family from Houston to Dallas with Xerox.

We settled in Plano, Texas, just north of Dallas. I had won the National Sales Demonstration contest, besting all sales reps from each Xerox branch office in the Office Systems Division. The finals were held at the Doral Resort in Miami, Florida during the Presidents Club annual recognition meeting for all the sales reps who had made their yearly quota, just like IBM had done. It came down to two finalists making sales presentations and product demonstrations on a new Xerox product that was in direct competition with IBM. The two semi-finalists were part of the show. I was voted best by the sales reps, branch managers, and "higher ups" in Xerox Office Systems, which got me promoted again. The new job meant a lot of air travel, hotel rooms, wrinkled suits and a lot of late-night entertainment.

Major Life Change

Divorce happens, but, thankfully, the wounds do heal. In my case, it took communication, understanding, giving, and forgiving… and the love from two wonderful daughters. There were many reasons that led to the divorce. For me, it was a combination of my immaturity, entering marriage maybe too early, lack of understanding and little self-knowledge—as well as wanting to "fit-in" in the corporate world. The marriage, itself, had no real conflicts, as we shared common beliefs and values. Under the pressure of the Vietnam era with the draft issues, losing a military commission, my anger at the course of events went so far to even have anger towards God Himself. I had the first real test and major disruption in life, career and even threat to my life itself. I disconnected. It took me a few years to get back with confidence in my life, career and understanding of God's will (plan) for my life.

I was still caught up in my personal advancement, and the false pursuit of happiness centered on the details of life, and only finding fleeting moments of happiness. I had yet to realize how to obtain enduring stability and contentment.

CHAPTER FOUR

THE SCREEN DOOR OPENS

It was 1977 and I had just moved into my grandparents' house in old east Dallas, south of Mockingbird Lane off Greenville Avenue.

A friend of mine, Herschel T. Phillips, III (whom I met when he was a helper/builder for his uncle and from whom I purchased my first house in San Antonio in 1971) had moved to Dallas, practically in my neighborhood, and had started working for American Airlines.

I, soon thereafter, bought that old house from my Dad. He and I agreed that we would have three different, independent appraisals made on the property. Dad and I agreed that we would take, not the low, not the high, but the middle appraisal—whatever that would be—as the sales price of the property. The middle appraisal came in from an independent appraiser, Keith Rowland, who I later found out was a friend of Herschel's. The three of us soon became golf buddies, playing regularly at Tenison Park Golf Club.

The old house was still full of my grandparents' furnishings, a lot of lace on the windows, furniture, rugs, space heaters, window AC units, even old mink stoles that belonged to Grandmoney and Great-Aunt B.B. It was fully furnished throughout, including Granddad's neckties and shoes. It was a classic, three bedroom-one bath model with hardwood floors, great rugs, a fireplace, living room, large dining room, breakfast room, kitchen, a knotty pine den/TV room, and a spooky old staircase, leading up to an eerie attic with a lot of old crap up there. I cleaned the place out and cleaned the place up and had one huge open house, garage and yard sale. Then I remodeled the place, updated the kitchen, and installed central heat and air conditioning.

The Screen Door Open Trophy

Tenison Park Golf Club in Dallas – Home of the SDO

My Xerox district office was just a few blocks from my grandparents' home (now mine) and that house was soon to become known as The Clubhouse of the Screen Door Open Golf Championship. We were creating our own golf tournament, Dan Jenkins' style, and a golf fraternity amongst friends.

It was autumn, in 1977, and we had just finished a round of golf at Tenison Park. We were drinking some beers at the Clubhouse (as my house was, already, affectionately known) when the idea came up of having a unique golf gathering of friends to play in friendly competition in Dallas, and specifically at the famous Tenison Park.

I had continued to show up at some IBM Hundred Percent Club meetings, just so I could play golf in some fabulous places with my IBM friends. I was also traveling to the Xerox President's Club, to continue playing golf with my friends from my sales days at Xerox. You don't lose your real friends just because you change jobs. I had personal friends from San Antonio with whom our golf adventures continued whenever

I was back visiting my folks. I had other golf friends from high school and college, even some local friends now that I had moved to Dallas. *What the heck!* Why not have a fraternal meeting of some golf buddies and play some friendly golf over some weekend in Dallas?

Herschel, Keith, and I went out the backdoor of my house (the Clubhouse), through the screened-in porch that led out to the back yard and looked at the space. "Hey, Meadows, you've got lots of room here for a huge scoreboard. Easy to build, make it 16 foot wide and 8 foot tall, use four pieces of 4'x 8' sheetrock, and frame us up a scoreboard," mused Keith.

"Yeah, why couldn't we?" I asked. "Sure, why not?"

Next we thought about entertainment. "We could go up Greenville Ave. to the Greenville Ave. Bar and Grill or the Greenville Ave. Country Club…"—a couple of very good watering holes—"for some local entertainment, when not playing in the… What shall we call it?"

"I know," Herschel said, looking at the back door… "It's **The Screen Door Open!**"

That was in 1977, when it all began. The idea was to create a fraternal order of golfers coming to Dallas, golf being the commonality, for a unique golf experience and entertainment. It needed to be a great time that would stand out in the minds of the participants and one that would make them want to return year after year. It wouldn't need to be expensive, just fun and memorable. Our plan was to undercharge—and over deliver a great experience.

Tenison Park Golf Club is a municipal golf course in Dallas with two 18-hole courses. It first opened for play in 1929 and today is famous for many things. Here's three of them: Lee Trevino, *Titanic* Thompson, and the United States Screen Door Open International-Invitational Golf Classic.

Tenison Park GC was built by Dallas banker E.O. Tenison after World War I as a memorial to his son who died in the war. The course has a storied history as Texas's most infamous hustler's course, the place where guys like Titanic Thompson and Lee Trevino earned their livings—and their reputations. The original West course was laid out by Jack Burke and Syd Cooper in 1925 and was followed by the Ralph Plummer-designed East course in the 1950s. Over the years, like the neighborhood around it, the course fell victim to neglect, the clubhouse got old and musty and its conditions deteriorated significantly.

Golf Hustling History at Tenison Park

Lee Trevino grew up poor, in Dallas, and as a kid did some caddying at Glenn Lakes Country Club in Dallas where the caddies played cards, threw dice, and played the makeshift three-hole course behind their caddy shack. After a stint in the Army, Trevino returned to Dallas and worked at Hardy's driving range. He would often work late at the driving range, hustling under the lights, then get up early and head to Tenison Park Golf Club where his hustle for extra money continued during the daytime.

Titanic Thompson crossed paths with Trevino in Dallas when Lee was 21 years old, around 1960. There they partnered in bigger hustles.

Titanic was born Alvin Clarence Thomas, in 1892. He grew up poor in the Ozarks, near Rogers, Arkansas. By the time Ti Thompson and Lee met, Titanic was almost 50 years older than Lee and in his 70s. He got the name Titanic when he won a proposition wager, as a young man of 24, jumping over a pool table with a 54-inch surface that was 30 inches off the floor. Snow Clark, owner of the Joplin, Missouri pool hall, said the kid's name should be Titanic, because "he just sank everybody." He got the name Thompson from a typo in a newspaper article years later. That was OK by him, as he wanted to travel "low-key" and under the radar.

He used the name Alvin Thomas when on the road hustling. He traveled in a Pierce Arrow with a pool cue, horseshoes, two sets of golf clubs (one left-handed, the other right) his guns, and a bunch of cash (often as much as a million dollars) in the trunk of his car.

Titanic Thompson's goal, his compulsion, was to prove he could beat any man at anything. And this he did, all his life. From the early years in the 1900s, Titanic Thompson won and lost millions of dollars in card games, shooting pool, rolling dice, throwing horseshoes, playing golf, and anything else anyone could think of in wagering (or proposition bets). He became notoriously famous, connected with Houdini, Al Capone, Minnesota Fats, Howard Hughes, Benny Binion (World Series of Poker), Legs Diamond, Nick the Greek, "Shoeless Joe" Jackson, Meyer Lansky, Ray Floyd, Lee Elder, Ky Laffoon, and so many more, all with true stories that would fill volumes.

By the way, Ky Laffoon's name appears in gold lettering on the list of winners inscribed on the wall in the Phoenix Country Club Men's Grill for winning the Phoenix Open held at PCC in 1935. Laffoon assisted Titanic Thompson in his golf hustles. He used to do some caddying for Ti, dressed up in bib overalls and playing a dimwitted country bumpkin role in the ploy. After Titanic fleeced his pigeon, he would say, "I'd bet you double or nothing that my caddy here could beat you! Want to go double or nothing?" Well, you know who won those wagers: Ky Laffoon. He went on to win 12 PGA golf tournaments, played on the 1935 Ryder Cup team, and finished 5th in the 1936 U.S. Open.

Titanic Thompson never played in golf tournaments. So, just how good was he? Ben Hogan said, "He's the best shot maker I ever saw. Right or left-handed, you can't beat him." Byron Nelson said, "No question, he could have excelled on the tour, but he didn't have to. He was at a higher level, playing for $25,000 a nine, while we played for $150." And Sam Snead, quite a hustler himself, called Ti "golf's greatest hustler."

Back to Dallas and Tenison Park and The Merry Mex, Lee Trevino. The stakes improved for Lee with Ti's involvement, for sure! Lee had developed his trademark hustle, using a 32-ounce Dr. Pepper bottle. Titanic saw and liked Lee, his spirit (he was a guy who often bet more than he had on him…), his style, and his unorthodox swing. So they teamed up on "their hustle." Like Ti, Lee had spent hours in practice and preparation. "I practiced almost a year before I got into a match with my Dr. Pepper bottle," Lee once said. "Then I played with it for three years and never lost."

Portraying Lee as the underdog, Titanic Thompson would say to his 'mark,' "See that little Mexican, over there? He's got no golf clubs, no shoes… too poor. He'll play you with a bottle. What'll you spot him, ten to one?"

It was Ti Thompson who arranged the match between Lee Trevino and Ray Floyd down in El Paso, Texas.

Ray Floyd vs. Lee Trevino

Lee had moved to El Paso, Texas and was the Assistant Professional (meaning he was part-time locker room attendant, picked up balls from the driving range, and serviced the golf carts) at Horizon Hills Country Club. "Welcome to Horizon Hills," said Trevino as he met Ray Floyd. "Let me get your clubs out of the car," said Trevino.

"I've got a game with someone here," Floyd said. "Yeah, me," was Trevino's reply.

Word had gotten around about the match and the locals put $18,000 down on Trevino and more on side bets in the "trash bets"— birdies, chip-ins, and such. Lee turned the front nine with a one-shot lead, which was still standing when they reached the 18th tee. And that's the way the round of golf finished: Trevino 65, Floyd 66. Titanic's side betting on Floyd, was down some $18,000 to $20,000.

Trevino backers agreed to play for the same amount the next day, but first they took Ray Floyd across the border into Juarez, Mexico for a late evening of women and tequila, followed by an early morning dove hunt. Thinking they had gotten Ray Floyd hammered that night, confidence was high among the Trevino backers.

Trevino, again, hung on to a one stroke lead, winning the second day with a score of 63 to Floyd's 64. Ti and Floyd backers were now down some $36,000. Floyd convinced them that he could beat Trevino and the third round was set for the next day.

There was talk that Titanic wanted to make the wager $50,000, but the amount is not really known. Guesses have it at a double or nothing bet. The final day was one gigantic fiesta with pickup trucks, radios blaring Mexican music that carried down the fairways, lots of beer and tequila, horns blaring, and drunks yelling.

Raymond shot a 31 on the front side. Lee made a birdie to close the gap to one shot, then made another birdie to tie the score. They were on the 18th tee, a 556-yard par five, reachable in two on the dry-hard fairway. Trevino hit first, lashing a three wood onto the green, some 15 feet from the hole. Horns were honking and Mexicans in the beds of pickup trucks were cheering, jumping, screaming, and pumping fists into the air! Ray settled over his second shot to the 18th green with a one-iron in hand. A one-iron! He hit it "Dead Solid Perfect" to 20 feet from the hole.

Again, it was down to the 18th green. Floyd rolled it in, for an eagle three!

Trevino eyed his putt from all sides on a green he knew very well. He needed this putt to match Floyd's 63. Lee settled over the putt and then the stroke and the putter sent the ball down its path. It took a dip into the hole, made an almost complete circle and then lipped out, leaving the ball resting half over the hole, half out… refusing to drop. Floyd won – Floyd 63, Trevino 64.

A three-day Mexican Stand Off—and certainly one of the most famous money games of them all!

1978
Screen Door
Open
Dallas, Texas

PLEASE ONLY 2 TO A CART
NO ALCHOHOL
SHIRTS MUST BE WORN

July 1978 - The First Screen Door Open: Tenison Park, the perfect venue

Eleven other guys were personally invited to the inaugural event. So, there would be 12 participants—11 special golf friends and me—in the first-ever Screen Door Open Golf Classic. Present was my longtime pal, Malcolm, who was then working for Xerox in Oklahoma City, Chad Alexander, Kappa Sig brother from Oklahoma State University, and two other Xerox friends, Joe Wyzkoski from San Francisco and Dick Taylor from Houston. Also competing were my former IBM buddies, Dan Shackleford from Ft. Worth, and Tony Lopez and Doug Messerlie both from New Orleans. Add in my Tenison Park golf guys, Keith Rowland, Mike White, and Tom Clarkson—and, from San Antonio, Bart Palm—and that was the field. I had two Honorary Participants that first year: Herschel T. Phillips, III from Dallas and George Allen from Houston. Everyone stayed at the Clubhouse (my house) on Richmond Ave. in Dallas, Texas.

We played golf at Tenison Park, with three teams of four golfers each in competition for two days. We had Bar-B-Q brought into The Clubhouse and lots of cold beer and we frequented the joints on Greenville Ave. There was a late night with single-digit-hour pizza delivery (2 am, if I had to guess) from a pizza joint, appropriately named Leonardo De Munchies, one of the greatest brand names of the times as well as the greatest pizzas ever. (No doubt on that score because our taste buds were ever so titillated by the herbs supplied by Herschel T. Phillips, the Roman numeral.) Everyone must have had a good time, because we did it again in 1979, with everyone returning. We chose to honor Ben Hogan in our second year.

The Old Course St. Andrews – The Royal & Ancient Clubhouse

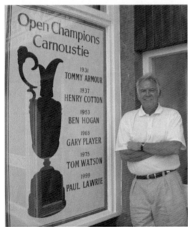

J. Mike – Carnoustie 2003
50th Anniversary of Ben Hogan's
Open Championship

The Claret Jug
2018 Open Championship,
Carnoustie

1997 – 20th Anniversary SDO Presentation at The Old Course
Mike Bixler with Greetings from Prime Minister Tony Blair

Shady Oaks Golf Club – Ft. Worth, Texas 1993
Jim Braswell - Ben Hogan - Joe Wyzkoski
40 years after Hogan's Open Championship

GTE Classic 2003, Ojai, California
Arnold Palmer – caddy J. Mike

Arnold Palmer's autograph
to J. Mike

Jack's 2005 Farewell to the Open
The Old Course, St. Andrews

Jack autographs £5 note for J. Mike

2015 – Palm Springs
Another Okie with J. Mike:
Johnny Bench from Binger, Oklahoma

2002 – Sherwood CC, California
J. Mike - Wayne Gretzsky - Jim Rankin,
8-time SDO Champion

Separated at Birth
Tommy Armour III and J. Mike
Champions Schwab Cup 2017, Phoenix CC

J. Mike at Dundonald Links, Scotland
2017 Women's Scottish Open

Sam Casano and J. Michael Meadows

Fundraising: J. Mike, Alice Cooper, My Diane

SDO Headquarters – Dallas, Texas – 1982

The Ed Hagan Quartet
Jammin' at The SDO

SDO in Juarez, Mexico, 1991
The DOOR PRIZE

Helicopters, Harleys, Horseback
Hot Air Balloons… what's next?

Forty Years of Friendship and Golf
Keith Rowland, J. Mike, Herschel Phillips

*2015 Golf in the Kingdom lunch at Prestwick GC, Scotland. Home of the first
Open 1860, the next 11, and the venue for a total of 24 Open Championships*

Mike Hyatt & J. Mike – First Tee "Railway," Old Prestwick GC, Scotland

*Sunday, July 29, 2018 on Golf in the Kingdom's Scotland Tour. Bernard Langer and
Phx CC friend, Jim Fishman, on the Swilken Bridge. A fine 2nd place finish in the
2018 Senior Open Championship for Langer. Friend Gordon Murray,
whose house is "The End House" overlooking the 17th Green – "The Road Hole,"
the 18th hole, tee to green, the Swilken Bridge, and The Royal & Ancient Clubhouse:
"Location – Location – Location," the number one rule of real estate… Not bad, Gordon!*

Official Transportation 1980

| *John Martin - Don McKinney* | *J. Malcolm Haney 1996* | *Jay Thomas* |
| *SDO TKO* | *SDO Acceptance Speech* | *... always with beer in hand* |

*"Because of the Screen Door Open,
my husband (Joe) was A.W.O.L.
on my birthday each year for more
than 25 years... and I loved it!
I laughed so much hearing about
the antics and surprises of
each SDO. It brought such
joy to the both of us."
Mary Margaret Wyzkoski
1943 - 2018*

The 1988 Screen Door Open

Pat Gallagher – Bagpiper – J. Mike
2014 Sidewinder Champions,
Phoenix CC

Jim Hromas and Mike Hyatt
1981 Screen Door Open,
Dallas, TX

Under Rule 23 (Loose Impediments) of the USGA, Jack Reynolds of New Orleans and
SDO Tournament host, carefully removed the impediment without moving the ball

"Hello? Yes, this is the President's office!"

"The Roos" of 1954-1957 – Kaiser Kangaroo Reunions, Rancho la Quinta, CA. 2012-2015
Left to right top left photo: Ricky Dugger, Jack Thomas, J. Mike Meadows, C.B. Hudson

Charlie and Me. Hmm? I think I could sell these golf balls back to the golfers!

Somehow a sponsorship became required for someone to receive an invitation to the event. This included a former participant's recommendation along with the participant's qualifications to be invited to the annual event. Qualifications included: having good standing in the world, being a jolly fellow of good character with a sense of adventure… and so forth and so on. What it basically meant was that anyone ever invited to an SDO could invite like-minded lovers of the game of golf and those who they thought would enjoy and appreciate the entertainment.

1979 Exxon Office Systems

That same year I received a call from the past head of Sales Training at Xerox Headquarters in Dallas, who told me that Exxon, the oil giant, was going to diversify beyond the oil business and jump into the Office Automation marketplace. I asked, "Is this the same Exxon whose product I use when I'm filling up my car?" "The same," he said. I then asked, "I think they are the largest organization in the world, aren't they?" The response validated that, "I think you're right."

Bob Fine, having been with Xerox for many years in the Copier/ Telecopier side of the business, said that he was going to take a lead role in Exxon's new initiative and that he would be responsible for bringing on people for sales positions, sales managers, and sales training opportunities. The bottom line was that I could, well, have any position that I wanted. I told him that "we could talk, but that I definitely wanted to continue living in Dallas." His next remark—"No problem"—sealed the deal.

On further investigation, I found that Exxon had purchased three start-up companies: Qyx (electronic typewriters), Qwip (fax equipment) and Vydec (word processors). The company was now ready to enter the Office Systems marketplace with Exxon Office Systems, investing $2 billion in a bid to become a major player in what seemed to be the growth industry of the new decade.

My questions and concerns were about advertising and promotion support. Bob indicated, "No problem." This was as solid as you could get, right? The largest organization in the world… Exxon. A sure thing!

We did talk, and I basically said that I wanted all three positions or nothing doing. Next thing, I found myself in Lionville, Pennsylvania at the first company Exxon had purchased, Qyx. I took the quasi-position as all of the above: salesman (lead salesman), sales manager (hiring other sales people), and sales training, whenever, and wherever needed. And all the while maintaining my residence in Dallas. I had been with IBM and Xerox in sales and was recognized as one of the best, promoted to District Training, followed by National Training with Xerox, so I figured Exxon needed me for all three positions—and I was right! I was in a major leadership position in developing the SYSTEMS Training for Exxon Office Systems.

July 1979 – SDO participants grow to 20

SDO T-Shirt

Malcolm, who was now working for Kodak, sponsored and invited John Hefley, our first-ever senior participant at 50 years of age. Jim Rankin, a Xerox guy from Ft. Worth, accepted his invitation. Tony Burke, Malcolm's brother-in-law, was extended an invitation and accepted. (SDO Trivia: Tony's wife, a graphic designer, created our classic trophy logo.) Malcolm had introduced me to Roy Clyde Walker, with whom we played golf in OKC with Stormy Williams, and we invited him, thinking that this was his kind of golf. We weren't surprised when he accepted.

I invited W.W. Pierce, who I had met in Lionville after joining the ranks of Exxon Office Information Systems, and again the invite was accepted. Bill Davison, our high school golf team member, accepted. Bart Palm invited his real estate partner and golf professional from San Antonio, Jack Harden, who also accepted. Mike Bixler, with Xerox in Leesburg and now living in Plano, was a perfect fit. Chad invited Chuck Hetrick, a dentist from Edmond, Oklahoma, who accepted (and who's been working in my mouth ever since.)

In Michael Murphy's 1972 classic *Golf In The Kingdom*, in Part II – The Game's Hidden but Accessible Meaning, he has a passage titled *Of a Golf Shot on the Moon* wherein he describes how "Alan Shepard and his golf pro, Jack Harden"—notice the name in the above paragraph—"had planned the thing..." and "What could have led the man to design that faulty club, smuggle it on board (the Kitty Hawk) with those "heat resistant" balls and risk some billion-dollar disaster from flying divots or tears in a space suit? What could have led him to such monumental triviality amid the terrors and marvels of the moon? The madness of the game had surfaced again, I thought, as I pondered his motives."[2]

Well, that golf club was a Wilson Staff 6 iron that belonged, back at that time, to our 1979 Screen Door Open Champion, Jack Harden, Jr. His name is permanently engraved on the SDO trophy. It was Jack Jr.'s golf club that his father, the golf professional at River Oaks CC, made into a break-down, telescoping club for Alan Shepard to fulfill his passion to hit a golf ball on the moon... "the game keeps giving us glimpses."

By the way, I saw the club in the USGA Golf Museum at the Golf House in Far Hills, New Jersey.

"There's No Business Like Show Business"

1946 by Irving Berlin
written for Annie Get Your Gun
Sung by Ethel Merman

So, let's go on with the show!

Steer Horns, Helicopters, Harleys, Hot-air Balloons and Horses?
I Know What You're thinking:
"I thought this was a golf tournament."

The 1979 Screen Door Open Golf Championship began with chauffeured limousines, but not the black, stuffy limos you're used to seeing. These were Texas Taxis—another of my Entrepreneurial Ventures—a fleet of white Cadillac Eldorado convertibles complete with longhorn steer horns as hood ornaments.

Helping make Texas Taxi unbelievably famous were *Playboy* magazine (which had us as the #1 thing to do in Dallas) and *People* magazine that ran a feature on Texas Taxi with a full-page shot of the Eldorado convertible, a cowboy, and two dazzling cowgirls and then a *full-page article* featuring the TV series *Dallas* which we appeared on at least a dozen times—smack dab in the middle of the magazine. We were always driving J.R. (actor Larry Hagman) Sue Ellen, and Bobby around Dallas, whenever they were in town. Texans love to do things up really big, so we provided just that opportunity.

SDO Tournament participants were greeted and welcomed to Dallas Love Field and DFW airports upon arrival by a Cowboy or Cowgirl driver, cigars, and beer. Not a bad greeting, huh?

Texas Taxi

An instant hit in Dallas, the cost to hire a Texas Taxi was $50 per hour (with a 2-hour minimum) and we had six of them. This was back in the days when drinking and driving was legal. You just couldn't drive drunk, that's all.

Back in the early '80s in Texas, drinking and driving was as common as 7-Eleven stores. The state had no law against quaffing a Lone Star or sipping on a Scotch and soda while cruising anywhere, and we had the perfect party, on wheels.

After the 1979 Screen Door Open, we ripped out all the carpeting in each Texas Taxi and replaced with boat carpet and drains. This sure made it easier to clean the cars… using a power hose, both outside and inside. Since part of our service was supplying Lone Star beer, you can well imagine the kind of cleanups that were necessary to keep the rolling stock in tip-top shape.

Texas Taxi Fleet

It was beginning to look as if the U.S. Screen Door Open was shaping up to be an annual "clam bake" type occurrence of camaraderie, entertainment, and golf, so we elected officers and formed committees for just about everything—Food and Beverage, Transportation, Invitations, Tournaments, History, etc. This was just for fun and basically in name only. Fictitious committees were also formed—Greens Committee, Membership Committee, etc. The only one true and valid committee became each year's Site Selection Committee, a highly sought after position within the committees because this selected group of helpers had to be willing to travel and help in selecting the next venue.

The 1980 Screen Door Open III had 24 participants. Now what shall I do?

Maybe it's time for a Hole-In-One Car. Nah, nobody is going to have a hole-in-one, but what about this… Someone will be closest to the hole, so we'll give away a car this year. Yeah, that's the ticket! And we'll invite Dan Jenkins, author of *The Best 18 Holes in America, The Dogged Victims of Inexorable Fate, Dead Solid Perfect, Limo,* and *Baja Oklahoma* (his works up until 1980).

Closest-to-the-Hole wins this Car

Dan's schedule would not allow him to attend and be our guest of honor that year, as some other commitment had him at another golf event, with not as good a name. (As he wrote in his letter to me that follows.)

It was some tournament that happens in the third week of July every year, known simply as The Open (the oldest of the four majors, held since 1860, and administered by the Royal & Ancient) had him committed there, at Muirfield in Scotland for the 109th Open Championship, which was won by Tom Watson. The Open got Dan Jenkins' commitment before the SDO could.

Dan did write a great letter to the Screen Door Open, from his own fabric-ribbon portable typewriter (easily identified by an old IBM typewriter salesman), which hangs in the clubhouse today. (The SDO clubhouse is now and has always been wherever I hang my hat.)

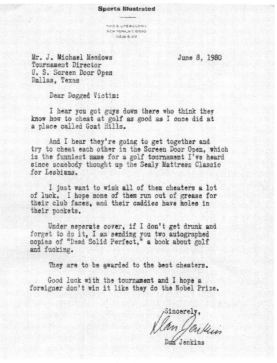

Sports Illustrated

TIME & LIFE BUILDING
NEW YORK, N.Y. 10020
PLaza 6-232

Mr. J. Michael Meadows   June 8, 1980
Tournament Director
U. S. Screen Door Open
Dallas, Texas

Dear Dogged Victim:

    I hear you got guys down there who think they
know how to cheat at golf as good as I once did at
a place called Goat Hills.

    And I hear they're going to get together and
try to cheat each other in the Screen Door Open, which
is the funniest name for a golf tournament I've heard
since somebody thought up the Sealy Mattress Classic
for Lesbians.

    I just want to wish all of them cheaters a lot
of luck. I hope none of them run out of grease for
their club faces, and their caddies have holes in
their pockets.

    Under seperate cover, if I don't get drunk and
forget to do it, I am sending you two autographed
copies of "Dead Solid Perfect," a book about golf
and fucking.

    They are to be awarded to the best cheaters.

    Good luck with the tournament and I hope a
foreigner don't win it like they do the Nobel Prize.

                                    Sincerely,

                                    Dan Jenkins

Dan Jenkins' Letter   1980

Dan Jenkins signing my copy of **Baja Oklahoma**

174

We added Pat Gallagher, formerly with IBM and (at the time) at Exxon with me, and Mike Hyatt from my OSU days. Mike and I had reconnected and he was living in Ft. Worth. The venue—yes!—still Tenison Park Golf Club. And the Clubhouse: still my house in Dallas. For that year's event we planned a formal evening (tuxedos) at Dave and Busters playing snooker, limos for transportation, and two days of Team Golf.

I had converted the spooky attic into one big open room, which somebody named "The Top of the Stairs Club," where (despite the July Texas heat and the lack of air-conditioning up there) W.W. Pierce, in his tux, put on one helluva Frank Sinatra impersonation, to the drunken delight of everyone. W.W.'s "Sinatra performance" became the standard for many more SDO events, with his final SDO performance, and his great comeback in 2014, at the Men's Grill President's Room at the Phoenix Country Club.

Dubya Dubya 1979   *Dubya Dubya 2014 RIP*

SDO IV 1981

This was also the year we welcomed Lee Weatherly of Dallas, and his marvelous mobile Bar-B-Q grill. He rolled that machine right into the back yard for the finest Texas-style food a group could ever expect, especially the B-B-Q chicken and grilled steaks. Dave Quisenberry, formerly of Exxon Information Systems, joined our group that year. This was also the year that the SDO became the first "USSDO International-Invitational Golf Championship," or USSDOIIGC for short. The committee added the big burly-bearded Scotsman, Colin McNee Ferguson, who was living in London, England and was my UK contact of Exxon International Office Systems. The SDO participation continued to grow.

| *Me & Colin* | *Colin in Dallas* | *Colin & Me* |
| *England 1979* | *SDO 1981* | *Scotland 2016* |

So, *now* what am I going to do? The construction of the gigantic scoreboard and a stage was added to the back yard of the Clubhouse. Across the top, flags from every state of the union represented by SDO participants were placed, along with the Union Jack (flag of the UK) in the center.

SDO Bar-B-Q in Clubhouse yard   *The Ed Hagen Quartet*

1981 SDO Transportation

I still had the Texas Taxis and the stretch limos, so these vehicles took us from the Clubhouse, cruising the six miles down Ross Avenue to downtown Dallas, to the Re-Union Plaza where there were helicopters waiting to deliver us to Tenison Park. The flight was another six miles "as the helicopters fly" straight to the golf course.

Helicopters

The old Clubhouse had been through a major renovation by this time. I had eliminated the wall between two bedrooms, making one large room that was 18 feet by 36 feet—and had been outfitted with 32 lockers. Yes, lockers like you find in golf clubhouses across the country. The low-gross winner of the SDO every year would occupy locker #1 the following year, upon his return to defend the Championship.

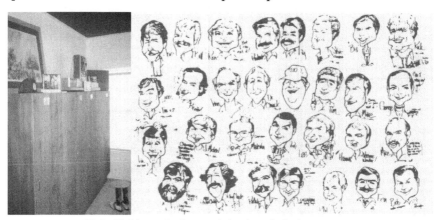

SDO Clubhouse Lockers and sketches of all players – 1981

1982 SDO… Dallas, Texas

We expanded to 32 participants in 1982, so the question of the day became: how are we going get to Tenison Park, this year?" Graham Ross from Scotland (an invitee of Colin Ferguson) brought his bagpipes for opening ceremonies and played them at the Greenville Ave. Country Club Bar & Grill and Swimming Pool, where Dick Taylor (accidentally on purpose) bumped Graham, kilt and pipes, into the swimming pool. Dick said, "I can't stand that screeching any more. It sounds like a hyena caught in a coon trap." Good thing bagpipes, being full of air, do float because ole Graham was wrapped in a wool kilt and wool socks up to his knees and was totally soaked… and sinking fast.

The following morning I gave every SDO participant a $50 bill. That raised a slew of questions: "What's this for?" and "I think you want me to give this to somebody?" And "OK, where is she?" I said, "I suggest you hand this over to your transportation representative this morning!" "What?" came the chorus. I had one last piece of advice: "And pick a pretty one."

All of a sudden, outside the clubhouse came a "loud-rumbling-overture-of-power." This was back before EPA Guidelines, when just one Harley idling sounded like: *cub-a-bucaw… cubaw…. cubabaw cubaw and bum.. bummuba… bum bummuba… bum.* Thirty-two Hogs sounded like nothing short of roaring thunder—and a lot of trouble!

Harley-Davidson, once a proud brand of motorcycles that were originally only owned by a legit band of bad-asses back in the day, began (sadly) to become more concerned with merchandising rather than building decent bikes. All of a sudden, with their marketing, it became acceptable for doctors, lawyers, and fat bald guys having a midlife crisis to ride a Harley. But, certainly not *our kind of guys*, this particular morning. Each one of these fellas, wearing mostly black and heavy black boots, were promised a "fifty-by-god-dollar-bill" each, a keg of beer upon arrival, and another keg of beer upon delivering us to Tenison Park.

SDO – High on Harleys

We (the SDO guys) were all wearing our shorts, T-shirts, and golf caps. Quite a contrast between the two groups of guys—golf guys and biker dudes! Though we were different, we had great fun socializing: 32 of them, and 32 of us, in the front yard of the clubhouse and, well, basically examining and admiring biker tattoos and drinking beer. There were lots of Harley-Davidson logo tattoos, and skulls and such. Several tattoos simply said: Born to Ride or Freedom. One biker rolled down his lower lip so we could see the tattoo inside his mouth. It read: "F#*K" Another biker had a simple **BFD** tattooed on one arm, and **WTF** on the other.

Each SDO participant got on the back of a Harley and off we roared, 32 Harleys and 64 brothers bonding in the moment. It was six miles through traffic, then entering the golf course from the green on #18 of the East course of Tenison Park, riding up the gravel cart path to the front door and first tee. Quite a head-turner, you could say! So much so that when we arrived at the front door of Tenison Park Golf Club people were flocking out from everywhere, even from off the golf course, the practice area, and coming out of the clubhouse to see what was happening. There was a group of Asian golfers who came out of the clubhouse and upon seeing them looking at all the Harleys, one of the bad-ass biker dudes pointed to his bike and yelled at them: "This ain't no Sue-Zooky, and it ain't no Cow-a-Suckie...It's a Haw-Ree-Davidson!" That's the 1980s for you...

SDO Clubhouse 1950

SDO Clubhouse 1982

The beer keg was brought to the course parking lot with permission of the head professional Jerry Andrews, who was always amenable to my requests, no matter how crazy they seemed. The bad-ass bikers stayed with the beer until the keg was dry as eight foursomes teed off #1 at 1:00, 1:10, 1:20, 1:30, 1:40, 1:50, 2:00 with the last inebriated group at 2:10 on a Saturday in late July of 1982. From the golf course we could hear bikers "thundering" away as they left us to play the first round of the 1982 Screen Door Open on Tenison Park East.

Many of the SDO participants were asking if the bad-ass biker dudes were coming to pick us up after golf. I asked them, "Did you give your biker that $50 bill?" The reply, "Sure did, just like you told us." My reply was, "If they got the money, they ain't comin' back to get you."

I had something else planned for leaving the golf course. When the last group finished their round and joined everyone in the Tenison Park Golf clubhouse, and after beers on the course and in the Tenison clubhouse, I said, "Transportation is here, and we have to go right now... Follow me!"

We left through the back door of Tenison, turned left and walked the distance of a good 1-iron, crossing E. Grand Avenue to a big open field where ten hot-air balloons were staged and getting blown up for the single largest balloon ascension in Dallas history. It took FAA clearance and a special permit for the mass ascension, since we would be flying into Dallas Love Field airspace. There were a few guys who refused and rode with the chase crews, but most everyone else was hollering and screaming with excitement. We took off, having no clue where we would land.

I liked ballooning so much that I bought the Blue Checkerboard one, took lessons, got a commercial license, and found myself an "aeronaut" and in a new business venture.

1982 SDO Transportation after golf and new venture for J. Michael

Challenging Times for Exxon Office Systems

Exxon International was having me do more training in the UK and the Netherlands. I left first for Birmingham, England and on to Den Hag to train reps in sales, product, and marketplace training on the Qyx product line. Something was happening in the United States with the entire company, while they continued to expand elsewhere.

All of a sudden, it seemed, Exxon Office Systems Company dismissed about a fifth of its workforce and closed a manufacturing plant as part of what it called an effort to streamline operations.

The layoff of nearly 1,100 workers proved to be an unsuccessful attempt to bring the Exxon Corporation's ailing office systems automation business into the black. Combined with layoffs of 600 workers a few months earlier, the new cutbacks reduced the company's work force from nearly 6,000 employees to 4,000.

"The moves are really designed to strengthen the company and to move us from operating in the red to operating in the black, which is our target by the end of next year," said the director of public affairs of the office systems company, which was based in Stamford, Connecticut.

Next the company said it was shutting its Orlando, Florida plant that manufactured the Qwip facsimile machine and would dismiss all but a handful of its 465 employees. Qwip production transferred to the Lionville plant, which was already producing the Qyx electronic typewriter. The 600 other employees laid off in that wave of cost-cutting came from all parts of the company, including headquarters.

The once-celebrated move of the nation's largest oil company into office automation had now turned into an embarrassment, in the view of many analysts. The office systems company, whose sales were estimated at $200 million in 1980, lost tens of millions of dollars that year, according to published reports. And the losses continued.

Although the company was a pioneer in word processors, electronic typewriters, and low-priced facsimile machines, it failed to update those products and was leapfrogged by its competitors, including Xerox, IBM, and Wang Laboratories Inc.

Management Problem

The company did not have follow-on products, and had nothing in development. Exxon also had trouble managing what were once small entrepreneurial companies, and most of the founders of Qyx, Qwip, and Vydec left Exxon after the oil giant acquired their enterprises.

Like Exxon, other companies (most notably the International Business Machines Corporation and the Xerox Corporation) also announced reorganizations and, in Xerox's case, layoffs, to help streamline operations. But those efforts were viewed by analysts as aiming to compete better and cope with a recession.

Exxon's moves looked, to me, like survival tactics, as all the while Exxon discounted any speculation that the company would withdraw from the office automation business. The "sure thing" I had banked on didn't last as Exxon came to the realization that not only do oil and water not mix, but neither to oil and electronics.

So, soon to be out of work, I started looking for new opportunities. In the early 1980s I had a couple of Commodities Trading Advisors (CTAs) who were in their mid-20s using our Texas Taxis, Rolls Royce, and stretch limo services and running their own financial investing company. They also had a commodities brokerage firm, Contemporary Financial Services, and a telex time-sharing company. (None of which, for the record, I knew anything about...) This was before I learned that the term "contemporary" means *ever changing*. The main kid, who will remain nameless, had to leave Connecticut, because the state wasn't big enough to contain his ego. He left "the back east" because Texas was the land of opportunity in the financial world. You don't have much of a chance to become a bank president before you're 50 in New York, but they're everywhere in Texas, and in their 30s. Dallas was perfect for his ego, for it was the land of one's ability and not of one's success.

Since I was from Oklahoma City, he wanted me to go with him and meet some individuals who wanted to go public with an initial public offering (IPO) in a corporation being formed to refurbish all the 747 aircraft engines in the world by reducing their excessive noise. This would be accomplished by building new engine nacelles (the encasements in which the engines were housed) so that all the 747s could meet the new FAA noise requirements in the United States. At that time, there was only one 747 allowed to fly in U.S. airways and that was Air Force One. The individuals involved, in Oklahoma City, were the past commander at Tinker Air Force Base (déjà vu, as my dad was first assigned to Tinker), the past CEO of Wilson Meat Packing, and a successful businessman from Edmond, Oklahoma.

Again, I didn't know anything about those areas of business. Come to find out, they wanted me to come along and play golf with the gentlemen at Oak Tree Golf Club in Edmond (the young executives didn't play golf) and be introduced as a business associate of Contemporary Financial. The kid was only 23. I would be his 37-year-old business associate, and a former IBM executive.

While driving from Dallas to OKC (at 100 mph in the kid's new Porsche with my knuckles turning white), I asked him a lot of questions about the commodities business and I learned about the term, "churning and burning." The term had to do with the fast use of other people's money in the buying and selling of contracts in the commodities markets. "A lot of commissions are made with each transaction, and we are the brokers. We make a lot of money in commissions," he explained. I asked, "Do you also trade your own commodities accounts?" He said, "Of course, and we never lose any money in our own accounts, we're on top of it every minute that the market is open."

He proposed that I come into his commodities business and raise money for the CTAs at Contemporary Financial Advisors. He needed more elders in his office, I guess. I asked him, "If you can, for sure, give the same guarantee to investors," —that being *that we never lose any money*—I think I could bring a lot of investors' money into... what's the name of it, again? Contemporary Financial Advisors?"

I really enjoyed meeting another entrepreneur, Tom Stewart, from Edmond, OK, who said whenever he found another new business opportunity, he wanted to hire me as VP of Sales and Marketing. Sounded good to me!

The kids opened an appropriately named bar back in Dallas, *Other People's Money*, while I went exploring new opportunities. *Other People's Money* was such a great name for all their enterprises.

In 1981 the board game *Trivial Pursuit* appeared in the United States, and was an instant hit—holding the rank of America's Number One Board Game for years. One day W.W. Pierce (Exxon and SDO participant) and I were eating Chinese food and drinking Tsingtao beers at the New Big Wong Chinese restaurant a half block away from the SDO clubhouse in Dallas. When the bill came, accompanied with two fortune cookies, the idea hit me. Why couldn't we do something like this, except put it into a great tasting cracker? Yeah, trivia questions… with the answers on the back of the slip of paper! Then one of us said, "Yeah, crackers with a trivia question, where the peanut butter usually is!" and "Yeah, that's the ticket!" You might be asking yourself just how many beers we'd had…

1984 World Premier of Trivia Bits

Turning the idea into a product was harder than we thought. We got together with a local chef who had baking facilities, hired some people, and started making cheese crackers by hand. The first problem was how to bake the two pieces of cracker with a slip of paper in the middle. "That's more difficult than baking a two-layer cake while they sit on top of each other," Mom said, "and you want to put a piece of paper in there?" Mom then asked me a very good question, "*Ma' kel*, what do you know about bakin'?" I had to answer truthfully: "Nothing, Mom."

We finally had a prototype. So, one of the big Dallas hotels, The Anatole and its Mistral night club gave us one very good announcement party on July 12, 1984: "The World Premier of Trivia Bits."

J. Michael Meadows
TRIVIA BITS™ Inc. P.O. Box 64874
Dallas, Texas 75206 (214) 871-0737

The phone started ringing at our new offices and we were off and running in our business, or so we thought. We were on the radio being interviewed around the country, on TV news shows, and in magazine articles galore. We were even featured in *Entrepreneur Magazine*, in the May 1985 issue.

With publicity came demand and with demand came the need for contracting with a "volume baker." Then we found the Richmond Baking Company in Richmond, Indiana, the nation's oldest cracker bakers. We showed them our prototype and the orders we had in hand. They tasted our crackers and agreed to "take on the product." The first problem was how to place a piece of paper on top of cracker dough at high speed, then fold it over and bake it. We found an engineering company in Wisconsin that had developed a hydraulic rotary placing device that could lay a "fortune-cookie-size piece of paper" on dough at a very fast rate, as in 16 pieces of paper per second. Next little problem was how to fold the dough over, in half, and on top of the paper resting on the bottom piece of dough. Another engineering firm came up with the solution: a row of "plows" which the pre-baked dough would slide over, while coming down a 4-foot-wide high-speed conveyor belt into the oven, and out the other side, dropping into our newly designed container that resembled half of a tennis ball sleeve.

With all this R&D adding up, the bank account was being rapidly depleted and all we could do was take out even more in loans, which we did. Every "test run" of the product, to get the taste just right or to test the rotary placing devise or the folding mechanism, cost us $5,000. The automated process began on the third floor of the baking company, where the dough was mixed in batches of thousands of pounds, spread and rolled out on the baking line. On the second floor, they were scored and ready for paper placement, going through the fold-over system and into the oven to test our system—and then actually bake thousands of crackers. It finally worked so that each baking run we produced, get this, was one million crackers, enough for about 18,000 single retail cans.

We had researched (meaning: we went to libraries, sat on the floor laughing our asses off with our portable dictating equipment) trivia questions and answers, coming up with more than 5,000 trivia questions and answers, by ourselves.

Trivia Cracker Marketing

It was bound to happen. The trivia craze was just too popular a phenomenon not to spur some ingenious games and gimmicks. So now it's here—the first snack cracker with a trivia question inside. The newly invented Trivia Bits not only tickled your taste buds but also tested your wits.

Found in your taverns

Entrepreneur Magazine wrote: "The tasty cheese crackers with a hint of cayenne pepper is the invention of former Exxon marketing executives **J. Michael Meadows** and **W.W. 'Bill' Pierce.**" We touted, leveraging our stellar business credentials yet we knew nothing about baking crackers. "Meadows says that he and his partner came up with the idea while eating a fortune cookie after a Chinese dinner at The New Big Wong restaurant in Dallas. It sounded like a simple idea, but the baking process was very difficult."

More Press Releases: "The American Institute of Baking assisted in developing the process so that the cracker stays crisp and the paper didn't stick to the dough. After the baking process was perfected, Meadows and Pierce researched all the trivia questions and answers. There are more than 5,000 questions and each is numbered for trivia collectors."

"The partners have been marketing the crackers as a bar snack to airlines, hotels, restaurants, and bars. American Airlines is tentatively scheduled to include them as in-flight snacks. Trivia Bits are now being sold to the public in various quantities, including large decorated cans for $14.95. They're available at the Trivia Bits outlet in the Quadrangle in Dallas, Texas."

We first went after bulk sales to hotels, restaurants, bars, and airlines. I remember a bar owner calling our offices once and complaining about all the crumbs being left on the bar, the tables, and the floor of his place. He said his customers were going wild busting up the crackers just to get to the trivia questions. He admitted some of the crackers were being eaten, but it was the mess the crackers were making and all the little slips of paper all over the place that drove his complaints. "Well, let me ask you this," I said, "how are your bar sales?" "Oh, way up," he said. My next question was, "Did you want to stop your next order, then?"

We could "see the light at the end of the tunnel," as it is said, and it wasn't a train. At the time, we were unaware of the fact that our biggest problem had been developing.

W.W.'s health was in trouble. He was facing his third or fourth open heart surgery, with arterial sclerosis that's typical in persons of older age and in his case was hereditary as his father was taken in his 30s. W.W. was not yet 40 years old, with another full open-heart procedure needed. This was such a critical time in our business, and in our 50/50 partnership. The prognosis was that he would not be back to work for months, and he said when he could work, it would have to be from home, recuperating, and in a bathrobe and slippers.

The business and partnership would be seriously challenged, and there was way too much risk involved. Our partnership agreements had a buy-sell agreement and I felt it necessary to call that provision. I said I was prepared to take it all, including the nearly $300,000 in debt we had amassed. And that's what I expected would happen. But I was in for another surprise—a shock, actually. I was stunned (and shocked, I admit, though I'd be the first to say that I have had very little shock me in life) when W.W. said he would take it all. Despite my efforts to talk him out of it, in rational pleadings and what I thought to be logical reasoning, he insisted on buying me out. W.W. and I stayed life-long friends and he was as close a brother as one could have.

July 1984 – "The Alamo Open" of the SDO

The first nine USSDOIIGCs [United States Screen Door Open International-Invitational Golf Championships] were all played in Texas. One special one, SDO #7, had a different Texas venue, however. We got up for the first round on the morning of a Saturday in late July in 1984, were picked up by stretch limos, and off we went. Someone yelled, "Hey, this isn't the way to Tenison!" To which I replied, "Nope, it sure ain't!"

The limos slowly drove through the Hyland Park section of Dallas, down Mockingbird Lane. Someone suggested, "I think Meadows has got us on Dallas Country Club…" as we passed the entry to DCC, but continued into the Preston Hollow area of Dallas and right past Mary Kay Ash's 12,000 square foot house. She was the founder of Mary Kay Cosmetics and we saw five pink Cadillacs out front. (No steer horns, however.) We proceeded on our way into the back entrance of Dallas' Love Field.

Entering the Private Planes Only area of Love Field we saw a 32-passenger DeHavilland aircraft, waiting for us. All limos drove right up to the aircraft and everyone got out, some very cautiously, and everyone was instructed to board. The flight crew began unloading the golf clubs from the limos and loaded them into the aircraft, as most guys stood around with a look that could best be described as disbelief. "What is going on here?" one of them finally asked. The pilots and crew were instructed not to say anything about where we were going. We taxied out to the runway, the craft took off, and refreshments were served.

Destination Unknown

Chuck Hetrick, my dentist buddy from Edmond, was a pilot himself and he quickly figured out two things. One, we were headed south, and two, we couldn't be leaving the country because we weren't in possession of our passports. (Those would be required for later SDOs.) Others started guessing: Waco? Austin? San Antonio? That's when the flight attendants started serving the margaritas.

San Antonio and Pecan Valley Golf Club, site of the 50th PGA Championship in 1968 (and all that history...) was our destination. After landing, our first stop was The Alamo, the birthplace of Texas Independence. When we got to the Alamo, my dad was waiting for us right outside the big wooden doors.

Dad had continued being active after retiring from IBM, opening a floor covering business in San Antonio and taking a photography course at San Antonio College. Perfect! I had a photographer for the SDO. Below is a picture of our Screen Door Open participants in front of the Alamo.

SDO at The Alamo   Photo by J.A. Meadows, Jr. (aka Dad)

Dick Taylor's father had just passed away, and the funeral was in Houston during the SDO Alamo weekend. I thought about Dick, his father and family. Dick was a dear friend to the SDO and all participants. I thought that I should be present at the funeral to represent the SDO and all the guys. I caught a SW airlines flight to Houston and got to the funeral service as it was concluding. I hugged Dick and told him that all the guys were thinking of him and sending him their condolences. After speaking with Dick's mother and brother and expressing my sympathy, Dick grabbed me and said, "There is nothing more for me to do here. Let's get on a plane and get to the Open." Dick and I returned to San Antonio and played some golf. Everyone was glad to see Dick.

1984 SDO at Pecan Valley GC – San Antonio, Texas
Plaque memorializing Arnold Palmer's "best ever 3 wood"
Left to right Phil Cornett, Tony Lopez, Jim Hromas, and Steve Plumbtree
Photo by J.A. Meadows, Jr. (aka Dad)

The question came up about the return flight and when we needed to get back on the chartered aircraft. That's when I told them that I had only booked a one-way charter, Dallas to San Antonio, as I had been able to find the aircraft on a dead-leg to the Alamo city—and at such a great price! "How are we going to get back to Dallas?" was the question they had for me. That's when I took a credit card out of my wallet, held it up and said, "Everyone's got one of these, don't you?" There was a brief bit of silence, and then everyone broke out in laughter! It was a great ending to a fabulous weekend in San Antonio, as Dan Jenkins wrote, "In a sunken oven of pecan trees and thick, baked Bermuda grass, on land so unpicturesque it makes you wonder why Mexico ever wanted to keep it or why Texas wanted it even for a shopping center."

Texas Taxi est. San Antonio, 1984

We (dba Texas Taxi) took the opportunity to sell a franchise to some investors in San Antonio, headed by none other than my first real estate venture partner Mike Johnson.

We had the opportunity to sell the entire limousine company, Texas Taxi (with assets comprising six white Eldorado convertibles, two black stretch limos, and a Rolls Royce). We did so and with good timing. Negotiations started just in time and right before the 1984 Republican National Convention, which nominated Ronald Reagan and George H.W. Bush. The offer was from a major limo company that was coming into Dallas and buying other limo companies. That was fine with me, as the novelty was already wearing off.

Sold 'em... lock stock and steer horns

So there I was, back on the street...again.

I remembered meeting, in the UK, the manufacturer of a product I had been keenly interested in called Flipstick®. It was a portable walking stick—pretty neat and slick, actually, having a handle with a button that you'd push and it "flipped" into a seat, not unlike the shooting sticks of old British tradition.

Flipsticks USA

A very handy accessory for sporting events... ah ha! The PGA Tour, little league games, nature walks, anything outside, and some inside possibilities too!

The product was made with a very high-quality aluminum tube, painted or shiny metal, with a flip mechanism of stainless steel and brass, a molded plastic seat (in a variety of colors) which could be silk-screen printed. Yes!

I went to Pershore, England and met with the manufacturer and negotiated the selling rights for the United States, including term of agreement, price, shipping requirements, and all that kind of stuff. Upon returning to the States, I was helped by a friend in Houston to find some Texas investors in order to get the business started. Successfully financed, I acquired a warehouse and office in Dallas, hired a secretary/assistant, and found a local silk screener.

I went on the PGA Tour and set up kiosks, testing the market, proving there was a market, selling each Flipstick for $20, at more than a 50% margin. I then contacted the big tournament names, made presentations and got orders for silk screened logos on Flipsticks for AT&T, GTE, The LPGA, and more. I had orders from different sponsors of golf tournaments around the country. I made up samples in the color red for all marshals at golf tourneys that were silk-screened with QUIET printed in white, on the seat, for the marshals to hold up when the pros were playing. I hired a couple of commissioned salesmen and was successful in getting a TV infomercial on air, selling the product at *only $19.95* via our 1-800 phone number, with a real fast talking announcer, you know the song: "*call now 1-800-555-1234… that's 1-800-555-1234 operators are standing by, so call now… 1-800-555-1234.*" We were featured in catalogues like L.L.Bean in 1989, and Horchow as well as many others, who took us on.

Reality set in. I simply could not keep up with volume requirements as we agreed upon with the manufacturer in England—sales just could not keep up. So I was out of business once again.

The SDO Trail Ride

Another SDO had a couple of letters added making the invitations read the SDO-TR. Bob Stevens from Arlington, Texas, who had been to a couple of SDOs, announced that he had the "TR" thing all figured out. On Friday and Saturday nights, July 15 and 16 that year, the Milwaukee Brewers were playing the Texas Rangers at home in Arlington Stadium, so he declared we must be going to a Rangers ball game. But not so!

Rode 'em down Greenville Avenue

Saturday evening, the 16th of July, 1988, after our round of golf, I announced we were going out to dinner—in lieu of the annual BBQ clubhouse dinner. We walked from the clubhouse down Richmond Avenue to the east one half block to Greenville Avenue for a stop at our first "watering hole." Waiting for us there were 30 horses, saddled up and ready to go, and a chuck wagon loaded with food. The TR? Well, that stood for Trail Ride. We all saddled up, except for a very few who elected to ride with the keg in the chuck wagon, and rode down the middle of Greenville Avenue to our next Trail Ride "saloon stop," each (of course) having hitching posts for the steeds. This also took a permit from the city of Dallas, for a weekend of horseback riding down the middle of one of the busiest streets in Dallas.

I got a call...

One day the phone rang. It was Tom Stewart, the entrepreneur, who I had met in Oklahoma City when he was working with the past Commander of Tinker AFB and former President of the Wilson Meat Packing Company, Oklahoma City Stock Yards. You may recall that we worked together in an initial public offering in a venture to build noise reduction nacelles on all 747 aircraft in America.

Now he was calling me on a new venture.

Tom asked me if I had ever heard of Spirit Manufacturing Corporation of Jonesboro, Arkansas. I told him, "I've never heard of Jonesboro,

Arkansas." He then asked if I had ever seen or heard of a Delta Toolbox. Again, my reply, "I can't say that I have." Tom told me that if I ever looked in the back of a pickup truck, I would notice a metal tool box, up at the front of the bed, right behind the cab...that was a Delta Tool box, made by Spirit Manufacturing. I told him I would start looking at the back of pickups more closely.

Next thing I know, several newspapers and trade journals have posted the following...

Meadows Named to VP Position   2/22/1989

The appointment of J. Michael Meadows of Dallas as vice president of marketing for Spirit Manufacturing Inc., the nation's leader in the manufacture and distribution of physical fitness equipment and recreational equipment, has been announced.

Meadows brings to Spirit an extensive background to the planning and execution of sales and marketing programs within corporate, small business, and consumer market segments.

He received a Bachelor of Science Degree in Economics from Oklahoma State University in 1968, and since served as senior marketing representative, IBM Corporation; district programs manager and as national sales training specialist, Xerox Corp.; marketing manager, Exxon Corporation, and as director of sales training, Exxon Office Systems Division, United Kingdom and the Netherlands.

Meadows has also served in various capacities at OSU, including adjunct instructor, Business Extension Department, lecturer for the University Marketing Department, and advisor to the College of Business Administration.

Tom Stewart, CEO of Spirit, said "Meadows, a creative and innovative business professional, comes to Spirit Mfg. with the drive, insight and ability to coordinate each aspect of our entrepreneurial activity for emerging growth."

The job came with a membership to the Jonesboro Country Club. That was additional good news as my first thought was: a new venue for the Screen Door Open.

Tommy Bolt, '58 US Open Southern Hills & Reprise '77

Born in Hayworth, Oklahoma, Tommy Bolt won the 1958 U.S. Open at Southern Hills in Tulsa, Oklahoma. I was 11 years old at the time, and beginning my familiarity with professional golf.

But by the time the U.S. Open returned to Southern Hills in 1977, I was very familiar with professional golf and Mr. Bolt. His reported temper gave him the nicknames of *Terrible Tom* and *Thunder Bolt*. I was also familiar with his swing and ball-striking ability. I went to the '77 Open primarily to see the man and his golf game. At 61 years of age, he still had very broad shoulders that tapered down to a 32" waist. I saw him play on Friday, after shooting a 75 on Thursday. He posted a 78 and missed the cut. But, at 61 years of age—my, oh, my—he was, in my opinion, Terrific Tommy Bolt!

A very close friend of Tommy's, Jim Dawson, from Chicago and Arkansas, had become a friend of mine through golf and golf travel to Scotland, England and South Africa. Jim invited me to a small Thanksgiving dinner at his cabin, outside of Hardy, Arkansas near Cherokee Village where Tommy Bolt and his wife Mary Lou lived. Jim and Tommy were very close friends. Only five or six people were there, but what a great time! Tommy and I held hands during prayer before the Thanksgiving feast. Tommy passed away on August 30, 2008 and Jim Dawson served as pall bearer.

Me, Tommy, and Malcolm

The U.S. Screen Door Open was played in 1989 in Jonesboro, Arkansas where Malcolm Haney and I, while playing a practice round, found Tommy Bolt. We played a hole with Mr. Bolt, after which we had our picture taken with him, his arms around us. He was smiling and repeating "sex, sex, sex," because he said, "Saying it, just makes you smile."

The SDO Monument

Jonesboro is located in far northeast Arkansas, some 140 miles (a 2.5 hour drive) from Little Rock. The nearest big city was Memphis, almost due south of Jonesboro (a 70-mile drive) just over the "Mighty Mississippi" river. Good thing Spirit had airplanes: a King Air or a Baron for our use, for Jonesboro is out there in *no-wheres-ville*. That area had very good Bar-B-Q and duck hunting, just about the best in the world. But—OMG—the mosquitoes where so big they could "flat-foot and kiss a chicken!"

1990 SDO – Terradyne Golf Club, Wichita, Kansas

In 1990 the SDO was held from July 20 to 22 at Terradyne Golf Club outside of Wichita, Kansas. Oklahoma State graduate and PGA Professional Grier Jones, (winner at Doral) was our host with golf clinics and a long-drive championship.

This was the year of the "SDO Road Trip." Most all SDO participants flew into Wichita, but there was one car that drove all the way from Dallas to the Terradyne Golf Resort, as the four passengers had nothing but time on their hands and they were in no particular hurry. In the car was John Raley, the unemployed former PGA professional, Ted Hartman, the unemployed "generalist" with a specialty in winning the long drive competition at every Screen Door Open, Jonathon Baird, the embodiment of knowledge in the widening fields of philosophy and psychology, and yours truly, the master of unemployment.

So, with time to discuss all the important matters of the world on the road trip, especially the prospects of new endeavors for us upon our return to "Big D," it was decided that a "We Tote the Note" car lot was a great opportunity. Yeah, another used car lot was perfect for Ross Avenue as there were only eighteen such lots on that boulevard already. "Except," John Raley said, "not one of them serves Bar-B-Q." Yeah, we'll do Bar-B-Q Fridays—with our own special sauce. You know... *"the Eagle Flies on Friday"* (Friday, of course, being pay day).

The Acme Motor Car Company

Driving out of the Acme Motor Car lot, looking up to the back side of the Acme Motor Car Company sign, you would have seen "Hope you make it Home!"

Oh, Yes... It's Ladies Night, Oh, What A Night!

Another wonderful tradition came about at the clubhouse with my pal, Jonathon Baird. One day, while we were having beers at this joint on Greenville Avenue—Stan's Blue Note, which had 101 different ales—J.B. said "Hey, I got it. How about this..." Uh, oh! Of course, I shuddered at the thought of another of J.B.'s ideas... yet this one, I thought, had merit.

He said, "Why don't we have *Monday Night Is Spaghetti Night at the clubhouse?*" My reply, "OK, but what's that all about?" J.B. continued, "Let's you and I be the only guys attending and we'll see how many young ladies will accept an invitation to our Italian dinner night." I said, "Sounds like a lot of work."

It seems J.B. had thought this through… "Oh, no," he said, "you see, we'll just buy the wine and the pasta." His thought was that (I was guessing) the girls will take over with making salads, garlic bread, you know—we'll let them run the show."

He was right. What a hit it was and the ladies loved it! It was another one of those things that goes on one's Something to Look Forward to List. This immediately became a monthly event.

The clubhouse (that's my house) had a very nice dining room with Duncan & Fife furniture, a buffet and china cabinets, so we could set a fine and elegant table for each dinner. The ladies loved it and took part in the event details.

I had a Sony "reel-to-reel" tape deck and some really good speakers set up. We would play just some cool mood music—you know, light jazz, Sinatra, Tony Bennett, that kind of stuff.

Spaghetti Night at the Clubhouse was a fabulous success… and the ladies began bringing salads, French bread, flowers, candles, hors d'oeurvres and desserts of all kind. It became a sort of "can you top this?" party with the gals seeing who could bring in something bigger and better for each dinner. It was an implied challenge: "Let's see you outdo this affair." Plus, the number of gals grew, having as many as a dozen attending each soirée.

What a great kitchen party it became! So many gals working to please just two guys. We would sit, sip wine and dine, listen to classy music and discuss the events of the past week and weekend. The ladies would talk about their dates and events they had attended… So much frivolity! All in a mostly cordial and (I must say) delightful environment, especially for Jonathon and me.

On one particular evening of a *Monday Night Is Spaghetti Night at the Clubhouse* gathering, one of our regulars, Colette DuVoss, had been a bit overserved with the fruit of the vine and feeling no pain, as she came out with, "Hey, f*#k Sinatra. Meadows, play some Rock 'n' Roll, will ya?"

That was the beginning of Monday Night Is Spaghetti and Boogie Night at the Clubhouse!

THINK about this…Life Happens While You're Making Plans

There's nothing like death to make you think about how short life really is and to get you thinking about the future. Due to this recognition of how quickly it can all be taken away, I have become much more philosophical and even more spiritual about studying life's purpose.

Dad passed away in 1990, not long after his open heart surgery in the mid-to-late '80s.

When he was going through all kinds of health tests before that surgery, the testing missed the fact that he had colon cancer, which eventually broke through the colon and moved into his other organs. Almost immediately after heart surgery the cancer became our concern, as it was rapidly advancing.

He was only 72 years of age when he died… the same age as I am now. (Young, right?) When Dad died I was 47. So at 72 years of age today, and some 25 years after his passing, I am thinking more about my own mortality and the future.

There are a lot of memories that I treasure about my dad. As a kid, I could never accurately describe what he did to make a living and support the family, which was his number one purpose in life.

He was a Systems Man for sure. Going to work for IBM in 1939 at the age of 22, he was trained to deliver the best customer service to all of Big Blue's (IBM's) clients, to respect every individual, and to seek excellence in every endeavor. Dad had a systematic approach, it seemed, to everything.

He studied systems and procedures and had the manuals from all his IBM training to which he referred often. The procedures of servicing clients and their computer systems left no room for guesswork. PM, or Preventative Maintenance, was key to providing excellence, he always proclaimed. This is maintenance that is regularly performed on a piece of equipment to lessen the likelihood of it failing. It is performed while the equipment is still working, so that it does not break down unexpectedly and so the "down time" is never a factor. This makes me think about Preventative Maintenance in one's own life.

He studied manuals on everything from our household appliances to cars. I believe he could build and fix anything.

His retirement came in 1975, after 36 years with IBM. His lifestyle as a steak, potato and eggs guy, along with being a smoker, was not the best for his health. I am now more aware of proper Preventative Maintenance for my own health and well-being.

At the time he faced open heart surgery, he did quit smoking... cold turkey, just stopped and never lit another cigarette. Funny, because Mom never quit smoking and she lived more than 17 years longer, always puffing on a Herbert Tareyton cigarette until her death in 2007 at 86 years of age.

I remember what Mom said to Dad just a week or so after he had quit smoking. He'd smoked, and inhaled for 59 years. She said, "Jim, *I tell you what*! Go get yourself a carton of Tareytons, or get a good attorney, 'cuz you are fit to be tied!" (Meaning: he was one *irritable* man.) They actually made it through Dad's nicotine withdrawal, with very little issue.

Knowing that he probably wouldn't be with us much longer, Dad "systematically" walked us through, step by step, his wishes for everything, after his passing. He was instrumental in laying out the details of procedures to be followed for the remainder of his life and how he wanted us to proceed afterwards.

Aging under God's grace, my dad continued his growth in spiritual maturity in the face of his bout with colon cancer. I am convinced that the older we get the more we need God's wisdom.

With Dad's instructions, Mom and I visited a couple of grave sites and selected what we thought was the most beautiful one in the Hill Country of Texas, under a lovely old oak tree near a babbling brook. Dad asked, "How much?" We presented him with the data (the proper term for the computer mechanic). He said, "No way! Here's what I want you to do: find a decent bare spot in the middle of the place, buy several plots and bury my body in one of them. I'll wait for Mom there. And after I'm buried there, plant a tree by me, and I'll fertilize it... the tree will grow and other people will want to be buried there. Then sell them our lots, unless any of you want to be planted there, too."

He said, "I'm not going to be there, so I don't and certainly won't care. I'll be gone. Now, don't make a fuss on viewing my body, I prefer you don't let anyone look at me after I'm dead. They'll have to just remember me the way I was when alive. OK?" There was only one reply: "Yes, sir!"

"Now let's write my eulogy, son," he said. And we did.

During this time, the most profound impact Dad had on me was his passion for studying the Word of God. I remember him studying the words of the letters written by the Apostle Paul.

He was very much immersed in his Bible Studies, specifically pertaining to Paul's writings, and his letters (13 books of the New Testament). I remember Dad saying that as the world changes the world will have a greater need in a relationship with our never-changing God.

This experience happened at a time when I still had questions pertaining to my life's purpose, a time during my frantic search for happiness, which was still centered on the acquisition of stuff and making money to pay for the stuff I had already bought but didn't really need.

I thought Dad was first and foremost a cerebral man—an intellectual person with a much higher IQ than I had. I thought he enjoyed studying for the sake of gaining knowledge alone. "This is not a theoretical exercise for me, son. It's a study of God, the living God, who has always existed and provided us with the manual for the application to any and all situations of one's own life." His words always made me **THINK**.

Margaritas, Mariachis, Matadors y Muchas Gracias Mexico

By 1991 I had leased the old homestead out and we no longer had the clubhouse located in Dallas. I was living in Jonesboro, Arkansas.

Going forward, our SDO venues changed every year. In 1991, the site selection committee had decided on El Paso, Texas. Well, that was the arrival destination… but our hotel accommodations and golf course rounds were across the border in Juarez, Chihuahua, Mexico.

The Door Prize

That year The Door Prize was won by Joe Wyzkoski, who had the thing shipped from El Paso to St. Augustine, Florida. "What is *that?*" Mary Margaret Wyzkoski asked the Fed Ex delivery service standing at her front porch.

The Hotel Lucerna and the Compestre Juarez Club de Golf

This was the first time we employed caddies. I met Juan Ramón Macias on the site selection and planning trip (with some other committee members), and he agreed to not only be my caddy and caddy master, but my transportation chairman and interpreter, as well.

It was a blistering July day and we were just south of the United States-Mexico border… and the Campestre Juarez Golf Club was alive with the SDO golf tournament.

Juárez, Mexico wasn't always as dangerous as it is today. Not long ago, Juárez was a booming destination for gringo tourists looking to hop over the bridge for cheap merchandise, strong drinks, and fun times. Outdoor festivals were big. Night clubs were always packed. Margaritas were plentiful—and legend has it that they were *invented* over there. Could there be a more perfect venue for the Screen Door Open International-Invitational Golf Championship? Just across the Rio Grande from El Paso, Juárez was a blue-collar center of a more than a million residents with production assembly lines cranking out everything from straw brooms, boots, and TVs to seat belts for American car companies.

You've probably heard of Juárez—and not because of its golf course, the Compestre, but because of its powerful drug cartels and bloody past. From 2008 to 2011, more than 7,500 murders were committed in this sprawling city that's just miles from El Paso. The appalling peak came in 2010, when officials recorded 3,075 homicides, or an average of about eight per day, cementing Juárez's ignoble reputation as the "murder capital of the world." Tourism tanked. Businesses shuttered. After dark, residents hunkered down in their homes, fearful of kidnappings and random acts of violence. You wouldn't want to go there now.

We were there in a different era, for sure, 20 years before the trouble began in Juárez.

Phil Cornett had been elected (forced, actually) into the position of SDO Hospitality Chairman because of two things: the homegrown tomatoes he would always bring for the opening night BBQ chicken banquet and the Margaritas and Tequila Sunrises he made during our weekend festivities.

On Saturday morning after a breakfast of Huevos Americano, along with the Margaritas, Bloody Marys, and Tequila Sunrises that Phil made to keep us in our perpetual fog of delight, we left for the golf club, Compestre Juarez.

Just outside of the hotel, Phil had to step over a prone Mexican man. He was lying (not quite, but almost…) in the gutter, and on his back. Phil, the ever-so-generous person that he was, poured the last few drops of his own tequila into the poor hombre's mouth. This caused the man to become semi-conscious, whereby he grabbed Phil by the ankle and said: "Mas tequila, por favor." Phil replied, "I don't have any more, but I'll go get you some." "Si," replied the man, "an wen jew cum bak, bring the mariachis!"

The golf course was beautiful and in immaculate condition. It had bent tiff greens and fairways with lots of grounds staff working the place. The golf course and many beautiful homes were enclosed by a big wall, guard gates, and security. Everyone had a caddy (well, actually, Hal Clifford had three: one carrying his golf bag, one carrying a big umbrella, and one carrying a chair.) We had other caddies and staff running beer, tequila, and burritos all morning, while we played golf.

Later that evening, after resting by the hotel's pool, refueling with tequila shots, napping and such, we were picked up by a rickety old bus and headed south, out of Juárez, into the Mexican country side, bumping down a dirt road, sometimes spilling an entire shot of tequila. The guys were quite concerned when we pulled up in total darkness to a wall with huge double-wide wooden doors. The bus sat in total darkness, headlights off, while I exited the vehicle. I told the guys that we were lost. It was a remote area in *no-wheres-ville*... our own kind of Margarita-ville. Several of the guys were having a very strange cultural experience in a very tequila-drenched situation. Then the flood lights came on and the wooden doors opened, swinging inward. We entered a circular bull fight arena. Ole!

Everyone received their own personal bull fight poster with their name printed in Spanish: Matadors: Miguel Prados... Juan Carlos Baird... Ricardo Martin... Joaquin Reynolds, etc. The tequila and beers were flowing. Then out came the bull, a "little fella"—but still a bull!—the size of one very large Great Dane, with little knobs growing on his head which would, one day, be big-ass horns.

Ole!

He was big enough though, that only four of the 24 of us had the nerve to take the red cape and get in the ring. No one was hurt, not even the bull, who did knock one of the guys through the air and on his ass. I did get into the ring myself, and the bull made a couple of passes at me, before a huge adrenalin rush fueled me enough to drop the cape, run to the wall and jump it, landing safely back in the stands of the bull fighting arena. Ole!

Tequila shots get you drunker faster, everyone knows that. And a couple of our intoxicated pals reached the ninth and tenth stages of drunkenness, never experiencing—only bypassing—the other eight as found in Dan Jenkins book *Baja Oklahoma*. Chapter 7, page 115, taken from my copy, which Dan autographed, his ownself, as follows:

To J.Michael –
If there wasn't a God, Baylor wouldn't lose football games
Dan Jenkins

In any event, here are the 10 stages of drunkenness if you're not familiar with them:

1. Witty and charming
2. Rich and powerful
3. Benevolent
4. Clairvoyant
5. F--- dinner
6. Patriotic
7. Crank up the Enola Gay
8. Witty and charming, Part II
9. Invisible
10. Bulletproof

– as written by Dan Jenkins

Two of our guys—out of left field, stage left—entered the arena, flinging themselves over the wall and landing on their feet inside the ring. They were both sans clothing (yes, naked as jaybirds, they were!) and each had their capes in hand and charged the little bull who seemed as confused as the rest of us.

These two Texas boys will remain nameless, for protection sake. However, the one who was *Invisible* went on to became a city mayor, and the one who was *Bulletproof* became a judge.

Taking one Tequila shot… —OK, fine, even a second shot …OK, but after the third—the ability to say *No* and understand your limit decreases drastically… which is the reason you *take* another, and just say *uno mas tequila, por favor* and then find yourself the next day, having maybe made a real bad decision. Damn you, tequila!

CHAPTER FIVE

PALMER – HOGAN – NICKLAUS

Arnold Palmer

Those who love golf almost always have an Arnold Palmer story, and you can bet your "mashie niblick" that I certainly have a story or two!

There was a TV Special that aired in 2015 titled *Arnie and Me* and I wish that I would have entered my story for that program. Here's the story...

Arnold Palmer: 1929 – 2016

In my investigation I have found that according to the U.S. Census Bureau, there are some 325,376,212 people in the United States. Of that number, they say that there are 117,620 people with the first name of

ARNOLD and that there are 182,105 people in the United States with the last name PALMER. It's reported that there are some 65 people in the US with the name ARNOLD PALMER.

I've been around two people named Arnold Palmer, and they *both* have presented thrills, excitement, and given me such great memories.

First, there was Arnold Palmer, the Xerox Corporation executive, circa 1970s.

When I was first hired by Xerox (and went to Xerox's International Center for Training and Management Development in Leesburg, Virginia) I met Mike Bixler, an instructor at the center. Mike has been a dear friend ever since. I have always loved Bixie's sense of humor. He can find humor in most things and makes laughter a priority in his life. Sometimes it's a bit warped… yet he's one of the funniest, happiest guys I know. So much so, that now when we call each other, we always begin with laughter, triggered by nothing more than the sound of the other's voice.

One day, while in Leesburg, Mike said to me: "You know, Arnold Palmer is here today! Would you like to meet him, maybe even have lunch with Mr. Palmer?" My head was spinning… "What?"

Well, "eager" is too mild an adjective in describing my enthusiastic, fervent, gung-ho, exuberance at wanting a second meeting with the KING himself. "Come on," Bixler said, and we walked down a few hallways to an open office door and walked into the office. There was a fellow sitting at a desk. Bixler said: "Arnold, I would like you to meet a friend of mine from Houston. This is Mike Meadows." I thought: "What?" I looked at the name plague sitting on his desk. It was engraved with the name Arnold Palmer, but he was definitely not the golf King.

When I was in Dallas with Xerox Corp., in 1976, Arnold Palmer had moved from Leesburg to Dallas to Xerox HQ, located in "Big D."

I was the Xerox Southern District Sales Training Specialist in the Office Systems Division in Dallas. You can imagine the number of people the District office would greet and entertain. I certainly had my own way of entertaining them, thanks to Mike Bixler.

We wore out the antic, and maybe even Arnold Palmer of Xerox Corporation, but he was always kind and a good sport of it all.

And, then, of course there is the golf legend named Arnold Palmer.

Arnold Palmer, THE KING, 1993...
and our reprise at Ojai Valley Inn and CC

The King and I
March, 1993
GTE Classic, Ojai, CA

In 1993, I was in Camarillo, California, employed by Western States Imports, the engineers and designers of Diamond Back Bicycles. I was VP of Sales/Marketing for their newly formed Fitness Division. We had designed and were producing and marketing the first piece of fitness equipment that would control heart rate. It was named the Preference HRT 2000 (Heart Rate Trainer 2000) and heralded the new millennium of the 21st century. By the way, if you can control heart rate (not monitor it, but control it) you can greatly accelerate maximization of cardiovascular fitness.

Trade Show

I had successfully been able to test my new Heart Rate equipment at the Aerobics Institute in Dallas and with Sir Peter Snell who was directly involved with many individuals (like Wayne Gretzky) in fitness training. Gretzky was training on the HRT, my stationary bike, in his home off Mulholland Drive in Hollywood, California.

I had also placed my bike with the Centinela Hospital Player Fitness Center, a traveling van that moves around following the Senior PGA Tour.

That year, the Senior PGA GTE Classic Golf Classic was being played at the Ojai Valley Inn and Country Club in Ojai, California. I had one of my bikes on the van, so I saw it as my way of getting into the tournament and get really up close to those PGA Tour professionals who were "working out" in the van. Even the older PGA golf pros tried to keep in shape.

Most of the golf pros arrive early or stay late to work out, keeping fit and prepared for the tournaments.

They hit balls on the driving range, putt on the practice green, and even do daily warm up exercises in their schedules of being on Tour. The Centinela Fitness van had been on tour with the Seniors since 1984 and was a 45-foot long trailer that expanded to 24 feet wide when parked. This van was parked right on the practice range for the pros at the 1993 GTE Classic.

Many of the golfers worked on sore shoulders, aching backs, "tennis elbow"… things like that. But almost all the players, at some time during the tournament, stopped in the van for cardio exercise. They were riding my bike for that reason and it was easier than running on a treadmill, with less risk for a knee injury.

When I arrived at the Ojai Valley Inn and Country Club, I spent time with all the pro golfers coming in to stretch and work out in the van. I met Larry Ziegler, Dave Hill, Al Geiberger "Mr. 59", Defending Champion Bruce Crampton, Tom Weiskopf, Isao Aoki and other professionals in the fitness van.

Larry Ziegler and Mike Hill   *Al Geiberger*

I met Larry in March of 1993 while he rode my stationary bike. In talking with him and Dave Hill, Larry said that his caddy wasn't going to make it to the tournament in time to caddy for him in the Pro Am the next day. "Larry," I said, "let me caddy for you, I would be delighted to do it." He said, "You're on!"

I came back early the next day to find Larry Zeigler on the practice range and his caddy had made it there in time to do his job and caddy for Larry. So I went inside the training van and spent most of the rest of the morning talking to the physical trainers on the van.

As the morning wore on, I could see that the practice area was now practically empty except for one lone golfer on one end and one on the other end, a huge crowd of spectators, and whoever else was around at 11:00 that morning.

Wait a minute, I thought… Then I asked the guys in the van: "You guys got the pairing sheet for today?" They did, and low and behold there's THE NAME: Arnold Palmer, with an 11:40 starting time. Ah ha… Then I thought, *I bet I know who that other lone golfer might be…* That guy with the little Ping carry golf bag at the other end of the practice range just might be… an amateur playing with Mr. Palmer!

Slow down, J. Mike… I was saying to myself as I approached the guy on the range, the one with the little Ping carry bag. I was having the same eager, fervent, gung-ho, exuberance of feelings—just like in 1976 at Xerox in the hopes of another Arnold Palmer personal encounter.

"Hello," I said, approaching him.

"Hi," he said.

"I'm J. Mike, and I believe you have the 11:40 starting time?"

"That's right, "he confirmed.

"Good, I've been waiting for you. I'm your caddy."

"I wasn't going to get a caddy," he said,

"Well, you're in the Palmer group, right?"

"Yeah…" he said.

"Well, you see, it's been taken care of… as Mr. Palmer does not want you to carry your own golf bag, much less to be raking bunkers, and all that stuff. He wants to enjoy the day with you and for you to have a good time, with him… and I assure you Mr. Palmer will not be carrying his golf bag! He does not want you to do all that kind of stuff. And again, sir, it has all been taken care of. You know what I mean?"

I'm trying my best without saying anything to convey a message to this guy, as in,

Hey, I've been sent to save you, it's a gift, just accept it.

"Oh, well, yes… I see now," he said.

Picking up the gentleman's bag, I said, "Mr. Palmer wants you to meet him on the putting green." The gentleman replied, "Yes, sir" and he followed me there.

Holy Smokes, I am going to be with The King, once again!

On the first tee, Mr. Palmer was giving instructions to his own caddy, who had Palmer's golf bag on a golf cart. His instructions included: "Never leave the cart and my clubs alone." Arnold Palmer would be walking with the four other players (the four amateurs) in his Pro-Am group while the caddy drove the cart—arriving at every tee, on the cart path, and then getting the cart back into the fairway, under the ropes, and around every green and then back on the cart path to the next tee. Arnold Palmer was still playing pretty good golf back then and was still the largest draw for spectators of anyone playing the game. So, that caddy had quite a job of maneuvering the golf cart and delivering golf clubs to Mr. Palmer. The crowd was huge.

I was carrying a small, light golf bag for my amateur in the group while Palmer's caddy had the challenge of trying to drive the golf cart around, in between, and through the spectators. Mr. Palmer, trying to speed up the play just a bit, decided that it would be a good thing if I would take over the responsibility of the flag stick, since his caddy wasn't going to be anywhere near the action.

"Son, what was your name again?"

"J. Michael Meadows, sir."

"What do they call you, son?"

"J. Mike, sir."

Photo is courtesy of Phoenix Country Club

After the first three holes—and after Mr. Palmer telling me something about walking in his putting line as we left the third green—he said, "J. Mike, don't you think you ought to put that flag stick back in the hole?"

"Yes, sir."

My, that was embarrassing!

My nerves were finally settling down and I was getting comfortable in my caddy role, primarily due to the graciousness of the King. I mean, I'm not sure I could put into words my feelings or those in the gallery who had close contact with him. The nobleness, grandeur, rareness, and splendor of this man, as unpretentiously kind a human being (other than my father) as I have ever met.

Mr. Palmer would even start conversations with me. On the 10th hole, walking down its slope from the tee, and feeling comfortable, I told Arnold Palmer that I had been at the 50th PGA Championship at Pecan Valley in 1968, inside the ropes, working back then for IBM Sports. I told him how I had been with him on the final day and that final 18th hole.

He looked at me and said, "You were there?" I spoke the following words at a really fast pace: "Yes, sir, I was, and I was almost on top of you when you got the drop from the TV cables and hit that unbelievable three wood, which took off like a jet airplane, rising up the hill and onto the green."

He said, "Man, that was 25 years ago, J. Mike. You were there?"

"Yes, sir, I was."

He continued, "You know, *that* was the best three wood I ever hit and probably the best golf shot of my life."

During the airing of that TV special, *Arnie and Me*, in 2015 and again after Arnold Palmer's passing, I saw an interview with Doc Giffin, Mr. Palmer's assistant for more than 50 years. In the interview he confirmed the statement Arnold Palmer made to me as we walked that fairway together, recounting that amazing shot he hit at Pecan Valley those many years ago.. I am so glad it is captured on film.

CHAPTER FIVE

The DNA of Ben Hogan

Ben Hogan had accomplished so much in golf before I was even aware that there was such a thing as golf. Before I was 3 years old, Ben Hogan had 37 tour wins, 38 second place finishes and 23 thirds. This was all before the near fatal car crash of February 2, 1949 and the unbelievable comeback including his record of the early 1950s.

In the spring of 1992, I was invited to play Shady Oaks Country Club in Ft. Worth, Texas. I was going there on a site selection trip in anticipation of making Ft. Worth the venue of an upcoming United States Screen Door Open International-Invitational Golf Championship. Mr. Ben Hogan was born outside of Ft. Worth, in a town named Dublin. In search of work (Ben's dad was a blacksmith) the family moved to Fort Worth, Texas.

When Marvin Leonard took up golf, for exercise at the suggestion of his physician, he played at River Crest Country Club and the Glenn Gardens Golf Club, both in Fort Worth. That's where he ran into two young caddies by the names of Byron Nelson and Ben Hogan. He developed a life-long friendship with both of them and provided Ben with financial assistance to pursue a professional career in golf and, later, to create the Ben Hogan Company.

Mr. Leonard also built and owns Star Hollow Golf Club, a one-hour drive southwest of Ft. Worth, his personal private golf course and clubhouse with a membership which is renewed on an annual basis. Star Hollow is a majestic 9-hole course, beautifully manicured and cared for, with two sets of pins and 18 different teeing areas. The place is known as Little Augusta, which should help you in understanding just what a special place it is. In the clubhouse, the staff serves the most fabulous hamburgers, featuring beef from their own cattle you'd see hoofing around in a nearby pasture.

A little more background…

Ben Hogan won the Colonial National Invitational in 1946, '47, '52, '53, and '59 (his last tour victory). Colonial Country Club in Ft. Worth is the one true Hogan's Alley, because of Mr. Hogan's membership and records there.

There is one other course that's known as Hogan's Alley: Riviera Country Club in Pacific Palisades, California. It earned that name for Hogan victories there in the Los Angeles Open in 1942 and the U.S. Open in 1948.

There is one golf hole in the world of golf known as Hogan's Alley. It is the sixth hole at Carnoustie in Angus, Scotland and the site of the 1953 Open Championship, won by the "Wee Ice Mon," the endearing nickname given to Mr. Hogan by the Scottish fans at that 1953 Open.

Shady Oaks Golf Club became Ben's home golf club. He was a Charter Member of the club built in 1955 by Marvin Leonard, the local Ft. Worth businessman who also built the Colonial Country Club in 1934.

Arriving early, long before our 1:00 pm tee time, I was hoping to find Mr. Hogan sitting in the 19th Hole. I think everyone who went to Shady Oaks hoped to have "a sighting"—maybe even an encounter with the man himself. I know I did.

I heard that he regularly had lunch at a big round table in the clubhouse, a special table reserved for him which overlooked the 18th green, with his back to the rest of the room.

I went to the bar and sat on a stool. I noticed the back of a gentleman dressed in a business suit. As the barman was coming over to me, I raised my hand slightly, very timidly, keeping it close to my chest, and pointed to the corner table at the window and the back of the man sitting there. Before I could ask, the barman said softly, "Yes, that is Mr. Hogan."

Oh my gosh! Just the two of us (me and Ben Hogan) in the 19th Hole at Shady Oaks. I was experiencing excitement and nervousness in just being there, steps away from the man himself... the man who held the top spot on my list of golf heroes. Most of us have heard many stories about the demeanor of Mr. Hogan. That is, that he was shy, withdrawn, distant, and uncaring, and not an especially friendly person. You'd hear that he really didn't want to be around people. I had no desire to find out first hand if these things were true.

Jimmy Demaret and Ben Hogan
Photo is Courtesy of Phoenix Country Club

A couple of interesting quotes I've run across… One from Jimmy Demaret, who was known to be Ben Hogan's best friend: "*The strangest thing is that Ben and I have never been close… Nobody gets close to Ben Hogan.*" The other from Sam Snead, who said caustically, "Hogan didn't like anybody except maybe his wife."

So, here is what happened that day in the 19th hole between me and Mr. Hogan: not much!

Every now and then I would look his way from my bar stool, watching him take a sip of a martini or raise a cigarette from an ash tray to smoke. I think I watched him for a good 10 minutes before he extinguished a cigarette, rose from his place at the table, turned and walked toward the bar and me. Oh, my! He stopped beside me and looked up at the TV over the bar where there was a PGA Tour event being broadcast. He paused for about 10 seconds and *all the while* I was staring at him. Then he looked straight at me. I made a nervous smile, and he said, "Hello," and then walked out of the room.

I immediately turned and slowly walked over to where Mr. Hogan had been seated and looked at the space he had just occupied. I thought, this is where he sits, where he eats, where he drinks, and where he smokes. Then, I spotted the club ashtray containing two Benson and Hedges cigarette butts, obviously just smoked by, yes… Ben Hogan.

Crazy, I know, but I took an ashtray containing the remains of two smoked cigarettes and thus had, in my hands, the DNA of Ben Hogan! Yeah! I carefully protected the stolen property until I could place some Saran wrap over those butts and put them on prominent display with my other cherished golf memorabilia. They disappeared quite some time ago, but it was such a hoot to show people those butts, and to say, "These cigs were smoked by Ben Hogan himself!" A lot better than taking a tee, golf ball, or divot, don't you think?

It was a different story about one year later, on March 24, 1993 when four dear friends of the Screen Door Open visited Shady Oaks where, once again, Mr. Hogan was sitting alone at his table in the 19th Hole overlooking the 18th green.

THERE HE IS! Another sighting...

Joe Wyzkoski, Jr., aka *The Polish Prince* and *The Wyz*, and Ralph Boccarosse, aka *Bocco*, both from Virginia, had planned a trip to Houston to play in the National Hole in One Competition at the Woodland Country Club in March of 1993.

Mike Hyatt, a member of River Crest Country Club in Ft. Worth invited the Wyz and Bocco to come to Texas a day or two early and fly into DFW. Mike said, "We'll have lunch and play Shady Oaks and even Colonial." River Crest CC was undergoing some construction and refurbishing and there was a reciprocal relationship between the two clubs, River Crest and Shady Oaks. A wonderful suggestion, they all agreed, and the date was set.

Needing a fourth, another of our old friends, Jim Braswell, aka *El Toro* and *Bras*, who then resided in Dallas, accepted the invitation from Hyatt for the round of golf. My dear friends were reuniting and playing a great golf course on a beautiful day, with lunch planned for after the match in the 19th Hole.

It was a great and special time for friends with a partnership match concluding on the 18th green with Wyz sinking a 30-foot par putt from above the hole, fittingly ending the match at "all even."

CHAPTER FIVE

Shady Oaks Standing Rule: Don't Bother Mr. Hogan

Walking off the green, Mike Hyatt, said: "There he is!" Well, that's enough to stop you in your tracks, isn't it? They all see Ben Hogan sitting at the big round table, all alone. Hyatt pleaded, "Please guys, we're going in there. Please don't do anything stupid. I am a guest and I would like to be able to return." To which Bras replied, "Hey, look, he's sitting at a big huge table (the special table reserved just for him) and it's empty, except for Hogan. Come on, we'll join him."

Hyatt, again, begged, "Please don't get me kicked out of here."

Despite Hogan's accurately perceived demeanor, sometimes people would walk over to his table and it often became a very awkward situation. My four friends entered the 19th Hole and noticed Mike Ditka (famous football player and NFL coach) being escorted to Mr. Hogan's table by one of the young pros they had met earlier in the pro shop. The four of them took a table as close as possible to Hogan's personal table and eavesdropped on what was being said. The young pro said, "Mr. Hogan, this is Mike Ditka. He's here to practice and he's going out to hit some balls." To which Hogan replied, "Hello." Then, nothing but silence. Mike Ditka stood there for a moment, in the deafening silence, and then walked away, befuddled. "What?" Wyz thought, "Hello? That was it? To Mike Ditka? Just a Hello? Boy, that is cold."

Hyatt, Wyz, Bras, and Bocco finished lunch and Hyatt suggested it was time to leave. Mike Hyatt led the way, but continually turned back to see that the other three were following him.. Walking out, and the last of the group, Wyz thought, *I'll never have this opportunity again.* With that thought, he walked right over to Hogan's table and said something very brilliant: "Uh, I came over to introduce myself." Mr. Hogan took a moment, looked Joe Wyzkoski, Jr. up and down, smiled, and then stood up and said, "Well, in that case, I'm Ben Hogan" and extended his hand.

With his mind now racing to think of something to say, Wyz said, "Mr. Hogan, can I get a picture of you and me?" Mr. Hogan took a moment, looking at Wyz, like sizing him up again and replied: "Do you have a camera, son?" "Yeah," Wyz said, "It's in my golf bag." Hogan replied, "Go get it!"

With that, Wyz almost knocking a table over, moved quickly through the 19th Hole and out the exit of the club. He saw Hyatt with an *OH NO, WHAT HAPPENED?* look on his face. Before a word was spoken, Wyz, very excitedly, said: "I got us a photo op with the man himself... come on! All ya'll are invited."

Hyatt and Bocco, timid, embarrassed or whatever, didn't move. But Bras said, "Are you kidding, Wyz?" "No, I'm not!" Bras said, "I'm all in, let's go!"

It took about eight seconds to get back inside, find a server and hand him the camera. Wyz said "There's plenty of film, take your time, don't shake, stand steady, here's the focus... are you ready?" He added a final admonition: "Don't blow this."

Very graciously, Mr. Hogan asked, "Joe, so how do you want to do this?"

Joe said, "Well, Mr. Hogan, if you'll just sit where you normally do, and Bras, you sit to the right, and I'll sit right here." As you can see, the picture certainly captured the momentous encounter.

Jim Braswell   Mr. Ben Hogan, age 80   Joe Wyskoski, Jr.

Then, in a very cordial conversation they talked of being at Shady Oaks and of Hogan golf clubs, because both the Wyz and Bras played Hogan clubs. Mr. Hogan said he had just approved the new golf club models at a production meeting that morning. My friends, Jim and Joe, both attest to Mr. Hogan's charm, friendliness, and kindness on that special day.

My buddies told Mr. Hogan that they were also going to play Colonial on this trip and asked if he would like to join them. "No, thank you," Mr. Hogan said, "I'm no longer playing golf." Joe Wyzkoski then asked, "Mr. Hogan, did you see me make that putt on number 18 earlier today?" The reply was, "No, I didn't, Joe. Just where was the ball on the green?" Wyz answered, "Some 30 feet above the hole." "That is not an easy putt," Hogan said, "Good putt, Joe!"

I'll rephrase that: That was not an easy thing for you guys to do... Good job, Jim and Joe!

Joe Wyzkoski (The Wyz), Jim Braswell (Bras), even Mike Hyatt and Ralph Boccarosse (not pictured) left Shady Oaks on August 24, 1993 with one great golf experience and a deep appreciation of the man whose golf swing and ball striking was as near perfect as mortal man could possibly achieve.

Mr. Hogan passed away four years later.

Mr. Hogan, 1960
Weeks Park Golf Course, Wichita Falls, Texas – The Texas-Oklahoma Jr. Golf Tournament
played since 1957   Photo is Courtesy of Phoenix Country Club

The Texas-Oklahoma Junior Golf Tournament, now one of the biggest junior golf tournaments in the country, has been played for more than 62 years.

Back in 1960 at the 4th annual tournament were two young players who actually would not meet each other for another 19 years. Jim Rankin (who would be SDO Champion in the years 1982, 1983, 1984, 1988, 1990, 1991, 1992, 2004, and 2006) was just 13 years old and living in Weatherford, Texas. Malcolm Haney (SDO Champion in 1996) and 14 years old, at that time was living in Oklahoma City, Oklahoma.

Both young golfers were at Weeks Park in Wichita Falls, TX for the T-O Tourney in 1960.

The 4th Annual T-O Jr. Golf Tourney had added prestige that year as Ben Hogan appeared to give a clinic for all the participants. Jim and Malcolm remembered how all the boys were sitting on the ground, Indian-style, when the black Cadillac arrived. Hogan exited the car, with his caddy, from the back seat. Malcolm reported, "Mr. Hogan was wearing tan slacks and the famous cap."

"Before starting the clinic," Jim said, "Hogan sent his caddy out 170 yards from where he would be hitting." Hogan then explained his method for hitting a *draw* (right to left golf shot), then a *fade* (left to right), while hitting a five iron. Each ball he hit would land at the feet of the caddy. Then, Mr. Hogan had the caddy walk out 10 more yards to a distance of 180 yards, explaining and demonstrating how to hit the same golf club, even a bit farther. (Hitting a five iron 180 yards, back in 1960, was really some kind distance for that club). Jim said he and everyone else were in awe of the man.

Following an afternoon of golf tips and instruction, they all went to a banquet at Midwestern State University where Mr. Hogan spoke on "the game of life." Each participant received a Hogan golf ball as a gift from Hogan.

On tour, Hogan had picked up the nickname *Iceman* because he would not talk to the galleries during tournament play. He explained that evening, to the youngsters, that he was not intentionally being unfriendly

226

or discourteous, but that he was so focused he forgot that they were there. (My, what concentration that would be…)

Hogan showed that he was a warm person by agreeing to put on the clinic and speak to the junior golfers without accepting any payment. He spoke of his current focus, which was on winning a fifth U.S. Open Championship. He won the U.S. Open in 1948, 1950, 1951, and 1953. He gave an inspiring and courageous talk on his recovery from a near-fatal car accident in 1949, and subsequent rise to the top of his profession once again.

Jim Rankin and Malcolm Haney were both participants in the 1979 United States Screen Door Open its second year, which honored Ben Hogan. They met in Dallas and discovered that they both shared this wonderful story of two kids playing golf in Texas and meeting Ben Hogan.

Jody knew him!

And knew his secret system, too!

I recently re-read a book given to me in 2004 by Mike Hyatt titled *Afternoons with Mr. Hogan*, by Jody Vasquez. Jody worked at Shady Oaks, in the clubhouse and as a caddy/ball-boy for Hogan, shagging balls that he hit during his lone practice sessions (at 75¢ per session) on a remote part of Shady Oaks. Jody started this job when he was 17 years old and was with Mr. Hogan most every day for four years in the 1960s.

During their 20-some years of friendship, Jody learned a great deal about Ben Hogan and writes more than speculation and hearsay about the man. Jody wrote, "He [Hogan] achieved a wonderful insight into playing golf and in pursuing perfection in life." Vasquez wrote about his character, values, and beliefs. It was as if he was revealing the very essence of my own father. Vasquez wrote, "The search for excellence in whatever you choose to do begins and ends with you." In his book, Jody Vasquez wrote of Ben Hogan: "As Mr. Hogan saw it, you either did things right or didn't do them at all." It was as if Valquez knew my father. And I believe that is the principle of commitment I try to apply to everything I do.

He (and my dad) believed that what other people thought of you was secondary or didn't matter, but that what you thought of yourself and your decisions to succeed were more important.

Go with Hogan – *IN QUEST OF EXCELLENCE*

Just mention the name Ben Hogan, and you think of Excellence and of one of the best to ever play the game of golf. He has been called "the greatest ball striker of all time." When the best living golfer of all time, Jack Nicklaus, says that Ben Hogan was the best ball striker ever… well, there you have it!

Tommy Bolt said, "Jack watched Hogan practice, but Hogan never watched him."

That makes me think of the often-quoted words of Vince Lombardi: "The quality of a person's life is in direct proportion to their commitment to excellence, whatever their chosen field of endeavor."

Life got off to a tough start for Ben Hogan. He was a small kid, living on the fringes of poverty in Ft. Worth, when his father committed suicide in their home. Childhood, for Ben, was cut short. Having to work to help support the family, he worked as a paper boy for a couple of years and then discovered the caddy job at Glen Garden CC, where he had to fight just to get the chance to carry a golf bag. He met another caddy, Byron Nelson, a popular, bigger, and outgoing kid. As a young golfer, Nelson was a "natural," a lot more so than Hogan. All of this intensified Ben's quest for excellence in everything he did: club repair, caddying, all his various odd jobs—and especially in playing golf, and (even more so) in hitting golf balls on the range.

As a teenager, he became a professional because he needed the money. His competitiveness kept him going on his quest. Obsessed, he hit golf balls for hours each day! It's been said that "Hogan Invented Practice" and he practiced more than any other golf professional, ever.

I suppose he became the embodiment of Practice Makes *Almost* Perfect, though he would tell you today that he never attained perfection. He hit hundreds upon hundreds of golf balls in each practice session, stopping to take notes on what made a ball do this or that. If he hit a bad shot, he would note what he had done wrong. He was most always alone, an introvert with few social skills, just a driven guy pounding golf balls.

It all started paying off when he discovered how to cure his hook. As a little guy, he got more distance and could hit it out there with the big hitters if he played a hook. However, a hook could get you in more trouble, too. As Lee Trevino would later say, "You can talk to a fade, but a hook won't listen." Ben Hogan had to find a way to control his drives. After hitting thousands of golf balls, he found a way to hit high, long drives that started slightly left and produced a slight fade to the right. Thus, Mr. Hogan became the greatest ball striker... but a man without much personality. He didn't care. He was simply in quest of excellence in golf.

In the '40s he was winning tournaments right and left, and the big ones, too! From the year I was born, 1946, through 1948, after serving in the war, he was on fire and won 37 tournaments. Everyone wanted Hogan's attention, autographs, and interviews. He didn't like to chit-chat and refused to talk to the press, so they made up untruths about him and published articles that described him as aloof, distant, uncommunicative, and stiff. There was never any small talk or bantering with the man, ever!

Ben Hogan – 1947
Photo is Courtesy of Phoenix Country Club

Then there was the near-fatal car accident of '49. Doctors said if he lived he would never walk again. Oh, yeah? Well, they didn't know Ben Hogan. They didn't understand this man's inner character, drive, and plain old gumption. He was determined to prove them wrong. Sixteen months after the accident, through determination and pain in rehabilitation, he won the U.S. Open, walking 36 holes on the final day to force a playoff and then another 18 holes the next day. He won the U.S. Open, one year and four months after the auto crash.

In my room called Hogan's Alley, with all sorts of golf memorabilia, books, and mounted Hogan irons (which have never been hit), is one of the most famous pictures of Ben Hogan ever taken: the One Iron at Merion.

He played in the 1950 Open, just 16 months after his car accident. This must be the most famous photo of the man, shot from behind as he looked up the 18th fairway to the green, hitting the one iron some 213 yards to the hole, on the 72nd hole of the Championship, after walking the final 36 holes that very day. There is a commemorative plaque in the fairway of the 18th hole that reads: *June 10, 1950 – U.S. Open – Fourth Round – Ben Hogan 1-iron*. It marks the spot from which he hit the shot onto the green, where he two putted, putting him in a three-way playoff the next day, which he won. Mr. Hogan never hit a one iron in competition again.

Legend says he did not have a seven iron in his golf bag at Merion, and when asked why he said, "Because there are no 7-iron shots at Merion."

You would be hard pressed to find a one iron today. The Butter Knife, as it was called, has been replaced with the modern hybrid, a cross between fairway metals and two and three irons. You'll find these hybrid clubs in most golf professionals' bags today. These clubs—not an iron and not a metal—are more versatile and forgiving and produce better shots than long irons.

The one iron was, arguably, the most difficult golf club to hit. Lee Trevino is quoted as saying: "Even God can't hit a one iron." However, the one iron has been responsible for a few other notable golf shots—and all by Jack Nicklaus.

Hitting a one iron 238 yards to the 72nd hole in the 1967 U.S. Open at Baltusrol, needing a birdie to tie the U.S. Open scoring record held by Hogan, Nicklaus hit to within 20 feet of the hole, made the birdie putt, and finished with the score of 272.

Nicklaus, again using a one iron, this time at Pebble Beach in the 1972 U.S. Open, drilled it into a blistering wind on the par 3, 17th hole. The ball hit the flagstick and dropped a few inches from the hole. The birdie helped him win that U.S. Open Championship.

One more time! Nicklaus, at the '75 Masters playing with Tom Watson on the final day and needing to keep pace with Tom Weiskopf and Johnny Miller, hit a one-iron second shot (242 yards) onto the 15th green, made birdie, and went on to win the Masters.

No one could hit a one iron like Ben Hogan or Jack Nicklaus. Period, exclamation mark!

Hogan had a few more years, amazing years, and many tournament victories. In 1953 his stamina was so strained that he struggled just to walk. But he still had an unbelievable year. He played in six tournaments and won five of them. For the good of golf, he traveled to Carnoustie, Scotland to compete in the Open Championship. He won that event—in spite of some tough weather and difficult course conditions. The Open of 1953 was the last major that Hogan won. The Scotts loved him (and, you will remember, nicknamed him the Wee Ice Mon.) Winning the British Open is considered the true mark of a world champion.

Hogan's Ticker Tape Parade New York City

When he returned to the states after winning The Open at Carnoustie there was a huge ticker tape parade for him in New York City. Ben Hogan had arrived.

There is no such thing as a Wrinkle Free Life… and Ben Hogan knew it.
From what I came to know of Ben Hogan, his secret was his System. And a number of lessons seem to jump out.

1. The value of a quest for excellence, in everything

This lesson is perhaps the most obvious and mirrors my upbringing, all my life teachers, beginning with my parents and with IBM, during the first 25 years of my life. It continues with me today.

Hogan knew he could never achieve perfection, but he was committed to becoming as close to it as possible. Striving for excellence should be the goal each one of us strives for.

2. Like Hogan, we should seek improvement

Hogan not only practiced like crazy in his early days when he was playing only mediocre golf, but he continued to practice far more than any other golfers even after becoming one of the best golfers in the world. Hogan said, *"I got enjoyment out of improving. If I just hold my own all the time, it didn't satisfy me. If you improve, you get a great satisfaction of accomplishment."* Maintaining the status quo was not Ben Hogan.

It is great to learn new skills, in golf—in writing—just to develop ourselves in new areas.

It's amazing to me that I am better at more things in my 70s than back when I knew everything, at age 20. I am committed to not making the same mistakes at 72 that I made at 32. Spiritual growth is my quest.

3. We will always do best when we are doing something we love.

That's when there is hardly any sacrifice at all. Hogan enjoyed practice (I, on the other hand, don't especially like practice...) In a TV interview Hogan was asked, "Why did you practice so much?" His reply: *"I had to— my swing was so bad."* The interviewer then asked, "Is that all?" *"No,"* Hogan replied, *"I loved it."*

4. He Dug It Out of the Dirt

It's almost unbelievable how good he was at hitting golf balls. Hogan is quoted as saying: "I dug it out of the dirt" or "the secret is in the dirt" or "it's in the dirt, go dig it out yourself." Ok… but what did he mean?

Many think it means get out to the practice range, hit thousands upon thousands of golf balls, and maybe you'll figure it out.

I don't buy that, at all. That's way too simple. There have been many thousands of people, amateur and professional since Hogan, who have worked just as hard and have had better equipment and instruction, never before available. Yet no one has gotten to the level of perfection in golf that we saw in Ben Hogan. We can study what he said and watch all the videos and dissect both his words and his swing mechanics, even talk to his contemporaries, in search of what he did that was different. They all have different ideas on Hogan's Secret: the pronating and supinating of the wrists, thrusting the knees, the right leg, the extra cleat in his shoes, and a sundry of other thoughts.

The book, *Ben Hogan's Five Lessons* came out in 1957 (that's 61 years ago, as I write this…) and its relevance today is still very significant, so much so that it is known as the Golfer's Bible.

What bugs me—and I just heard it from an instructor the other day—is this: "We don't teach that way today" or "Well, that was fine then, because he was strong, flexible or whatever… but this is now and you should do it this way." Or, "Yes, Hogan wrote this or said that, but here's what I think he meant." This sounds to me like a lot of stuff coming out of many pulpits, today, about how "God wants to be your best friend" or "God wants you to be financially prosperous."

5. Ben Hogan's introverted personality?

Fact: introverts can rise to heights of excellence that most extroverts cannot. We cannot totally blame Ben Hogan for being a quiet man, given his very difficult childhood.

Hogan could never have been a Jimmy Demaret or a Lee Trevino (who both were showmen, and loved to talk and joke around). People called him shy, but one of his peers stated, "He could be gracious or he might ignore you." I would remind you of the "Two kids and Mr. Hogan" story and, my friends Jim and Joe with Mr. Hogan at Shady Oaks, where Hogan's charm and grace were personified!

I think Ben Hogan had such an analytical mind that he did a lot more thinking than talking. And, at first, he didn't realize that he'd come across as unfriendly. Remember when he explained it to all those kids (my friends) in 1960 in Wichita Falls, Texas?

Go with Hogan

Why would you accept information or instruction on Ben Hogan's swing from anyone who couldn't come close to making that swing? Why would you not listen carefully, even study what the greatest ball striker in the history of the game had to say about the swing and not follow it precisely? After all, his teaching and theory *has* been referred to as the Golfer's Bible. I believe Hogan carefully committed to and meant every word he ever uttered or agreed to have printed in that book.

I have even heard that "He didn't write that book," yet in 1985 Ben Hogan was quoted by Neil Seitz of *Golf Digest* as saying, "I would write it the same way I wrote it in 1957."

It is a book, just a book on golf… golf's most remarkable instruction book.

The Bible is a book, life's most remarkable instruction book. It is life's instruction manual.

The Ben Hogan Secret is marked by a methodical plan or procedures and repeatability. Hogan said, "There are no shortcuts in the quest of perfection."

Jack Nicklaus said, "Learn the fundamentals of the game and stick to them. Band-aid remedies never last."

Byron Nelson, President Dwight Eisenhower,
Ben Hogan, and Augusta National Chairman Cliff Roberts

The Hogan Secret is found is his words in *Ben Hogan's Five Lessons: The Modern Fundamentals of Golf,* the systematic study of the golf swing.

I think it's pretty obvious. His "secret" was in his ability to use a deeper and more sophisticated approach to learning the game. And he would have been an even greater golfer had he focused a bit more deliberately in practicing the skills of putting. (He wasn't a great putter.) Hogan had unbelievable focus and ability to go into a higher cognitive state for learning.

ProFund and Golf in the Kingdom

In the early 1990s, returning to Oklahoma City and Edmond for some golf (and a dental check up with SDO participant Chuck Hetrick, DDS) and a whiskey with the cigar-smoking, Ricky Dugger (SDO), and a lunch with Phil Cornett (SDO), the "land man" of oil and gas, I met Hal Clifford, another oil and gas man. Hal had gone to a different high school in Oklahoma City, Casady High School, and then on to the University of Oklahoma. Hal and Phil had offices in the same complex. Over a few lunches, I got to know Hal Clifford mainly because Phil wanted to request that the SDO committee invite Hal to the next Screen Door Open. Hal soon became a regular SDO participant.

During this time, Hal Clifford was Chairman of the Fellowship of Christian Athletes in Oklahoma, and was called by Mike Keleher, former Financial Development Director of the Josh McDowell Ministry of San Diego, California. Mike was looking for funds for a start-up venture, providing a new fundraising service in support of Christian ministries and Christian education.

Clifford was interested in finding a new and better way to use golf for FCA fundraising. He flew out to California to meet with Mike, learn more about the concept, and actually see a golf marathon played as a method of fundraising.

Hal was not only impressed but was convinced that this was a superior fundraising method. Upon his return to Oklahoma, he changed the format of an upcoming FCA golf tournament to a golf marathon. Hal's first golf marathon for FCA raised over $78,000—a significant increase over the previous FCA record of $10,000. Hal, further convinced of this phenomenal and superior method of raising funds, became a representative of the newly formed ProFund organization.

Hal called me about helping in the new venture with Keleher, now being headquartered in Edmond. The only problem was that, at that time, I was living on Maui, Hawaii. Timing was pretty good, as I was definitely coming down with a strong case of "island fever."

Tropical Paradise… *or a big lava rock*

While playing golf with my neighbor in Camarillo, California after WSI (Western States Imports, designers of Diamond Back Bicycles and the HRT stationary bike) was purchased by a Taiwanese-based company with a factory in China, my friend asked, "Hey, would you like to go to Maui and sell posters?"

"Well," I answered, "I would like to go to Maui, and I pretty much think I could sell anything, even posters. What's that all about?" Keep in mind that with the sale of WSI I was, again, a guy without any prospects.

"A friend of mine has some sort of art stuff going on over there. I'll get you a meeting with them. They have an opening on Maui," he said. "Can you give me your resume?"

Next thing I knew, I found myself in a board room, somewhere near Los Angeles. Around the board room table sat, I presumed, the big shots of Martin Lawrence Galleries. I was there for an interview, in regard to their Maui art gallery. I had done my homework on them. I knew how many art galleries they had worldwide, their sales, distribution, product line, etc. I also knew what questions to ask... kind of like this:

"So, I am here interviewing for a sales position for your gallery in Lahaina, HI on the island of Maui. Looks like everyone has a copy of my resume in front of them. Since this is, again, a sales position, let me ask: What qualifications, skills, and experience are necessary to be on the team in your gallery on Maui?" They talked, I listened. And I asked questions, leading them to the conclusion I wanted.

My attitude has always been: "When interviewing for a position, always go for it because you can always turn it down." They seemed very impressed with my sales background with IBM, the National Sales Training position with Xerox, and the International Sales Training experience with Exxon.

I said something like this, "I'm 47 years old, divorced, have loved living in Southern California, where the weather is very conducive to playing golf. I have never been to any of the Hawaiian Islands, but I hear golf is great there. It would seem likely that there would be the opportunity to play golf during the day and be at the Martin Lawrence Art Gallery in the evenings. I see that your store is open every day until 10:00 pm. So, it stands to reason that your art products sell mostly during the evening hours along Front Street." There were smiles all around the board room table.

Then came the final question, "What do you know about selling art?" I immediately responded, "Selling is an art." They responded immediately with this offer: "I want to send you to Maui for a few days, meet the people at the gallery, even work there a few days. Look at the lifestyle, play some golf, and see if you want the position. And if you do, it's yours." What a deal, an all-expense paid trip to Maui. I couldn't say "no" to that!

Of course, you know I was hooked when I stepped off the plane at Kahului airport, and I think the management people back at ML Galleries HQ knew that would certainly be the case. I was on the island of Maui, looking at the Pacific Ocean, which was completely different from the shoreline of Southern California.

The island breezes, the smell of tropical flowers everywhere you go, magnificent colors everywhere you look. The Aloha Spirit was so inviting, so welcoming! After the week on the island and a great experience, I said, "I'll take the position." They (MLG) shipped me to Maui, lock, stock, and barrel, shipping my car, furniture, everything.

Living on the island of Maui was fantastic, unbelievable, and absolutely wonderful… *at first*. It was like an international move, without the hassles. English is spoken, they have the same monetary currency, and the weather and golf were great. No, they were perfect.

I knew the living costs would be higher, but I could buy from the fresh fruit stands and eat where the locals ate and limit myself when it came to the expensive tourist spots. I would actually be eating better: fish, chicken, and rice… oh yeah, Spam, too. The island's love affair with Spam began in World War II, when GIs were served the salty luncheon meat because it didn't require refrigeration and had a long shelf life. I think it is still part of army surplus on the island.

And let's not forget those breathtaking sunsets! I really liked it, all of it—*at first*. It is a healthier place to live, so my first major decision was to stop any and all consumption of alcoholic beverages. It was easy for me to do and successfully accomplished for the twelve months of abstinence to which I committed myself. It was definitely a slower and more relaxed way of life.

My 1971 Porsche 911-T had been shipped over and I bought a rag-top Jeep Wrangler to cruise around in. Gas was $1.85 a gallon back then; expensive; but it's not like you did a lot of driving around on the island. Today gas on Maui is about $5.00 per gallon… ouch!

CHAPTER FIVE

Once I got my Hawaii plates on the Porsche and my Hawaii driver's license, I became what is called a Kama'aina—Hawaiian resident regardless of racial background. That meant I got Kama'aina (local's) rates everywhere, as in reduced green fees at all golf courses, about $30- $50 a round versus the very expensive tourist rates.

I couldn't help wanting a place to live that had a view, so I leased a place at The Masters, Kaanapali Hillside, an unbelievable place—and what a view! From my balcony, I overlooked the upper Kaanapali golf course, down to the ocean, where I regularly could see whales. Straight out, over the ocean view, was the island of Lanai. And looking over the ocean view to the right was the island of Molokai. The monthly lease payment was the same as my monthly base salary, so I would need sales commissions for everything else. No problem.

Working was fun, *at first* wearing Hawaiian shirts and slacks, and shorts. I worked the evening hours of 5:00 – 10:00 pm, six days a week. That's when the tourists were walking the streets of Lahaina, the old whaling town on Maui. Everything cool was on Front Street. In fact, the ML Gallery was showcased on the corner of Lahaina Luna Road and Front Street, in the middle of all the night time action. After the tourists finished their golf or ocean leisure activities surfing or boat trips, whale watching, or sailing out to Molikini for snorkeling, they would go to dinner at one of Lahaina's fine restaurants. Following dinner they would walk along the streets for some shopping. And, *"I tell you what..."* they are going to buy something, that's for sure! Believe it or not, Maui is one of the world centers for art.

The Maui lifestyle was different and meeting people was difficult. I think that was because it is a transient sort of place, meaning people would come and go. Not only the tourists but gypsy-like people were attracted to some time-out from mainland living. Tourists were in for a week or so and then went back home. Those living on the island, seemingly, were not real keen on making friendships as most were working in the tourist businesses and likely to leave at any time, as well. Maui seemed a place where people were trying to find themselves. And maybe that's what I was doing, too.

Maui, Money… Mistakes

The longer I was on Maui, the more claustrophobic it became. It became too much of a slowed-down life style for which I was too young. I felt disconnected. Every time I took a trip back to the mainland, I wanted to move back.

I wasn't into any of the ocean activities, mainly because of my life-long "swimmer's ear" difficulties. What I did was play golf and go to work and sell people artwork. Driving the Road to Hana is a beautiful drive, but how many times are you going to take that trip? I wasn't being challenged and began to ask myself, "What was I doing?" Had I come to Maui as a quick fix to something? For the adventure? The slower, more relaxed way of life was getting to me, and I felt like I was searching for answers. I would have my answers soon.

After a year, the Thomas Kinkade Company approached the gallery director and me with the idea of opening a Thomas Kinkade-owned gallery in Lahaina, on Front Street. Kinkade had 350 franchised galleries across the country, and at one time 4,500 retail outlets. This Lahaina store, as I understood it, was to be his (Thomas Kinkade's) showcase studio/gallery for the sale of both his original artwork, as well as Kinkade limited-edition prints. The company would lease and revamp the property at 855 Front Street, turning it into a first-class gallery. They would hire the two of us to run the gallery and hire an administrator/gallery manager as well as a few more salespeople at hourly wage plus commission.

The Thomas Kinkade Company would play an active role in overseeing the design of the gallery and be present for the grand opening. We met with the Kinkade people and agreed to employment contracts. I was getting the early stages of "island fever."

Kinkade was an Evangelical Christian and is known as the Painter of Light, but actually he was, to me, the painter of "Twee" —excessively or affectedly quaint, pretty, or sentimental paintings with cheesy cottages, gates, and gardens.

On each original he would place the following: "John 3:16" and a picture of that little "fish" symbol ✗ you see on bumper stickers, next to the "I ♥ Jesus" one… or even, next to the "I ♥ my cat" bumper stickers.

He also would hide in every painting the letter N, which became a kind of Where's Waldo? gimmick, having everyone looking for the N, the first initial of Kinkade's wife's name, Nannette.

Thomas Kinkade was a great mass-marketer. Whether or not art should be mass-marketed is the topic of another discussion. Before the time of e-mail and iPhones, the Kinkade Company was producing limited and numbered, computer reproductions.

I don't think that #47 of 1,450 is very limited. Nor is producing the very same thing but labeling it a Gallery Proof (GP) or an Artist Proof (AP) justifies the additional $2,000 to $4,000 in sale price. When they ran out of the 1,450 limited editions of a print, they started over in the "printing on canvas process." So, I figure that someone else also has a #47 of 1,450 of the same print, hanging on a wall someplace. They could factory-manufacture more than 500 prints a day that Kinkade never touched. I was having difficulty getting into this process.

Kinkade once said, "When I got saved, God became my art agent." I've heard that Andy Warhol said: "Kinkade was the natural heir to the apostle of mass production." And that Kinkade reportedly called himself Warhol's heir. News… or fake news?

Tom Kinkade came to Maui for the Grand Opening of The Thomas Kinkade Studio & Gallery on Front Street in Lahaina. I was there, along with the crowd, and a native Hawaiian high priest, in full array, to bless this new place of business. This was a traditional Hawaiian religious person of Polytheistic and Animistic beliefs and practices doing his "blessing thing" in the Christian artist's place of business, with every piece of artwork having the artist's personal hand written "John 3:16" inscribed along with that "little fish." I found that to be very interesting. No, a *disappointment* better describes it, as Thomas Kinkade made no mention of his art agent.

Ole Tom was a bit puffy looking, red-faced, and sweating profusely. It was obvious to me: alcohol and drugs. The guy was a human, just like you and me, but what I saw was a near worship of him—and he had a following, because he used the "I am a Christian painter" to sell his art. But he was fraudulent, as many court judgments state. He was purveyor of kitsch prints to the masses.

I almost fell for it, too, ushering people off the street into our climate-controlled viewing room, lowering the lights except for the ones to maximize the light in the art and the "Kinkade-ness" of the whole place… to produce the Kinkade experience.

I had the experience of being around the guy, a painter and a Christian. I have no problem with either. As a Christian, I am saddened by his fall, his sinfulness, and the continued cover-up. Yet I know "for all have sinned and fall short of the glory of God." (Rom: 3:23 NAS)

In the years before his death (he died of an overdose), Kinkade's business and life took a battering. There were allegations of malpractice, and his company declared bankruptcy, unable to pay its creditors following a series of court judgments ordering him to pay hundreds of thousands for defrauding the owners of two failed franchises. Following his separation from his wife and spiraling alcoholism and drug use, Kinkade's behavior became erratic. He allegedly caused scenes in Las Vegas and engaged in what he termed "ritual territory marking" at a California Disneyland hotel, urinating on a statue of Winnie the Pooh. He was arrested, and thus his private behavior became public. (Or so *The Guardian* reported…)

As I see it, Kinkade's art skill is at best, technically OK, but I find it monotonous. The popularity of this art tells us something about his customers and fans, about a desperate yearning for nostalgia that pervades parts of American life, and for a return to the safe glow of some imagined past, some place that does not exist. "It's not the world we live in," Kinkade said of his own paintings, "it's the world we wished we live in. People wish they could find that stream, that cabin in the woods." I absolutely agree. In fact, the paintings are disturbingly idyllic, which allows the public to escape from the world into unreal places.

The "Truth on Tom?" **I think Thomas Kinkade forgot about who he said was his art agent!**

I saw his art as avoiding the real world, and delivering a false message. And, yet, Kinkade followers believe it to be "Christian Art."

By the way, the next time you're at the Louvre Museum, standing in front of the Mona Lisa or in front of any painting you like, anywhere, take a picture of it on your iPhone, e-mail it to Kinko's, and they'll be happy to put it on canvas in the Kinkade fashion (same process) for you at a cost of $49.

Better yet, send a favorite picture of a place you've been, a great photo of your family or any special picture, and send it via email to Kinko's and get it printed on canvas. It will warm your heart.

Returning to the Mainland

I was scheduled to be back in Dallas for the annual "Potato Skins Classic," a golf tournament hosted by former IBMer, Exxon Office Systems, SDO participant and my friend, Pat Gallagher. I told Hal Clifford I would come up from Dallas to Oklahoma City (OKC) and see him.

During my return visit to Dallas, I ventured up to "Edmond America" to see Hal and Mike and determine what mutual interest there could be with this new ProFund venture. Clifford and Keleher had opened offices in a beautiful two-story place with executive offices downstairs and a telemarketing staff upstairs. Hal became very excited about the process, as he was Chairman of Fellowship of Christian Athletes of Oklahoma and wanted to use the ProFund system for the entire organization. It was so successful that he took it to FCA Nebraska, who has used the ProFund system and has been successful with it for years. In fact, in their book, *INFLUENCE, The History of Nebraska FCA,* there is an entire chapter related to Hal and ProFund. It was Hal who found financing for the start-up of ProFund.

ProFund 1992 – Present … 25 years plus of a Successful System

They (Mike and Hal) were developing a specific product for a specific market: a fundraising campaign, involving golf, but not the normal scramble-style golf tournament. They invented the Golf Marathon.

I could see that this new concept could raise some significant dollars for any non-profit in less time (less than 90 days) and with fewer people (only 25-40 volunteer golfing participants). It could raise more money for a cause than any other fundraising campaign or program, unless of course, an organization could get someone to whip out a check book and scribble a check for $50,000 to $100,000—or even $300,000. This could alleviate the charity's need to go through the process of writing and submitting grant requests, or making decisions on what fundraising activities they are going to do each year.

The ProFund message to non-profit organizations was in the form of a question: Do You Want to Have a Golf Tournament or Are You Trying to Raise Money?

Here's typically the difference:

Golf Tournament	vs.	Golf Marathon
$6,000 -$10,000 (if you're lucky)	vs.	easy $30,000 - $100,000 (or even more)
Months in planning	vs.	Completed in 60 – 90 days… and one day of fun

Charity Golf tournaments are not really golf tournaments. They are typically "scramble golf events" in which the charity organization attempts to enlist 144 golfers (a very difficult task to begin with) who will pay an entry fee (typically around $200). You and I can do the math: 144 golfers x $200 = $28,800 from entry fees and they (the enlisted golfers) play a scramble format, meaning everyone in the foursome hits a ball from the tee. Then the foursome picks the best golf shot and all four hit from that spot, repeating that program until the ball is holed. The lowest team score wins the "scramble event."

Golf Tournament Expenses? Astronomical!

THE GOLF COURSE WINS, **not the charity**.

The golf course charges a per-person charge to play on the course, and the organization feeds every player and provides refreshment on the course. There are gimmick prizes, and each participant gets "a goody-bag full of stuff"—golf balls, tees, a towel, a shirt, a cap, sun block... the list goes on and on. The organization sells Mulligans, allowing Nudging and Fudging, for a price. "But it's for a good cause."

Then after the golf event, when the Executive Director or whoever is at the podium thanking everyone and presenting the slide or video show of what the organization's mission and vision is all about, the golfers are wanting to get on with the golf awards, and (more to the point) "Open the bar!"

You see, most of the golfers have done absolutely nothing for the cause and have most likely not even committed their own dollars for the cause, because someone or some company has purchased and sponsored a foursome—with an $800 donation—and given some employees the day off to play golf. Most entrants are Scramble Junkies, Sandbaggers, Nudgers and Fudgers, having loaded their team with what I call Tour Scramblers at the expense of the charity involved. "What was the name of that charity we were playing for?"

The Way to Raise Significantly More Dollars for Charities in Less Time—and Exceeding All Expectations

The original, successful working model of the Golf Marathon had ProFund assisting the charity organization in the recruitment and enlistment of Key Dedicated Volunteers (typically 25 to 40) who became the Campaign Volunteers—and the total amount of people needed, not 144 golfers!

This new process had no sale gimmicks of any kind. No candy bars or peanut brittle, no raffles, no auctions, no script, no banquets, no galas or golf tournaments. No intensive time commitment that normally took up to a year for a charity organization to plan. I thought, "Wow, no ice sculptures, hot air balloons or circus elephants are needed to raise significant dollars for these organizations... and there are hundreds of thousands of non-profit organizations across the country trying to figure out how to raise dollars, fast." The Program was quickly becoming a proven, validated, viable means of raising significant dollars for charities in a short period of time. The reality hit me: practically every nonprofit organization, large or small, was ProFund's marketplace.

Always anxious to seize opportunities, ProFund had my attention. I proposed that they hire me as an outside consultant, hired on contract to go into the different regions, already established, and observe and work with their representatives. I wanted to see how they prospected, presented, and managed the services of ProFund. I would travel with the reps, ask questions, see board presentations, visit with clients and potential clients, directors of development and board members. This is exactly what I had done for Xerox and Exxon Office Systems on a national level. We signed a contract and it didn't take me that long to be able to see an unbelievable product and service for "the marketplace." That marketplace is all not-for-profit, 501(c)3s, organizations, and for that matter, any worthy cause with the need to raise significant dollars in 60 to 90 days.

I remembered that I had been on my first board of directors of a non-profit organization in 1970, the Patrician Movement, headed by a large Catholic Diocese of San Antonio. The Patrician Movement was one of my IBM accounts. Being a 22-year-old "business executive," I accepted their invitation to be on their board. I thought: *Yeah, I'm one of the board of directors for this organization and won't that look good on my resume.*

I went to regular board meetings and listened to the reading of the minutes of the last board meeting, old business issues, new business issues at the patient residence, the outpatient concerns, and looked at financials. I had no idea what it all meant. I was served a great lunch at every meeting, and (oh yes) they would talk about fundraising thoughts, ideas and ways to get the community involved. I, of course, didn't have much, if any, money of consequence back then (that I could part with, anyway) but I got to be on the board of directors. Some importance in that!

Someone should have helped me understand why I was on their board. Like most boards, they did not have any formal means of clarifying the purpose of being a board member—which is something I have found to be a major fault of many nonprofit organizations today.

CHAPTER FIVE

I will never forget what happened after one of the board meetings. Saying good-byes and excusing myself after the board meeting and lovely lunch, I was heading out to the parking lot and preparing to get back into my day, when an old fellow board member (about my age today) walked up to me, put his hand my shoulder while walking the rest of the way to my car with me and said, "You know J. Michael, we asked you to be on this board because of *those three initials.*" Then, my brief thought: *Yeah, those three initials, J.M.M., I think I'll get my white shirts monogrammed with them on the shirt pocket and even on the cuff of some white shirts, too.* He continued, "We know IBM has a great employee matching gift program for employees working with charities." It then hit me hard! How completely awful I felt, thinking that being on the board was all about *me.* How utterly ashamed I was. How small, how totally small of me. I had not picked up on the fact that the reason they wanted me on the board was for my help in *F U N D R A I S I N G !*

Remembering this first board experience and my other board positions with other non-profit organizations, I was blown away with how ProFund was the answer to any non-profit organization that needed to be more effective and efficient at raising dollars.

During my in-depth observations of ProFund, what I found was simply amazing:

The Near Perfect Business, according to Warren Buffett.

I had studied Warren Buffett's "Durable Competitive Advantage" as he described in looking for The *Near Perfect Business* (knowing nothing is perfect).

Buffett's near perfect business:

1. Has a near lockdown on competition
2. Is a service/system that really never changes, even in economic downturn
3. Is a service that organizations are willing to pay for
4. Has no need to redesign itself or its product

5. Has a long-term history of making money (*This would soon prove itself*)
6. Is one that continually takes us down the path of success, yielding a successful career (Mine… for the past 25 years)

I bet on the above list with ProFund and it has been win, win, win, win…quadruple winners ever since: the Charitable Cause, the Volunteers, ProFund, and the ProFund Associate.

I presented my results to Mike and Hal, with my new and unbridled excitement in ProFund.

Here are some things I discovered…

1. I found that most of the "sales people in the field" were inexperienced in sales and were only working as a part-time means of making a few extra dollars. Most were linked to a ministry that had used ProFund in their fund-raising efforts, and being successful with the ProFund program, they wanted to be a part of ProFund, but only on a part-time basis.

2. Those who were working as independent representatives could not make very much money representing ProFund, especially, part-time.

3. There was no formal training, not much in the way of communications or accountability and therefore most representatives had little commitment in the endeavor.

The list of challenges went on and on. Then I presented the System Solutions that I would create and implement to ensure success in helping non-profits to be more effective and efficient at raising significant dollars for *whatever* cause!

After my quick assessment, I put everything I knew thus far about ProFund to the test. I was able to pick up the phone and contract with several charities—immediately—for our NO RISK WAY TO RAISE MORE DOLLARS IN LESS TIME EXCEEDING ALL EXPECTATIONS! We can still make that promise today, getting even better results.

My proposal to Mike and Hal was very specific in the ways to create the dynamics to take ProFund to the next level of growth with me heading Sales Training, Marketing, Decentralization, Compensation, and Accountability with Regional or District responsibility. ProFund would do these things while decentralizing. "I'm moving west and will take over the Western Region of ProFund, and live in the Phoenix/Scottsdale area." I did just that. I moved to Phoenix, driving my 1978 yellow GMC pickup truck from Dallas.

Then, we started growing! Our typical campaign had only 28 volunteer/participants who were easily raising from $30,000 to $56,000 in less than nine weeks' time—and even as much as $325,000, raised for charity in a short 90 days!

I hired a computer programmer to write the programming language to be able to manage each fundraising campaign, giving each client their own custom campaign management website. Each participant in the campaign could post pledges, communicate with participants and donors, send automatic newsletters, send pledge fulfillment notices to donors, utilize credit cards for donations, send auto-emails of thanks with charity logo to each donor when payment was received that included a statement of tax deductibility. The website showed a leaderboard of how the campaign was doing, and how each individual participant was doing, and so much more. We had a first class, "slam dunk"-cannot-fail system of raising significant dollars.

And it is so well organized and developed that I can present it on a cocktail napkin and often have for the last 25 years. There have been more than 6,000 ProFund campaigns for non-profit, 501(c)3 organizations, and other worthy causes, raising hundreds of millions of dollars.

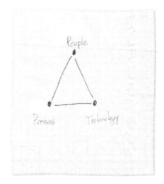

If you can't put it on a cocktail napkin it's too difficult to explain!

Speaking of a slam dunk… we use the ProFund System for clients who would like to have a basketball campaign. Our "Hoop it Up Campaign" (attempting 100 basketball shots) with six teams of five participants per team was raising $75,000. We then created other campaigns with Campaign Management Websites for Bowling (100 frames), Go-Kart Racing (100 laps), and Driving Nails (pounding 100 nails).

We had so many charity clients coming on board that we could hardly keep up with them, while adding more ProFund associates to the business. One of our first clients was Fellowship of Christian Athletes in Nebraska with whom ProFund conducted its first major fundraising campaign more that 25 years ago in 1993.

In the 2009 book, *INFLUENCE, A History of the Nebraska Fellowship of Christian Athletes,* the author, Arthur L. Lindsay, writes that FCA was able to raise over $1 million with ProFund through 2009, the year the book was published. Today, FCA Nebraska continues to experience success with the ProFund System.

Facts:

- A typical Campaign raises $50,000 to $100,000 with many raising even more, and with only 20 to 40 total participants (the total number of people involved).

- Complete, turnkey start-to-finish in just 60 to 90 days or less

- Totally volunteer based, no organizational staff required
- 95% effort is spent on fundraising
- 95% plus collection rate
- 90% or more of the funds come from new donors
- Dedicated ProFund Consultant and staff to ensure success of the organization
- All materials, training/development delivered by Profund consultant
- Clients are provided their own customized campaign-management website which is continually updated/refined with new technology advancements
- Bonuses: a Can't Fail System and great fun for your team of volunteers as they experience teambuilding with a group of volunteers who *ask* to be part of the next campaign, reducing turnover.

J. Michael Meadows
President

ProFund
www.profundwest.com

During this time, one of the many organizations that I have become involved with is Alice Cooper's Solid Rock, through the friendship of its executive director, Jeff A. Moore.

The idea for a teen center was born out of Alice and Sheryl Cooper's desire to address the needs of today's youth. Alice Cooper along with friend Chuck Savale envisioned a Christian, nonprofit organization dedicated to reaching teens through concerts, music venues, dance, and art programs.

Founded in 1995 by long time Arizona resident, rock star, and father, Alice Cooper, Solid Rock has had its primary mission to help meet the spiritual, economic, physical, and social needs of teenage youth in our community.

Executive Director, Jeff Moore said, "The goal is to provide a relationship ministry, in a safe place where teens can develop their talents in an organization based on Christian values and to create an atmosphere that allows teens to build confidence and discover their passion through the multifaceted music industry."

Alice Cooper said, "We are fulfilling a vision we've had for several years in providing teens and children with a central place to learn, have fun, and explore their creativity in a supportive environment."

During its first 10 years Solid Rock raised approximately $1.2 million and donated it to Valley area organizations such as Neighborhood Ministries, the Navajo Christian Foundation, and Grand Canyon University's Scholarship Foundation.

Beginning in 2006 I became involved with helping raise some of the funds to establish the youth center. Today, Solid Rock has a 28,000-square-foot youth center, in Phoenix, including a dance academy, a LeRoy Neiman Art Studio, teen game/meeting facilities, recording and practice studios, video/production/editing studio and a 500-seat performance auditorium.

I am proud that the ProFund Process has raised some $400,000 for this cause.

By the way, Alice Coper is a great guy and community leader with great passion for youth ministries. And, he currently carries a 6 golf handicap.

J Mike   Alice   My Diane

Golf in The Kingdom – Incorporated, 1994

For those who love the game, a trip to Scotland is a virtual necessity. It's taking a step back in history and taking a step up for one's appreciation of what the game was, is, and ought to be. I have now, personally, been the escort and tour guide to more than 1,000 lovers of the game, in groups of eight to 24, on the golf trip of a lifetime.

In the early 1960s I had seen newsreels, probably on ABC's *Wide World of Sports*, about the British Open. At the time, I knew nothing about Ben Hogan and the great year he had in 1953, after a near-fatal car accident in 1949. After all, in 1949 I was just three years old and in 1953, a mere seven years old.

But in 1960, entering my high school years and now playing golf, I saw newsreels about the British Open (now commonly known as The Open) and about Arnold Palmer winning the British Open in 1960 and 1961, with his caddy Tip Anderson. I had seen tape-delay coverage of the 1964 British Open Championship, on ABC with Jim McKay, being won by "Champagne" Tony Lema and caddy Tip Anderson, on loan from Palmer.

When I first saw these newsreels and golf scenes of the The Old Course at St. Andrews, and the majestic R&A building sitting there, I thought, *I could never get over there.* But I didn't think that for long, as my next thought was, *Yeah, I can! I've just got to figure out how to do it.* On my Golf Bucket List, right up there at the top, was to play Golf in Scotland, meet Arnold Palmer, and make a hole-in-one.

My first Scottish Golf Holiday was made possible by Colin McNee Ferguson, the big burly Scotsman. While living in London, I met Colin when I was doing some sales and product training for Exxon Office Systems, UK and The Netherlands, between 1979 and 1984.

He and I played golf in England and Scotland, played the Open Championship Courses: Old Prestwick, Royal Troon, The Old Course at St. Andrews, (check that one off the Bucket List!), Carnoustie, and Muirfield (with friend and member, Tony Fasson) and other various jewels in the crown of Scottish golf, including Colin's grandfather's club, Monifieth. In England we played Walton Heath, a Ryder Cup venue, with Colin's brother, Ian, and The RAC club in Surrey, being joined along the way by like-minded lovers of the game of golf. I know I have left some out, but that was more than 25 years ago.

Colin and I met a gentleman, David Bell, whose father lived on the Scores (a wonderful place behind the R&A) in St. Andrews. David had recently bought a building on North Street which had formerly been student housing for the college kids of the St. Andrews University, est. 1403. His plan was to convert the student housing residence into a hotel, named the Sporting Laird, and add a restaurant on the lower level. This he did as well.

David wanted me to meet Jock, a friend of his from a few doors down. Jock was a pub owner on the corner of North Street and Golf Place, which was just a nine iron from the 18th green of The Old Course.

I was delighted to meet Jock, who turned out to be Jack Willoughby, "a good ole Texas boy" and graduate of Texas A&M University. He had been in the oil business off the east coast of Scotland, near Aberdeen, and had just acquired the Dunvegan Hotel and Pub.

I had entertained business executives on golf trips before, and my mind was spinning. I now had two good contacts in the hotel business and it was David's intent to offer golf packages, including ground transportation, should I want to partner-up with him. I would be the U.S. sales agent for Scotland Golf Tours. Jack had the most famous Pub, for sure, in St. Andrews (and quite possibly in all of Scotland) along with an upstairs hotel with eight rooms that could accommodate 16 golfers, staying in the heart of St. Andrews.

Everything was put in place for business. On my return (which was back to Dallas), I quickly incorporated Golf in The Kingdom, a U.S.-based golf tour company.

At the time, I was still living on Maui. I invited David Bell to the Island and he came from Scotland, to "shore up" (yes, pun intended) the details of the tour business. While in Maui, he obtained the nickname Whitey when we went out on a boat, sailing to Molokini. He soon became known as Pinky, as the lad burned quite easily under the Hawaiian sun. We established our Golf Tour business while on the Island of Maui.

As President of Golf in The Kingdom, Inc., I have had the pleasure of creating and delivering custom-designed golf tours for groups of eight to 24 golfers and have personally escorted each tour—and more than 1,000 golfers over the years—to Scotland, England, Ireland, China, and South Africa.

I am also very fortunate to have been able to attend The Open Championships at Turnberry Ailsa, Lytham St. Annes, Royal Birkdale, Royal Liverpool, Royal Troon, five Opens at the Old Course, St. Andrews, and three at Carnoustie.

The Open Championship had its beginning at Prestwick in 1860. The idea came from the prominent members of the Prestwick Golf Club, after the preeminent golf professional of the time, Allan Robertson, of the St. Andrews club and ball maker (and the best player back then) passed away. Who would take his place and be the Champion golfer? The notes of the handwritten minutes of the meeting where the decision to host a championship was made, state "… and it shall be OPEN to the world." Between 1860 and 1925 the Open has been contested at Prestwick 24 times. I did attend the Palmer Cup at Prestwick in 2006 where the best college players in America took on the best of Europe.

These Championships are played on the most exalted, prestigious, and renowned courses in the United Kingdom and Ireland.

Nicklaus – a Family Affair

Every year during Masters Week, I think of the Jack Nicklaus victory at Augusta in 1986, and what was maybe the best nine holes of any major ever played. We are so fortunate to have this all captured in wonderful color and available to view at any time. I have *my* recording.

Nicklaus, with his son Jackie on the bag, had a first round 74; not too impressive. That was followed by a second round 71 and an even lower third round of 69, giving him a tie at 9th place going into the final round.

Even after Jack birdied the ninth, tenth and eleventh holes, CBS was not paying too much attention to him. Then came the bogey on the par three, number 12, which kept the cameras off Jack. But he reached the par five, 13, in two and two-putted for his birdie. Par on 14 for Jack, while the cameras were all over Seve Ballesteros and his eagle on 13. (The noise from the crowd was deafening!). Seve was now two strokes ahead of Tom Kite and Jack was four behind as he headed for the 15th tee.

It was looking like Seve Ballesteros was certainly "the heir apparent." Jack's second shot to the par-five 15th landed and rolled by the cup to within 12 feet of the hole. Jack made the eagle putt and Jackie jumped twice as high as Phil Mickelson could ever jump. I was glued to the TV, and so was just about anyone who ever watched a golf tournament. On the par three #16th, Jack was contemplating a four, five, or six iron. He went with the five and hit it so pure, that he didn't even watch it fly through the air. He bent over to pick up his tee, while Jackie yelled "be right!" Jack knew, and simply said, "It is" and started walking to the green. The ball hit the green, checked up, slid left... almost going in, and stopped less than four feet from the hole. Birdie!

Jack and Jackie

Everyone knew about the putt on 17 and it's one of the most iconic pictures in the history of the game. I put it right up there with Hogan's one iron in my list of golf's most dramatic golf pictures.

On 18, Jack hit a three wood off the tee, leaving a shot of some 175 yards. The next shot came up a bit short leaving a "40-foot" up hill putt. The first putt rolled to within six inches, was tapped in for par and father and son walked off the green arm in arm, to wait.

The Golden Bear

I have had three special occasions to be in the company of Jack Nicklaus.

The first occasion was a week or two following his great Masters victory in 1986, and the timing could not have been more perfect. I had just received, by mail in Dallas, the four copies I had ordered of *The Augusta Chronicle* newspaper's full Sports section, dated Monday, April 14, 1986. (That was 32 years ago…) Of course the paper had the iconic picture of Jack and that birdie putt on the 17th hole of Sunday's final round and his victory of April 13, 1986.

Looking at the *Dallas Morning News* sports section, the day I received the Augusta papers, I saw a piece on Jack Nicklaus coming to Dallas and presenting a tour of his newly redesigned Dallas Athletic Club's Blue Course. This was where Jack had won the 4th of his 18 Major Championships, the 1963 PGA.

My four *Augusta Chronicle* sports sections had the four front pages of Jack Nicklaus and four second pages and pictures, as well. I had ordered these four copies from Augusta with the intent of giving them away at the 1986 Screen Door Open. This was my plan: Two front pages were for Low Gross and Low Net. Four second pages would be presented to the four different flight winners. A front page would be presented to the winner of the Dirt Bag, awarded each year to the person in last place in the SDO. I thought I'd keep one front page for myself.

Upon my discovering that Jack was soon to be in town, I thought, *Wouldn't it be great if I could get all these newspapers autographed? Hum!*

I kept thinking of a way to make that happen. The tour of the new Blue Course was for members only, but I wasn't going to let that stop me.

Upon my arrival at the DAC I was stopped at the gate. Well (as I've said…) I wouldn't let them stop me. While slowly rolling by the security personnel, I held up the Augusta newspapers, and said, "These papers on Mr. Nicklaus' victory at the Masters, just arrived and I have the responsibility of getting them to him." They waved me through.

I caught up with a small group of people (maybe 50) on the Blue Course, walking with Jack Nicklaus. He had a wireless microphone around his neck and P.A. system with speakers mounted on a golf cart. It was a very personal and intimate occasion for some really big shots of the club, I presumed. Jack was describing each hole along the front nine holes, with explanation of his thoughts and why he had made the changes he did, and so on and so forth.

Upon finishing his description of a newly designed hole of the course, he would move to the next tee, answer any questions and sign some more autographs.

As soon as I had the chance, I approached Mr. Nicklaus with my copies of the Augusta Chronicle with his picture of the putt on the 17th green of the final day's play of the Masters.

I am… one, not supposed to be there, and two, planning to be almost shoving these papers in front of Jack and asking him to sign eight autographs. That might seem a bit bold, but this was my chance. As I came close enough for Jack to see me, holding the front page of the paper in front of my chest, he gave me a huge smile and waved me over to him. That's when I explained why I had so many papers and was seeking eight autographs as special awards for the SDO. That's when he said, "That's a great name for a golf tournament, The Screen Door Open." I got the eight autographs.

My second occasion to meet Jack Nicklaus came in the early 1990s, upon his appearance at Sherwood Country Club. This is the course he designed for David Murdock, Jack having carte blanche with Mr. Murdock's money. The course had opened in 1989, but was still in the middle of refinement, as in spending over $6 million to dig up and move some 1,600 oak trees around the golf course and property, just south of Thousand Oaks, California. These were not little trees, either. Some were more than 50 feet tall, were hundreds of years old, and many weighed well over 100 tons each. Tree experts were consulted, several saying, "We won't know if these transplants are a success for 10 or 15 years." Others were saying, "You can't do this, many will die." Murdock's tree consultants gave no guarantees that these centuries-old oak trees would live for more centuries. This being in California, the actions were certain to bring out the animal rights groups and environmentalists, and the wacky environmentalists, too. One guy took to tree sitting in the branches of one of the giant oaks and refused to come down.

Nicklaus supervised the entire project himself, hole by hole, with the course layout, placement of rocks, water routing, tree placement, everything. Today, some 28 years later, it seems it all worked out and is the crowning jewel of all Nicklaus-designed courses.

I met Jack again, this time at Sherwood Country Club, meandering my way onto the property during one of the Franklin Templeton Shark Shoot Outs of the early 2000s. He was headed my way, in a golf cart, when I unrolled my 24x36 print titled Golden Moment. This is a print of The Putt on the 17th hole of the Masters Championship of 1986. Smiling, once again, he stopped the cart and said, "I have to sign that." I asked, "Do you remember me at the DAC in 1986, where you signed all those Augusta newspapers after your Masters victory?"

"How could I forget," he smiled and said, "Thank you."

The third occasion: Jack comes to me!

The year was 2005, a Golf in The Kingdom Scotland Tour. During the Open Championship, which is contested on the Old Course every year ending in 0 or 5, we (the golfers on our 2005 tour) happened to be playing at Kingsbarns, which is located south of St. Andrews, no more than a 15-minute drive away. This course was opened in the year 2000. After the discovery of a very old nine-hole course there, Kyle Phillips and Mark Parsinen redesigned the property into an 18 hole course. They also later developed Castle Stewart way up high in the Highlands of Scotland, near Royal Dornoch, Nairn, and Old Moray (all on the Moray Firth of Scotland). Kingsbarns is ranked #54 in the world by *Golf Magazine* with a view of the North Sea from every hole, "So Spectacular!" This is such an awesome, majestic, and unbelievable Championship Links Golf Course!

We try to always play Kingsbarns on Sundays, so that it doesn't interfere with our opportunity to play the Old Course, through the bloody Ballot system imposed on The Old Course in 1995. The Old Course is closed on Sundays, by law. My 2005 Golf in The Kingdom tour group (4 foursomes) were making the turn at Kingsbarns (one of the few Scottish courses we play with the ninth hole turn returning to the club house, having a tiny little refreshment stand on the 10th tee).

All of a sudden, while getting a hot dog and beer following the first nine holes, we heard a helicopter approaching. It landed beside the clubhouse and out popped Tom Watson and Jack Nicklaus, who walked right up to us on the #10 tee.

We were a bit stunned to see these two great Open Champions headed our way.

They were the ones who broke the ice:

"Hey, how you guys doing?"

"Uh, great."

"How do you like the course?"

"It is just unbelievable, and so beautiful!"

Jack and me - he signed the new 5£ note for me

This was the year that the Royal Bank of Scotland produced a new £five (pound) note commemorating Jack's final appearance and play at the 2005 Open Championship. The note features the Golden Bear's logo, and two drawings of him in his last victorious Championship round on the Old Course of 1978. It also features his winning scorecard. The Royal Bank of Scotland has been producing its own bank notes since 1727 and Nicklaus is only the third living person to be honored this way, after the Queen and Queen Mother.

Knowing that the new notes were coming out, I had my scouts out at the local banks buying the new notes for me, and I had some with me. That was lucky! I asked Jack if he remembered me from the Dallas Athletic club in 1986 and again at Sherwood CC. He said: "How could I forget!" This was Jack's farewell to the Open Championship 2005 at The Old Course, St. Andrews.

The 20th Annual SDO, 1997 – played on the Old Course, St. Andrews Scotland

The Home of Golf… Birthplace of the Game…The Cradle of Golf

On the occasion of our 1997 Screen Door Open in Scotland 20th Anniversary Dinner at The Home of Golf

A speech was given, in the honor of the occasion and here are "some observations" by Mike Bixler:

"Good evening, gentlemen,

I have been thinking about the difference between golf and other sports.
Let me ask you the following:
Have you ever seen a golfer spit into the face of a marshal? Or
Kick a photographer in the groin? Or
Walk up to a competitor and taunt him before he putts? Or
Get arrested for being in a hotel with three hookers and a pile of cocaine?
Have you ever known someone to show up at a major tournament with orange hair, tattoos, and body piercing? I think not (except for ole Rainbow Head and his John 3:16 shirt).

You know, golfers don't yell at each other or start fights
No, when I think about golf, I think about:
Crenshaw winning his second Masters the week Harvey Penick
died.
I think about Norman and Faldo embracing after Norman's total
collapse.
I think about Jack Nicklaus winning his final Masters in 1986
and Jack waiting to greet Tom Watson at the 18th green at Pebble
Beach, after Watson's chip in on the 17th won him the US Open.
I think of Ken Venturi's walk down the 18th fairway, winning
the U.S. Open in 1964, at Congressional, after nearly collapsing
in the near-100-degree heat and humidity of the 36-hole final day
of play.

And, of course, we all think of our personal experiences in golf,
the weekly round with our friends, solitary walks in the early
evening, or peak experiences like the Screen Door Open. We all
share one thing: great personal experiences of being in the game
of golf.

Most importantly, we have found great companions in golf, which
leads me to J. Michael Meadows. As great as all the excitement,
pageantry, and competition that we have experienced as a result of
the SDO, the greatest gift has been friendship.

Not only has J. Mike's effort over the years allowed me to maintain
my relationships with guys I used to work with, friends of mine
before the first SDO, I have met my best friends as a result of this
great event.

Which leads me to my next topic.

Over the years, I'm sure we have all had opportunities to get
famous people's autographs. I have probably had more chances
than most people because of all of my travel. Fact: I have never

asked anyone for an autograph except Dan Jenkins just prior to the 4ᵗʰ SDO when I requested signed copies of *Dead Solid Perfect*.

In fact, if you will bear with me for just a moment, here is a list of some of the people who I've had absolute lay-down situations to get their autograph— and didn't ask for any autographs: Alfred Hitchcock, Jack Benny, Brian Wilson, Mel Torme, Forrest Tucker, Mickey Mantle, Jim Palmer, Bobby Layne, Ted Kennedy, Muhammad Ali, Jack Nicklaus, Mitzi Gaynor, BB King, Barry White, Sean Connery, Bart Starr, Pat Summerall, Jackie Stewart, Richard Branson, Joe Theismann, Joe Paterno, Jim Plunkett, Doc Severinsen, Paul Newman, Jane Seymour, Doug Sanders, Dave Marr, John Tower, Dick Enberg, Joe Namath, Bill Walton, Hume Cronyn and Jessica Tandy, John Riggins, Gale Sayers, Jim Ryun and many, many others. Again, I have never asked for an autograph, other than Dan Jenkins.

But, a few weeks ago I was at dinner with some business people, in a small restaurant in London, when a party of two couples came in and sat down next to us. We talked about it at our table, which is normal, I think, "Hey, look who just came in and sat down over there."

I then started to think about the SDO and J. Michael, in particular, and decided that I had to "risk all" to get this person to acknowledge our SDO trip to Scotland.

As we got up to leave, I knelt down between this guy and his wife and told him that I have never asked for an autograph before, and that this was for a special person and occasion. I then explained that this special person and very good friend has hosted a group of friends and golfers for the past 20 years and that this year we were coming to Scotland, to The Home of Golf, St. Andrews, Prestwick, Royal Dornoch and to the other fine "Jewels in the Crown of Golf." I said that this friend of ours, deserved a bit of recognition for all of his work, and therefore I was interrupting his dinner and imposing on him for his signature.

He laughed and said that certainly you, your friends and host, deserve to be properly welcomed to the United Kingdom and he graciously signed the back of my $1,200 receipt for dinner.

J. Mike, I would like to present you with a small token of our appreciation… for your friendship and the joy you have brought to our lives each July for the last 20 years.

The newly elected Prime Minister of the United Kingdom, Mr. Tony Blair, from Edinburgh, Scotland, sends his best wishes to all of us participating in the 20th United States Screen Door Open International-Invitational Golf Classic."

The Prime Minister's Best Wishes

CHAPTER FIVE

There have now been 40 USSDOII Golf Championships which began in Dallas, Texas and have been played in Oklahoma, Kansas, Arkansas, Mexico, Scotland, New Mexico, Louisiana, Arizona, South Africa, and China. Any one of which could be another book, or movie, but there hasn't been a big blow-out SDO in a while. Guess that's 'cause all my rowdy friends have settled down. The friendships made from the SDO are forever. There is rumor on another gathering of the brothers, those still having good standing in the world, jolly fellows of good character, sense of adventure, and so forth and so on.

CHAPTER SIX

IT'S A MAD MAD WORLD

The term *mad* can be used in several ways. As an adjective it can mean very angry, which no doubt we have all been at some point. Also, as an adjective, it can mean mentally ill, insane, or crazy, as in "Are we going mad?"

What's crazy about golf? Lots of things seem to be mad or insane to me in golf.

Golfers are to play by the rules on courses designed to make it difficult to hit a golf ball in the fewest possible strokes with environmental restrictions like bunkers, water, etc.

Unless you are a PGA professional golfer and playing at the highest level, under scrutiny of the cameras and rules officials, you are most likely playing under what I consider to be the generally accepted Fudging and Nudging with the Rules of golf. **I am guilty of some of these infractions, myself!**

Infractions of the rules of golf have become so commonplace, so routine, that no one questions them. Let me give you some examples:

Fudging and Nudging with the Rules of Golf

Let's ask these questions:

How you gonna play it?

How *have* you been playing it?

The *Mulligan* is first on my list of Fudging and Nudging with the rules of golf.

First a little history of the *mulligan*…

Legend has it that the *mulligan* is a sports term believed to be coined after one person, D.B. Mulligan, of Canada, who became a member of Winged Foot in Mamaroneck, New York sometime in the late 1920s to early '30s.

Seems Mr. Mulligan had a regular foursome and one day, on the first tee, he said, "I was so provoked with myself that, on impulse, I stooped over and put down another ball. The other three looked at me with considerable puzzlement, and one of them asked, 'What are you doing?' I replied, I'm taking a correction shot."

One of his playing partners asked him what he called it. "Thinking fast, I told them I called it a *mulligan*." Henceforth, they had an unwritten rule in the foursome that you were allowed another shot on the first tee if you weren't happy with the first. "I'm taking a *mulligan*" spread fast, and the name with it.

Another story has it this way: Buddy Mulligan was a locker room attendant in the 1930s at a country club in New Jersey. On a slow day at the club Buddy got to play with an assistant professional and one member, who allowed another shot, after Mulligan's poor drive, since the others had been practicing before play.

Thereafter, Buddy Mulligan proudly boasted around the club about how he was given an extra shot. The members loved it—and began giving themselves a *mulligan* in honor of Buddy. (This, by the way, is the way NBC's *Today Show* ran the story of the Mulligan in 2005.)

My friend Mike Hyatt is a member of River Crest CC in Ft. Worth Texas, where there used to be a sign on the first tee which read: No Mulligans! The sign has disappeared over time, relaxing the whole of golf's integrity, once again.

Today, the *mulligan* has worked its way into the American culture of a "do-over"—for anything, a chance after a failed first attempt.

When playing in my regular Saturday game, we are allowed a *mulligan*, but only one in the entire round and only on the first tee. And if you take a mulligan on the first tee, you must play the second ball, the *mulligan*. It's still part of the generally accepted standards of Fudging and Nudging. We don't play "a *mulligan* a side" nor do we play "carry over *mulligans*." As Ben Hogan said: "I play golf with friends, but we don't play friendly games."

Many golfers all over the world are playing golf for fun and not in any competitions. The rules are often relaxed in some of the social, fun settings by agreement of the players, which has become acceptable in such groups. But it is important that in any non-official competitive game of golf, all players are in agreement as to how they are going to play and under what rules they will govern their play.

In Scotland they do allow a *mulligan* on the first tee. However, they call it "Hitting Three." Over there, where they made all the rules, the Scotts do not recognize or acknowledge the *Mulligan*. "Nae (Scottish brogue for *not so*) for true golfers," they say. All golf shots count, even the one you take on the first tee. You hit it, you own it. We should all forget the *mulligan*, in my opinion. It's insane.

More examples of Fudging and Nudging... have we all gone mad?

Winter Rules, another infraction of the rules of golf, is almost universally accepted. This practice came about while playing on golf courses that were not in the best of conditions, thus allowing a player to move the ball to a more favorable position, or "nudging it." So, if your ball is lying on a patch of bare dirt, you may move it a certain distance and place it on a nice tuft of grass. But how far a distance is one allowed to move the ball? That's crazy!

"We always play winter rules," some will say. These golfers move the ball around even on beautifully conditioned courses, in the fairway or in the rough. So, if you're going to play winter rules everywhere on the course, you might as well move the ball out of the way of that hanging limb, which is obstructing your swing... right?

After you've taken a lifetime to find your ball in the deep grass or underbrush of the rough, you might as well place it in a new location and get a better lie. Taking relief (golf term) and improving your lie has taken on so many different meanings in the interpretations within the rules of golf that very few actually know most of the rules of the game.

We should always play the ball down (in the place that it came to rest), unless the course has given written notice or placed a sign regarding rules of play for that day.

Many of the ways amateurs are playing golf today could not survive the PGA or LPGA rules officials, and for sure not the Royal & Ancient Golf Club of Scotland. The R&A is the ruling body of golf worldwide, except for the United States and Mexico, where this responsibility rests with the United States Golf Association (USGA). The R&A works in collaboration with national amateur and professional golf organizations in more than 110 countries.

The R&A cooperates with the USGA in producing and regularly revising the Rules of Golf, and the two bodies have issued the rules jointly since 1952. The Rules of Golf are revised on a four-year cycle and, with the revision that became effective on January 1, 2012, was the first time a single, common set of Rules applied throughout the world.

In amateur golf today there seems to be little or no guilt (and hardly any accountability, or even protest) from other players in matters related to the rules of golf. "After all, it's just a friendly game" is the conventional wisdom and, because it is, nobody speaks up. Thus, everyone's attitude has come to this: "I am going to take as much advantage as everyone else is taking." Therefore, let's not ruin the day by being zealots and being so rigid about the rules. Really? We *have* gone mad.

Even if social golfers don't observe all the Rules of Golf in their casual games, it is recommended that they spend some time to learn them. Who knows when they might be invited to play in competition, where they would want to know how to play by the rules.

The *"Gimme"* may be the biggest, most controversial issue in Fudging and Nudging with the rules of golf, and it's mad.

The *gimme* is a putt that the players agree can count automatically without being played. Here's how this one works: When a player has only a very short putt left to play, he or she may be granted (most do not wait for it being granted, they just take it) a *gimme*. The stroke is counted, but the golfer doesn't need to hit the ball and hole it.

There is a really wide range of rules (and simple acceptance) on *gimme* putts. They range from "pick it up if inside three feet... it speeds up play" to "No, never! There's no such thing as a *gimme*."

It is the biggest controversy in the complete disregard of the rules of golf in allowing someone to not complete the objective of the game—which is using a golf club to strike the ball, causing it to go into the hole.

Another part of this controversy comes with the phrase *inside the leather*. When the term first came up, it referred to the grip of the club itself. You see, grips used to be made of leather (some may still be today) and *inside the leather* meant the length of the actual grip, which is only a measure of some ten inches, which is not much at all—and is a distance from which it is almost impossible *not* to make the putt. While it is very rare not to be able to make that distance of a putt, it has happened, even on the professional tours.

Scott Hoch in the 1989 Masters missed a two-footer for the win.

Doug Sanders missed a short putt at the 1970 Open Championship Old Course.

Ben Hogan, in the 1946 Masters, missed a two-footer.

Brad Snedeker, in the 2009 BMW, needed just to two-putt from 15 feet... but he four-putted.

Hale Irwin had a tap-in at the '83 Open and completely missed the ball.

Craig Stadler, in 1985 on the Ryder Cup team, missed a 14-incher.

Stewart Cink, with literally a tap-in, missed (that short of a putt) in the 2001 U.S. Open.

IK Kim in the 2012 LPGA Kraft Nabisco missed a really short, one-foot putt.

These incidents are all recorded and available for your review. I don't member anyone saying: "Hey, Stew, that was good."

The *That was good*

Here again, it's mad, unless it's match play. Anything other than "all putts must be holed," is simply unacceptable and is breaking the Rules of Golf. However, we all have had our regular group games of two or more foursomes, right? We are all playing each other, or teams are playing other teams in other groups, in front or behind us. It is widely suggested that you get the "How we gonna play this?" talked out on the first tee. "Are we giving putts today?" and "Are there any rules of golf that we won't be playing by today?"

We find ourselves giving a putt to someone, *even after the putt was missed*. What is that all about? Are we being kind, sympathetic, caring and compassionate in trying to eliminate the golfer's pain? Or is it because we will probably want the same consideration on the next hole? We even say "that was good" when someone misses a short back-handed putt. My friend Malcolm has always said: "We play golf this way: the nonchalant putts count the same as the 'chalant' ones do."

We tend to give each other the short putts. So much so, that we don't say anything when someone *gives himself* a putt... more than likely a fast, downhill, left to right breaking three-footer.

Today the term *inside the leather* refers to the distance between the top of the head of one's putter, up the shaft to the bottom of the putter's grip, which is not an exact or standard distance at all. It is usually somewhere around 25 inches - only two feet and one inch. But sometimes it's longer because not all putters are the same length.

To actually measure to see if the ball is *inside the leather* one must place their putter head inside the hole and lay the putter shaft along the surface of the green to see if the ball is actually between the putter head and bottom of the grip. The problem here is that very often the edges of the hole are damaged in the process. Some golfers, purposely, try to get a greater distance built into their personal putters.

Over time, the meaning and measurement has become loosely interpreted and often, merely a descriptive term. "That's *inside the leather*," as in just a statement, with no effort at measurement, and so the player just picks up the ball. Because it seems to be within a makeable length. *Really?*

In match play competition it is commonplace and considered good sportsmanship to concede short putts to your competition. It is *strictly* a match play occurrence.

Putts are never conceded in stroke play competition, as it affects the rest of the playing field.

In match play competition, one player may concede the putt, the hole, even the match, because the competition is strictly one-on-one, or two playing partners vs. another pair of golfers.

Players, in match play competitions, should never to ask, "Is that good?" One should merely walk slowly to his or her ball, while carefully listening, as the competitor just might say "That's good."

What about when someone concedes *a gimme*, but the player goes ahead and putts it anyway? So much for the *gimme* used to speed up play, huh? What about protecting the others who are playing in the game? I believe others playing in the competition need to be protected. What if the player misses the putt that had been conceded and takes the *gimme* anyway? Shouldn't that player be assessed a penalty for putting? I think it should be this: If it has been conceded, and not picked up, and the player putts and misses, he should have the score that was actually incurred on the hole.

But, "...that was good." Someone misses an attempt to make a putt and either the opponent or the player says after the miss: "That was good." What? "It was inside the leather, even though I missed it." *What?* Well, guess what: 1. The putt was not conceded before you putted and 2. you missed the putt.

Have you and a partner ever played in competition against another team, a twosome, in your group of four, and one of your opponents picks up, or gives a putt to his own partner? Again, putts are only conceded in match play competition, and only are conceded by the *opponent*.

Everything, rule-wise, should be settled on the first tee, before the first ball is struck. For example, everyone agrees to being allowed a *mulligan* on the first tee (in my group, if you take a *mulligan*, you play the *mulligan*— it is not your choice of the two tee shots).

Lifting of a golf ball to identify it is one of the most irritating things I see, all over the golf course. A golfer has a ball in play, which he picks up... yes, lifts the ball out of its current position. The player takes a look at the ball and then sets it back down, and often in a better position than they found it. This is carried out under the guise of the need to identify one's golf ball.

This is a tough one to believe, especially if you see this from your opponent or companion golfer in your regular game, doing it more than once during the game. You see, golf balls are marked on two opposite sides, by the manufacturer, visible right out of a new box, a *sleeve* of new golf balls. On opposite sides of each ball are the brand name and a number. Plus, most golfers use a Sharpie® pen to mark the ball by filling in the dimples in a pattern, even marking a ball with one's own initials, or lines and images, in order to help in the identification and easy determination of "Just whose ball is this anyway?" Lifting a golf ball from its position and replacing it should be done only under the Rules of Golf.

Most rules infractions occur simply because many players do not have a basic working understanding of the Rules of Golf. Golfers playing at any level of competition do have the responsibility to learn the Rules of Golf. It is a good idea to spend some time and learn the Rules, which will help you avoid some embarrassing issues regarding the game.

Here's the rule on lifting a ball in play...

The player may *touch* or bend long grass, rushes, bushes, or the like, but only to the extent necessary to identify the ball. The player must announce his intention to lift the ball to an opponent, other player, fellow-competitor or marker, and mark the position of the ball, before lifting.

If he is still unable to identify a ball thought to be played by himself, he may then lift the ball and identify it, provided that he gives his opponent, marker, or fellow-competitor an opportunity to observe the lifting and replacement, and that it is replaced in a close approximation to where it was found. Never touch an opponent's ball without permission, or you may open up a huge can of worms with someone who knows the Rules of Golf regarding lifting the ball.

I often see golfers picking up any golf ball in the fairway, even one that is clearly not their own ball, look at it, and drop it back in the fairway, or wherever it was before they lifted it. That, too, is a no-no.

I regularly play in competitions at my club in both match play and medal play (stroke play against the field of other players) where they always have a Format and Rules sheet, as a handout, before play begins.

In large red letters will be the words:

The Ball Must Be Holed!

Or

In Partnership format, the Ball used as the Team Score must be HOLED!

The documentation will also have:

Tournament Rules:

- USGA Rules Govern all play except when modified by Local Rules
- Refer to the Local Rules for additional information
- After completion of play, please turn in your signed scorecard immediately to the scoring table located at the Scoreboard

These are not match-play tournaments, because you are playing against the entire field of golfers, or at least those in your flight. Therefore to play a *gimme* in these competitions is a serious breach of the rules. Yet, unfortunately, it happens quite regularly.

Fluffing the lie or improving the lie of a golf ball is in the same category as *mulligans*, the *gimme*, playing OB like a lateral, etc. Do what you want, but you're only fooling yourself. Sorry… in my opinion, that's cheating yourself.

Some of what is being done is simply done because someone does not know the Rules of Golf. Ignorance of the rules is no excuse. I was recently playing, in competition, with someone who placed his foot behind the ball and pressed down the grass behind the ball. I said: "You know, according to the Rules of Golf, you cannot do that." Guess what? That person said, "I didn't know that" and thanked me. "Well, you know now" was my response. You can only enjoy the game more when you play by the rules. A player is not allowed to improve his or her lie unless so stated. Winter rules, summer rules, clean and place through the green… These things are not entitlements, and shouldn't be done automatically. I see life the same way. Play it as it lies!

Nudging and Fudging is prevalent everywhere golf is played. So much so, that these companies have produced commercials which use humor—related to cheating at golf—to sell their products and services.

The Aflac Insurance Company has their iconic duck cheating at golf. The duck kicks the ball away from a tree, then hides a ball under its wing, drops the ball onto the green and uses the ole foot wedge, nudging the ball into the hole.

Federal Express has the *Don't Count That* television commercial in which a golfer says to his caddy (no less than eight times), "Don't count that" while playing golf and he, too, uses the ole foot wedge. It is making fun about the lie, and slipping from the truth, until we are deluding ourselves and those around us.

So, I question "golf as a microcosm of life," and golf as a teacher of ethical behavior. It should, don't you think?

A buddy and I have paired up in a recent event or two. I recently sent him an email regarding the next partnership event. His reply message stated that his handicap has been steadily going up. He said: "Good news for the tourney, huh?" I replied: "Not really, as the committee will use each person's lowest handicap of the previous year." Not that my buddy would "sandbag," intentionally…

"Sandbagging" in golf — it's mad

Sandbagger as a golf term would make some sense if it had something to do with sand in sand traps or (as the Scots say, "bunkers"). We all know what a sand bag is, but how did bags of sand enter into the lexicon of the game of golf?

First, the word doesn't come from the type of sand bags we're all familiar with. It's not the defensive sand bags—those used for flood control, lining foxholes, and so forth—but the *offensive* ones that give us the golf word *sandbagger.*

Gangs and street toughs of the 19th century used sand bags as a weapon of choice. Take a sock or small bag, fill it with sand, wrap it tightly, and you have quite an effective weapon.

But the word didn't go directly from its gangland origins into golf. There was an intermediary step in there. *Sandbagger* was actually a poker term before it found its way into golf. In gambling it means someone who misrepresents his ability in order to gain an advantage.

Titanic Thompson was, by far, the best *sandbagger*—in poker and in golf.

Say you're in a poker match and you're dealt a fantastic hand. If you place a huge bet right off the bat, you might scare most of your poker mates into folding. Instead, you might choose to bet small amounts, hoping to keep your opponents in the match, increasing the pot and lulling your opponents into a false sense of security. The poker *sandbagger* would pounce late in the game, clobbering the other players with his good hand and rake in the pot.

The poker player, in other words, misled his opponents about how good his hand was… until it was time to whip out the figurative "sand bag" and beat those same opponents with it. Widely accepted, sandbagging in poker is an accepted part of the game and a common strategy.

Golf and gambling have always gone together, and the poker use of the term eventually crossed over into golf, and especially golf handicaps.

Any golfer who *deliberately* misleads others about his ability in order to gain an advantage— to win a bet, for example—is a *sandbagger*. Such *sandbaggers* might also be called bandits or hustlers.

Sandbaggers and Golf Handicap Indexes

More specifically, a *sandbagger* is a golfer who artificially inflates his handicap index in order to better his chances of winning tournaments or bets.

Here is how he does it: He inflates his handicap index by selectively leaving out his best rounds of golf when he posts scores for handicap purposes. Another is to, more simply, lie about the scores he is posting, claiming higher scores than actually shot. In this way, the golfer drives up his handicap index.

Then, when the *sandbagger* enters a tournament, he may claim a handicap index of 17 when, in fact, his real handicap might be a 10. So, this *sandbagger* has just bought himself seven extra strokes off his gross score, and improved his odds of winning his flight or the tournament.

This form of sandbagging is also known as "handicap building."

A *sandbagger* is considered by many to be the one of the lowest forms of cheaters. Golfers who are found to be *sandbaggers* are often ostracized and always looked down upon. Sandbagging can lead to the end of friendships and even to a golfer getting black-balled at other tournaments—or even kicked out of a club.

There are even more rules interpretations that wouldn't survive the R&A, professional tours, and should not survive in men's golf associations or club tournaments, but we see rule infringements all the time. It's what many do.

While we're on the subject of BS...

Here's some Golf BS that needs to be changed!

I make a hole-in-one and have to buy everyone a drink? That's BS!

It's a tradition, you say? I ace the 5th hole and a guy on 17, who I don't know, gets a beer on me? Even the guy walking in from the parking lot is told, "Hey somebody made a ONE on #5, have yourself a drink on him!" To which he (a stranger) responds: "Make it a double!" I've only had five hole-in-ones, so far, *but come on!*

At some clubs, everyone who is in the hole-in-one club pays $5 or $10 a month so the pot builds up until someone makes an ace. Let the golfer keep that money and let everyone buy their own drink!

The Pros can't use range finders? That's BS!

Think about it. You want to speed up the slow pace of professional golf? We have the players and caddies stepping off yardage and looking at books on the course. Then all the talk between them about the yardage book and what distance was walked off and then blah, blah, blah. Let them use the latest in range finders! There are those that calculate distance with slope, and give true distance required for the shot. Shoot it (with the range finder...) and there's no doubt about it. They've got it down to 176.2 yards. What would Hogan think?

Why have a different number of playoff holes for the U.S. Open, PGA, The Masters and The Open? That's BS!

I don't get it! The U.S. Open has a two-hole playoff if there are ties after 72 holes of competition. But there's a three-hole playoff at the PGA, and a four-hole playoff at the Open Championship. When there's a playoff at the Old Course, it's played on holes #1, #2, #17 and #18. Then, if there is still a tie at the end of the playoff holes, it goes into sudden death.

In my opinion, The Masters since 1979 has done it right: a Sudden Death Playoff. That's it!

MAD: Mental Attitude Dynamics[3]

In my Prologue, I wrote of a well-known sports psychologist, consultant, and author of many books who wrote about the importance of having a strong mind and preparing his golf professional clients mentally for competition. He confesses that his clients often say, "A different book helped me for a while, but it doesn't seem to work well anymore."

I agree with him that our most underused asset is our mind in winning the battle within ourselves. We become what we think and we must become confident. He emphasizes the importance of commitment to the process of strengthening one's mind and working on our **THINK**ing. He could not have written a better commentary on being a good golfer. Zig Ziglar nailed it, saying, "You Gotta Stop the Stinkin' Kinda Thinkin'."

The process is ongoing, too. Like physical fitness, you work out, exercise, and reach a level of fitness. If you stop the process of keeping fit, you become "soft in the middle," and weakness creeps in, both physically and mentally.

There has been a great deal written on the mind and golf.

My good friend Kerry Graham, a life member of the LPGA Teaching and Club Professional Membership and Member of the LPGA Hall of Fame, has studied the power of the mind throughout her long career in golf.

I have often joined her on the practice tee for a "mental golf tune-up." She would tell me, "Let's discover how you learn and focus." I asked, "Are you talking about me personally or everyone?" Kerry made it clear that everyone learns and focuses in a unique way and the trick to a better mental golf game is discovering that uniqueness.

I never hit very many balls on the practice area with Kerry. She helped me determine my individual golf learning style, and guided me to develop strategies for the way I learn. She keeps the instruction more focused and simple than other golf instruction I have had. She's definitely got my learning style down pat, and I continue to improve my focus, confidence, and consistency.

Through Kerry's book *The Power of Mental Golf*—and especially in reading the chapter Get to Know Your Brain—I was able to re-discover for myself *my preferred learning style*, which confirmed everything we had worked on. I was amazed at how her Learning Assessment, (offered in her book) was so spot-on as to how it mirrored the work we had done on the range. By the way, from the Assessment and analysis in the book, I found that I am very visual in the (V-R) Visual Right classification. I now have an understanding of my best learning style, the cues for better learning and focus, and my areas of weakness in learning and focus so I know what to avoid.

If we can understand how our own brain processes information, Kerry's teaching process can further guide us in using that personal information to better manage our brain. In her book, *The Power of Mental Golf*, and by taking the Learning Assessment at www.powermentalgolf.com you will be able to apply this information about your Sensory Strengths and Brain Processing Preferences to discover your Golf Learning Type(s).[4]

If you are already working with a golf instructor you will be able to share this book and information, learn about yourself, and be able to give explanations to that golf instructor on how you learn and focus best.

Adding this to my practical application of MAD, Mental Attitude Dynamics, makes both the game of life and the game of golf more pleasurable.

MAD determines one's life and character

While I grew up in a strong environment of mental attitude dynamics and have studied the Doctrine of Mental Attitude pertaining to spiritual life, I also am aware of the term *mad* in the following definition:

God and Sports Performance – it's mad

We see and hear from "religious" Christian sports figures all the time. Many will cross themselves, making the sign of the cross, during televised sporting events. Baseball stars will cross themselves, even kiss the cross worn around their neck and point skyward, each time they get into the batter's box. I've often wondered *how long will that religious act be in effect?* Evidently not for the entire game; more like an inning or two. Doing the ritual, every time the player gets inside the batter's box, seems a little excessive to me. And it begs the question: Why not with each pitch? I guess it's an individual thing, but can you imagine a golfer crossing himself at every tee? Or before each and every golf shot? (Par is generally 72, so 72 signs of the cross a round?) I don't know, maybe that's good until you get to the green. Talk about slowing the game of golf down even more!

Many stars make public statements, thanking God for their victories. We don't seem to see or hear much praising of God from the losers, however. That might be because they don't often interview the losers. I, personally, don't think God has much to do with sporting event results.

Hitting a triple or a home run is often followed by looking and pointing skyward to the heavens. We are to be grateful and give thanks for everything, except being thrown out at first. I've often wondered about stealing second or third base and then kissing the cross or pointing upward. What... for *stealing?*

Bubba Watson has been quoted as saying at Augusta National after winning the Masters, that he was thanking his "Lord and Savior, Jesus Christ." He also said, "The Lord couldn't care less whether I win or lose. What matters to Him is how I play the game." I agree with Bubba's "what matters" statement.

In today's world, it seems that these actions and statements are viewed as inappropriate by many, even offensive to others. Under my rule of "live and let live," I am OK with it, as it lets me know a little more about the person. I am able to move on without being offended. I can see how some people see it as a bit awkward, kind of like talking politics while opening Christmas presents.

In golf, however, unlike other sports, there have been multiple PGA Tour Bible Studies, led by well know players, evolving from the 1960s with such names as Babe Hiskey and Kermit Zarley, as well as others.

Other noted Tour players (I do not personally know them) who are characterized as being Christian or "religious" are Scott Simpson, Aaron Baddeley, Tom Lehman, Web Simpson, Corey Pavin, Betsy King and lots more. It seems that a sub-culture of Professional Christian Golfers has developed where you'll find Bible discussion groups, Bible Coffee chats or fellowship sessions where scripture is discussed, and personal faith testimonies being given at outreach group meetings.

I certainly question it. "It's not a genie," Lee Jansen said.

"I've seen guys come to Bible study for a few weeks thinking that if they can get that right in their lives, they'll play better. That's not the way it is."

My question is: Get *what* right?

You can't pick up a Bible in desperation, close your eyes and thumb through the pages, place your finger on a page—on a verse—and then, SHAZAM!, truly think that God is talking to you and this is the precise verse or message He has for you.

In Quest of Perfection

If you have interest in golf, you have probably watched some golf tournaments on TV, and it's likely you've watched some or all of the Majors—The Masters, The U.S. Open, The Open, and The PGA Championships—where the best golfers in the world, men and women have been working/practicing the game for most of their lives in ways we could never really imagine. They come walking off the 18th hole with scores of, say anywhere between 67 and 71, and are then interviewed. We, as viewers, have just watched these professionals hit unbelievable golf shots, shot after shot, that seem to us so perfect, that we cannot fathom how they do it. We can only dream of being that good.

In the interview, after their round, these professionals tell us that they are not where they want to be. They are not unhappy with their performance but will always talk about improving, and working on their game. Very often they admit to a trend of missing some important shot, a shot that they intended to hit differently.

All golfers, professional and amateur, hit bad shots in every round they play. Ben Hogan said he only expected to hit two or three really good shots per round. Arnold Palmer was quoted, in the *Desert Sun* newspaper in 1966 when asked his prediction for the winner of the Masters, as saying, "He who makes the least mistakes."

The lowest score in a Professional Golf Tournament, for 18 holes of play, is the score of 58 posted by Jim Furyk. There are only eight other scores lower than 60, and Jim Furyk owns two of them.

Al Geiberger posted the first ever score of 59 on June 10, 1977. Here is how that unfolded: He hit 14 out of 14 fairways and 18 out of 18 greens—ball-striking perfection, tee to green. But it would take more than that; he had to make a lot of putts. And he did. He had 23 putts total, a number that included a lot of birdie putts. But, he also missed some birdie putts, had no hole-in-one, though he holed out for an eagle from off the green on one hole.

There has never been The Perfect Round of Golf, and there never will be. What would that be? A birdie on every hole? Well, that would be a score of 52 on a par 70 golf course. But that score, when shot, could have been lower, with a hole-in-one or an albatross two on a couple of par 5s.

In interviews, just how many times does a professional say, **"It could have been better."**

Here is the most recent example... **and it's mad.**

October 8, 2017 Headlines:

"Ross Fisher breaks the Old Course scoring record in disappointing fashion"

What did I just read? "... in disappointing fashion?" How in the world could breaking the course record at the Old Course be a disappointment? First, a little history ...

The iconic Old Course of St. Andrews, Scotland is known the world over as The Birthplace of Golf, The Cradle of the Game, and The Home of Golf. It is the most famous golf course in the world, period, over and out! The Old Course, St. Andrews, Fife, Scotland is the most famous course with most golfers around the world.

History tells us that golf has been played there for some 600 years, back to 1400 AD. Today, St. Andrews Links Trust manages one of the largest golfing complexes in the world. Scotland golf became a way of life and part of the culture and economy there, before anywhere else… players, caddies, golf club and golf ball makers, etc.

Golf was banned in the Middle Ages in Scotland in the year 1457, as it was becoming popular. King James II thought that golf was taking the place of archery practice and forewarned of the need of being prepared militarily, as the Brits or someone else, were surely coming to invade, once again. The ban was continued by King James III. King James IV ended the ban in 1502 saying, "What the hey…" and became a golfer himself.

Playing golf is still banned on Sunday at The Old Course, unless of course, when the links management committee says it's OK for the Open Championship or the Alfred Dunhill Cup, or whenever they say it'll be OK to play The Old Course on a Sunday… which isn't very often.

Then there was Mary Queen of Scotts (1542 –1587) and her love of the game, before being beheaded by Queen Elizabeth I. Mary was a superb athlete of her time, at six feet tall, and a fine equestrian, who loved golf. She was accused of playing golf just a few days after the death of her husband, King Francis II of France. *Must have been a big no-no back then.* Just what is the correct mourning period before one can get back to the golf course? I wonder.

Mary Queen of Scotts is credited with originating the term *caddie*, as she played in France and had the military cadets carry her royal golf clubs.

A few other interesting tidbits about The Old Course:

- Old Tom Morris was the greenkeeper of those double greens… #17 arguably the most difficult par four in the world.
- Bobby Jones walked off the course, finding it so difficult.

- Sam Snead, flying over St. Andrews, looked out the airplane window and said, "Look at that abandoned old course down there… " not knowing that it would be the site of The Open Championship in every year ending with a zero or five.
- It's also known as the "Valley of Sin."
- The 18th green is the burial site of witches from past centuries.

OK! Enough Old Course History… And back to my point, the attitude…

"Ross Fisher breaks the Old Course scoring record… in disappointing fashion."

What did I just read?

Ross Fisher went to the 17th tee (of arguably the most difficult par 4 in the world) being 11 under par on the Old Course on Sunday, October 8, 2017 playing in the Dunhill Cup Championship. That event was played over the three courses of Carnoustie, Kingsbarns, and The Old Course. His tee shot on #17 was superb, a slight fade down what is known as The Road Hole. His long-iron second shot to the tiny, narrow green (that was protected by the famous Road Hole Bunker) rolled over the green and— UH OH!—crossed the gravel foot path and stopped on the three-foot strip of grass between the foot path and the rough black-top road, just before the wall. What did he do? He made an incredible up and down flop shot, Phil Mickelson style, making a score of "par four" on the hole that yielded only two birdies all day long.

He then went to the Tee of the easy par four 18th and drove to within 25 feet of the green. He putted and left the ball just four feet from the hole, uphill… right to left, and then missed the short birdie putt on the low side. Anyone could read the look on his face: Bewilderment.

He had two putts (and took them both) to set a new, all-time scoring record, by two shots, on THE OLD COURSE, mind you, and he still owns the course record today. It was the lowest score on THE OLD COURSE in 600 years of play, even with missing the birdie putt. And, it's two shots lower than the lowest score ever, in 600 years!!!

The press wrote, "....in disappointing fashion." Fisher, himself said, "I was playing all right, but I'm not going to complain too much with a 61."

All I can say is, "I hope not, Ross!"

You can't Keep It Out of the Rough

In the rough lies of life, and even in the fairways of life, we will find ourselves with hindrances, obstacles, obstructions, barriers, blocks, restraints, and more. There will be difficulties, no matter our status or position in life. Many situations confront us in which we will have to decide, on our own, how to handle each one. Learning to handle and manage these impediments and restrictions will make you a better person, even a better golfer.

In golf, the objective is to play on courses designed to make it difficult for a golfer to hit a golf ball in the fewest possible strokes with environmental restrictions: bunkers, water hazards etc. and where hitting a ball into a hole the size of the top of a pint of Guinness seems very unreasonable. Many amateurs, including myself, study, learn, and apply what we glean from golf instructors or golf instruction books and play the best game we can.

There are many people who play golf, without much focus on improvement. I think it is true in life, as well… and that is OK as long as it doesn't interfere with the freedoms of others..

Ben Hogan is quoted as saying: "The ultimate judge of your swing is the flight of the ball."

Just like the quality of our practice is measured in golf by the scorecard, so too, the quality of the practice of our faith is measured by how we react to the ups and downs of life.

Life can never be perfect, for we know we can never achieve the perfection of Christ Jesus. But we can spend our life on its fairways inside the game that HE designed for us, individually, in grace and in freedom, for the reflected glory of HIM and for our spiritual maturity. Many

Christians, in life, seem not to care about or only see human viewpoints in their Christian Way of Life.

Professional golfers have spent lifetimes developing and learning at a level we amateurs cannot comprehend. And they are always "fine-tuning" their game, looking for improvement, working toward perfection. The game of life, too, is not about perfection, for we know that no one has ever walked on the face of the earth in perfection, save one... The Lord Jesus Christ. **Jesus says in John 16:33: "In the world you have tribulation, but take courage; I have overcome the world" (NASB)**

In life, what is the objective? To play and live life, to study and learn, and apply that knowledge inside the formulated plan that God has for each of our lives. We have the ability to advance as far spiritually as we want. Are you advancing spiritually?

MAD: Mental Attitude Determines one's life, character and spirituality

I grew up in an environment of strong mental attitude, even pertaining to the spiritual life. In one's spiritual life there will be a constant struggle in thinking between two viewpoints: Human Viewpoint and Divine Viewpoint. So, there is always spiritual conflict based upon your thinking patterns.

You cannot fight in the spiritual conflict without Divine Viewpoint. If you only have Human Viewpoint you are a casualty to the conflict.

As a Christian, your spirituality comes from God the Holy Spirit, His ministry of it, when He controls it. Who is controlling your life?

CHAPTER SEVEN

YOU CAN'T THINK
WHAT YOU DON'T KNOW

Since childhood, the mysteries that have surrounded my life have had me experiencing coincidences that I could not understand. They were real and left me knowing that there was another side to life for me to discover. I have recognized that there have been many combinations of events, things that seemed to be chance happening, but I knew were more than just coincidence. Some call this Synchronicity of the Soul.

I remember Dad saying, "Son, there is an absolute science to all things, even spirituality. And, there isn't anything mysterious at all. It is only mysterious according to the level of awareness we have. The higher our level of awareness, the more the mystery is resolved." I wanted to understand the system that was operating behind the scenes.

In seeking truths, the divine viewpoint provides me spiritual wisdom. Maintaining the divine viewpoint is my challenge in today's world.

I knew I wanted to get answers to two questions: *Why am I here? And where am I going?* In other words, *What's next?*

What this means is that I am going to have to go "open kimono" with my valued readers and friends to reveal my personal beliefs.

Some readers will ponder over them, may not agree at all or only in part, with some of what follows. Many may find humor in my presentation of certain points.

Ok… just what makes me tick? My Faith

Mom and Dad were rooted in their faith, and that faith was at the core of all that radiated from every area of their lives—and they simply lived it! This stood out clearly and was very prominent in my parents' character, which I grew to love and admire. We were a Christian family and I grew up in a traditional Christian household. Dad prayed the same prayer at our evening and Sunday meals when the entire family sat down together at the family dining table: *"Our heavenly Father, thank you for another day of your grace… thank you for your many blessings… thank you for your love and watch-care over us. We ask you now, to sanctify this food to the nourishment of our bodies, in Jesus' name, Amen."*

And because we were an active Christian family, in harmony with all the other facets of our lives, we went to church.

As I wrote in my Introduction, "I am not a theologian, though I have studied under a few good ones. I am not unfamiliar with the Bible or Biblical Doctrine and have some insight or understanding in the application of Doctrine in my own life." I wanted to learn and knew there was more for me in living my Christian life.

I decided as a young boy to **GO WITH GOD,** placing my faith in His plan of salvation for me. Salvation enters you into the Plan of God and gives you a new identity, a spiritual species, with new potentials… ah ha! That's what Dad meant: new possibilities.

I am saddened to hear a Christian parent say that he or she wants their child exposed to all kinds of religions. How often do we hear this? *"When the child is old enough, he or she can make up their own mind."* I believe that something is dreadfully wrong when Christian parents are not sure enough of the truth of their own faith, that they let their children make this crucial decision on their own.

It seems to me that no responsible parent would make such a comment about any other aspect of a child's education.

Christian parents are supposed to give them that help and guidance. But today, thanks to our *"loose-leaf Bibles" (open up the three-ring-binder Bible,* allowing the removal of sections you don't like, or dropping in what sounds better) otherwise responsible parents let children make their own spiritual choices, *because* we don't know what truths to teach, or we believe only a few things in the Bible actually apply to us today. I also call this "Cafeteria Theology," where people believe you can just pick out what you like and leave the rest behind.

I heard the Gospel and accepted it, by faith, in what I believe to be God's plan of Salvation for me and all mankind.

And, you, no doubt have heard the following at least once, haven't you?

The Salvation Message:

God, the Father, sent His only Son to satisfy that judgment for those who believe in Him. Jesus, the creator and eternal Son of God, who lived a sinless life, loves us so much that He died for our sins, taking the punishment that we deserve, was buried, and rose from the dead according to the Bible. If you truly believe and trust this, acknowledging Jesus alone as your Savior, declaring, "Jesus is Lord," you will be saved from judgment and spend eternity with God in Heaven.

I knew one thing: I certainly wanted to go to Heaven, and be with God.

As I have written earlier in this book, as a kid I had not experienced anything very difficult in my life, nothing that had caused me to question God. That came later. I was just a kid going to school, Sunday school, church, and vacation bible school, playing baseball, and (as I got older) taking up the game of golf.

To Go with God Requires Faith, that's all!

The Bible says *faith,* the size of a grain of mustard... that's not very much, is it?

At that point, I knew practically nothing else about being a Christian. I barely knew the gospel. But later I learned that knowledge must be acquired and we acquire spiritual knowledge with accurate teaching of the Word of God, the Bible.

I learned that it is not about earning a relationship with God. It is not about doing good deeds or just being "a good person." All that is OK, even good, but we do not become Christian simply by joining a religious institution, by following some tradition in religious ceremony, or by being born into a Christian family. I believe I am very blessed by it and know many others who feel as I do.

For the record, I am not a Holy Roller, Bible Thumper, Speaker in Tongues, Born Again emotional fanatic... in no way am I. I do, however, favor thinking in terms of "What would Jesus do?"

As a young boy, I really loved Sunday school, learning about Jesus, and singing. A favorite: *Jesus loves the children of the world, red and yellow, black and white, they are precious in his sight. Jesus loves the little children of the world.* Not to overlook: *Jesus loves me, this I know, for the Bible tells me so* and messages like: *Do unto others... Love thy neighbor...* and so forth. All were wonderful principles that seem to drift away for some of us, over time.

At this early age, I didn't have some major revelation or a "rock bottom" crisis moment in my life where I had reached a feeling of total depravity and believed, therefore, the only way out was in turning my life over to the Lord. No, that wasn't the case. But as a boy of 9 or 10, I could consciously grasp God's Plan of Salvation for me. By the way, I did not experience instant happiness, either. No warm and fuzzy feelings. Nope, I was already a happy kid, due to my life's circumstances. And I didn't have a dynamic "radical transformation" in my life. I believe that has all been set aside for me at the end of the journey, when everything will be transformed.

Message on Faith

I began some 50 years ago with the Bible Doctrinal teachings of Pastor R. B. Thieme, Jr., then known as Berachah Tapes and Publications, based in Houston, Texas. The basis of my personal convictions, represented in this book, are based on my studies in Bible Doctrine. In addition, I have referenced other Biblical Scholars and Authors, as footnoted.

I would like to encourage readers to seek the grace ministry of R. B. Thieme, Jr. and visit his website at www.rbthieme.org. There is never a cost for any of his material.

God, Faith and Grace

Faith is the most basic system of perception. Faith is a system of thinking common to all mankind and is one of three systems of perception. The two others are Rationalism and Empiricism. Rationalism: "there is a way that is right." Empiricism: "truth and knowledge are based on one's senses." However, Scripture says: "for we walk by faith and not by sight."

Faith is the only non-meritorious system of perception and is, therefore, chosen by God as a means of response to His Plan. Faith is the only system equally accessible to all men and is compatible with Grace. Your faith should not rest on the wisdom of men… on human cosmic philosophies and/or human viewpoint rationalism.

It was later in life, in college, when a light bulb came on. I thought, *Jesus saves; OK, I've got that part … what now?* Ever since my college days I've been interested in what the Bible says. But there was so much information, I had many questions. There's the Old Testament and the New Testament, so how can I put this all together and really know what the Bible wants me to believe? It's the Bible! So, it must fit together somehow and can't be contradictory, can it? Is it really consistent?

Later, through personal difficulties and wanting to turn to God, I found that I didn't really know God. I had an attitude of resignation in all that was happening to me. I had an attitude of defeatism, a "so be it" mentality. There were times when I'd say "I give up" and "I guess this is God's will for me."

I have learned that as one begins to know God, we Christians will be constantly struggling between the divine and human viewpoints in our daily lives. I am keenly aware of what has been happening around us.

Billy Graham's daughter Anne Graham said:

"For years we've been telling God to get out of our schools, to get out of our government and to get out of our lives. And being the gentleman He is, I believe He has calmly backed out. How can we expect God to give us His blessing and His protection if we demand He leave us alone?"

More recently, Anne Graham, at her father's funeral, said that she would continue to proclaim the gospel of the New Testament, giving hope to the world.

The word *Hope*, to my understanding, comes from the New Testament and means "absolute confidence."

Ben Stein, a professed Jew (who has absolutely no problem with me being a Christian and vice versa) wrote the following:

"In light of recent events... terrorist attacks, school shootings, etc., I think it started when Madeleine Murray O'Hare (she was murdered, her body found a few years ago) complained she didn't want prayer in our schools, and we said okay. Then someone said you better not read the Bible in school. The Bible says thou shalt not kill, thou shalt not steal, and love your neighbor as yourself. And we said: Okay.

Then Dr. Benjamin Spock said we shouldn't spank our children when they misbehave, because their little personalities would be warped and we might damage their self-esteem (Dr. Spock's son committed suicide). We said an expert should know what he's talking about. And we said: Okay.

Now we're asking ourselves why our children have no conscience, why they don't know right from wrong, and why it doesn't bother them to kill strangers, their classmates, and themselves.

Probably, if we think about it long and hard enough, we can figure it out. I think it has a great deal to do with, 'we reap what we sow.'

Funny how simple it is for people to trash God and then wonder why the world's going to hell. Funny how we believe what the newspapers say, but question what the Bible says. Funny how you can send 'jokes' through e-mail and they spread like wildfire, but when you start sending messages regarding the Lord, people think twice about sharing. Funny how lewd, crude, vulgar and obscene articles pass freely through cyberspace, but public discussion of God is suppressed in the school and workplace.

Funny, too, how we can be more worried about what other people think of us than what God thinks of us.

Are you laughing yet?" [5]

CHAPTER SEVEN

Knowing about God vs. Knowing God

How it began for me, and for that matter, how it begins for everyone…

Belief or Non-belief in God

Believing in God or a divine being is a pretty universal concept. I can't remember ever meeting a person who was really a declared Atheist. Although, I have a friend who says: "All my life, I have been Agnostic, but lately, I'm not sure." That's funny… and yet the Bible harshly dismisses the atheist in one verse: "The fool (unthinking person) hath said in his (mind), there is no God." (Psalm 53:1)

The Bible does not seek to prove the existence of God… It declares HIM. (Gen. 1:1)

Knowing: You cannot know God or the will of God apart from knowing the Word of God. For those who only "know of God" and do not know God, J.I. Packer wrote: "Disregard the study of God, and you sentence yourself to stumble and blunder through life blindfolded, as it were, with no sense of direction and no understanding of what surrounds you."[6]

You don't learn about God from nature or sincerity. You have appreciation for His creations, but that is not knowing God.

"Nothing will so enlarge the intellect, nothing so magnify the whole soul of a man, as devout, earnest, continued, investigation of the great subject of the Deity." [7]

OK… but what to do? Where does one start with knowing God?

The following are the "7 Propositions, Points A. B. and C," as well as "The Essence of God" study notes directly from my notebooks as studied from recorded tape cassette class studies: *Introduction to Basics 1969* and *Basics 1969* by R.B. Thieme, Jr.

Seven Propositions to study and learn The Plan of God

Points A. B. C., the essence of God, and Spirituality

    A. Introduction

    B. 3 Phases of God's Plan

    C. The Believer Must Get Organized

A. Introduction. (This is not to prove, but to state)

This allows you to assess the status of your belief system.

You may answer Yes or No…

It's everyone's choice. You are free to answer as you choose to do so.

1. God exists (eternal existence) **Y / N**

2. Therefore, it is only fair to say that God reveals **Y / N**

3. God reveals in a way that makes sense, organized sense, because He is organized **Y / N**

4. Therefore, God has a plan **Y / N**

5. God has a plan for me **Y / N**

6. I owe God a hearing (I am not being asked to join up, sign up, buy anything, give money… no offering plates and no gimmicks) **Y / N**

7. The opportunity comes from the Word of God: the objective is to develop the Plan of God for your life **Y / N**

I began my studies with two assumptions: 1 – that the Bible is true and that it is, in fact, our only absolute standard of truth; 2 – that the God who is spoken of in the Bible exists, and that He is the Creator of heaven and earth and all things in them.

B. There are three phases of God's Plan (from the Bible)

Phase 1.   The Cross (plan of salvation)

The Cross is everything God had to do so there could be compatibility with man in time and eternity. (Refer to Who and What God: the Essence of God)

Phase 2.   The Believer in Time (right now and forward until death)

God's Plan is to give every believer His happiness, which is completely different than human happiness. (See Happiness)

Phase 3.   The Believer in eternity (It all begins at the Cross when you enter the Plan of God.)

Only your volition can retard execution of the Plan of God in your life, Phase 2.

C. The Believer must get organized in order to receive God's organized, perfect plan. Disorganization, which is caused by mental attitude sins, means a believer cannot take in the Word of God.

God is not who we think He is, but who He reveals Himself to be in the Bible. Man has been molding God to fit man's needs, but—sorry—it doesn't work that way.

Knowing the essence of GOD

The Essence of God is found in God's Word, the Bible, which is the only book from Him, by the way.

God is One in essence, three in personality. The three members of the Godhead are all equal and none is subordinate to the other:

God the Father – the author of the plan
God the Son –executes the plan
God the Holy Spirit – reveals the plan and guides and directs
God's people.

God is…

Sovereignty – the sovereignty of God has given man his own volition, and even if man rejects God's Plan, God's Plan will continue. (Dan. 4:35)

Righteousness – absolute perfection. He doesn't choose between right and wrong, because he can't choose wrong.

Justice – it is impossible for God to be unfair. (Deut. 32:4; Isa. 45:21)

These two essences—Righteousness and Justice—together, are known as God's Holiness and the basis through which we address and contact with HIM.

Love – perfect and maximum: The Love of God will/can never conflict with his Holiness. He will/can never conflict with His Integrities of Righteousness and Justice.

Eternal Life – He has always existed: Eternity Past through Eternity Future.

The THREE Os, which are relative to space and creation:

Omniscience – a term of theology whereby God innately/inherently knows himself and all things possible and actual.

Omnipotent – His is all powerful and able to do all things in accordance to his Holiness: integrity and sovereign will.

Omnipresent – God is present, everywhere at the same time, all the time, and everywhere.

Immutable – He is neither capable nor susceptible to change. This doesn't mean God does not act.

Veracity – God is absolute Truth and infinitely Faithful.

More on the subject of knowing

I know about my house, as an example of knowing, and know how to attend to it, how things work, what things I need to fix, what I just leave as is… and I know when I need some expert help.

I have never been in my neighbor's house, so I don't know about his house, except that it is there. I say, "I know the neighbor," but only because I recognize him. I see him often, but I've never met him. My only thought about him is: I wish he would slow down while driving through the neighborhood because I am concerned for the safety and well-being of the children.

Obviously, to know another person is a bit more complex than to know about some "thing," like a house or any inanimate object. People must reveal themselves to you in order for you to know them. People have secrets that you may never know. You can be in the company of another person for years and still say, "I really don't know him or her very well" because it is a matter of how much they've opened up to you. God does reveal himself through HIS WORD.

Our knowledge of other people depends more on them, than us. Our knowledge of them is determined by how much they open up to us, and how much they allow us to know about them. Just think about all the friends you have and how very, very close you are to some of them. (And I hope that you have lots of friends in your life.)

Earlier, I wrote that I did not know God. This was an awakening to me in 1970, when I was experiencing a difficult situation in my life and all I had were thoughts of *Why is this happening God? Why me God? Why now God? What are you doing to me, God?*

I have been a Christian for many years, and have known a lot about God and godliness, for a long time. One can know these things, even without knowing God. I am able to discuss the essence of God, the Godhead, what and who is God, eternity past, eternity future, sin (the barrier to God), Salvation, Faith, the Christian Way of Life, and even more because I have studied theological knowledge for several years, but only as an intellectual endeavor.

I enjoyed the subject matter, but found the intellectual knowledge made me sinfully proud and boastful, and I held it over other Christians, like I was better than they were. Why? Because I didn't know God apart from my intellect of Him.

It has become obvious to me, like it has for Dinesh D'Souza who writes: "Most Christians have taken the easy way out. They have retreated into a Christian subculture where they engage Christian concerns. Then they step back into secular society, where their Christianity is kept out of sight until the next service. There is religious truth, reserved for Sunday and days of worship, and there is secular truth, which applies to everything else." He continues: "This divided lifestyle is opposed to what the Bible teaches. The Bible tells Christians not to be of this world, sharing its distorted priorities, but it does call upon believers to be *in* the world, fully engaged. Many Christians have abdicated this mission."[8]

What then, exactly, is the Christian life? Is it going to church? Is it doing good stuff? Is it developing and regularly using some holy language? Do you stop hanging out with your friends? Is there a list of Dos and Don'ts? What exactly is Christianity? And what, exactly, do I do as a Christian?

Let's find a Church.

Church Hopping… *in which I'm very experienced*

Drive down any thoroughfare in most any town and you'll see church after church. I have even attended some churches to get the *feel* of the place. Unfortunately, people choose where they want to go to church based on how that church makes them *feel*.

Many churches are replacing true Church Age doctrines pertaining to the ministries of God the Holy Spirit with emotional stimulation, rock and roll bands, and ecstatic experiences like the Charismatic Movement from the '60s and '70s, or whatever will be next.

We should not allow our experiences and feelings to lead us astray or prevent us from searching the scriptures daily for truth.

I will never forget the experience when I went to a Contemporary Worship Service at a church that had more than just one type of service, in order to interest or lure people into whichever made them "feel" better. Today, it's all about "feelings." Upon seating myself in the auditorium, sanctuary, or whatever they call it, I couldn't miss noticing the two huge screens, hanging high and up front, which made me assume that scripture, doctrines, or biblical history were going to be projected and taught. I was definitely mistaken about the screens. Next, I saw the huge stage with a couple of electronic keyboards, three guitars, a full drum set and five stand-up microphones.

Then out came the band members, and five vocalists. Uh one, ah two, ah three… yes, indeed, rock 'n' roll and the screens were lit up so we could follow the bouncing ball for an audience sing-a-long, singing about some kind of "worthy and awesome" God. With the first beat of the drum, many people jumped up and were somehow, I was told, being spiritual and/or being filled with the Holy Spirit. There were a lot of hands waving and eyes closed, as people swayed back and forth with an unconscious look on their faces.

After some 20 or 30 minutes of rocking, swaying, and following the bouncing ball (i.e. being spiritual) a young man with long, blondish hair, wearing a Tommy Bahama shirt, came out from behind the curtain, with a microphone around his neck, and told everyone something about how God wanted all of us there to be more financially prosperous, even more than they could ever imagine … "pad dum - thum"… went the drum. And (I am not kidding) a woman appeared out of the back somewhere and ran down the aisle waving one of those long ribbon things like some of the women Olympic gymnasts use in their routines.

The gal who had invited me to church that day (I'll confess, it was an internet date) asked me after the service, "How did you feel about the worship service?" I replied, with confusion, "Uh, entertained?" She said, "Didn't you get into the spirit? Didn't it make you feel good?" My answer was another question, "You mean like a football game, as in rah-rah-sis-boom-bah?" She then said, "You're not spiritual." And I had to reply to that, with these words: "I know lots of people who are truly spiritual, and most likely more spiritual than anyone in that room today. And do you know what? They don't feel especially good!"

Suffice it to say, she never asked me out again.

So, now, when I'm driving down the road, after my daily bible study, and I see the sign: "11:00 am Contemporary Worship Service" or other interesting contemporary signs, I just keep on driving to the golf course because by definition anything that is "contemporary" changes all the time. It's The Church of Wuz-Happenin'-Now.

Here are more examples of man molding God to fit his needs and be up-to-date and current, in what I call "Creativity and More Modern Churchy Stuff."

Funny? Cute? Or, maybe, sad?

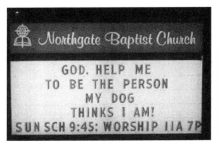

I am a dog person, but really? Church?

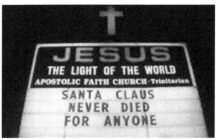

I don't get it.

What? Warnings from God?

Salacious, or what?

Gas pumps and tire sales coming soon!

Don't forget…pick up your **I ♥ Jesus** bumper stickers on your way out! Suggested placement…right next to your **I ♥ My Cat** bumper sticker.

My question, of course would be: Which one do you ♥ more?

What Is Spirituality?

Church pulpits are filled with those who say spirituality is derived from your relationship with your fellow man. For example: "If you're right with others, then you are right with God." Pleasers of Man say what they think the listener wants to hear (to listeners who think that's what they want to hear) even if it isn't the truth. Many are in pulpits to build their own kingdoms here on earth, soliciting so many offerings: love gifts, donations, contributions… all in the name of God, compelling people to give, tithe, serve, or do something apart from free will and volition.

If you are a Christian, and have Christ as the center of your life, you have to decide what your momentum is going to be. Most people think in terms of being good, as meaning being spiritual. There are lots of people who are good, appear to be good, and think they are good. Being good is ok, but it doesn't count as being spiritual.

Spirituality is determined by control: *The Old Sin Nature versus the Holy Spirit.* [9]

As long as you live in your present body, the Old Sin Nature will coexist with the indwelling Holy Spirit as a permanent resident of the body. This results in a great struggle for dominance in the life of every believer.

Spirituality isn't observing a set of rules, or staying out of the watering holes, or being moral, not smoking, not drinking, etc. Spirituality is not being pious, or using phony phrases: hallelujah, brother, sister, or "praise God." If there is anything phony, it is someone trying to say who is spiritual and who isn't.

Spirituality is a difficult subject because too many people have a religious background, some pet area of holiness, a pet forte of self-righteousness… and it takes a lot of growing up to get away from that.

Most Christians haven't a clue as to the work of God The Holy Spirit. "Your understanding of the Holy Spirit affects your concept of living the Christian life."[10] It is an extraordinary thing that those who profess to care so much about Christ should know and care so little about the Holy Spirit. The Holy Spirit is God and is not diminished by being said to be the Third Person of the Trinity, having every attribute of the divine essence. Get this: There would be no gospel, no faith, no church, no Christianity without the work of the Holy Spirit.

Growing spiritually and knowing God can only be accomplished by the learning of Biblical Doctrine, under the control of the Holy Spirit, and the application of this knowledge to the life you live. So where do you go?

Most Christians go somewhere (a church) where it makes them feel good. But "feeling good" is not Christianity or Spirituality.

It is the responsibility of every Christian to decide where he/she will go to learn the Word of God. I decided that if there is a God, the Word of God must all fit together and make sense. So there must be a system, a related system without contradictions.

Much of the doctrinal vocabulary and material in this chapter of the book was created by my Pastor-Teacher of many years, R. B. Thieme, Jr. As Pastor of Berachah Church for 53 years, he developed unique vocabulary, illustrations, and biblical categories to clearly communicate the infallible truths of God's Word. He should be credited with the following concepts and terminology: the old sin nature, grace as the policy of God, rebound, the rebound technique, rebound mechanics, faith-rest life, ICE (Isagogics, Categories, Exegesis), divine viewpoint, top and bottom circles, three categories of sin, four components of the soul, corrected Scripture translations (when marked).

God mandates that you think divine viewpoint—the mind of Christ—a perspective of life based on the infallible Word of God. When Bible doctrine is the foundation of your thinking, you will have confidence and stability under all circumstances, an orientation to grace, an inner happiness that produces capacity for life, love, and blessing, and a relaxed mental attitude toward people. [11]

Growing Spiritually with God

It is every Christian's responsibility to **THINK.**

"Behold, I send you out as sheep in the midst of wolves. Therefore be wise as serpents and harmless as doves." (Matt. 10:16)

I just read a piece written by Dietrich Bonhoeffer (a German pastor, systematic theologian, anti-Nazi dissident, who had a plan to overthrow Hitler, even kill him.) His "After Ten Years" in *Letters and Papers from Prison,* I believe is as relevant today as it was in 1943 when Bonheoffer was imprisoned and later hanged.

Paraphrasing Bonhoeffer's words, Patrick A. Meadows, PhD Princeton: Bonhoeffer argues that stupidity is an even greater enemy of the truth than is malice because stupid people can become foolish tools of any strong political or religious power in the public domain; therefore, they can also become unwitting agents of evil. Furthermore, he maintains that one can overcome stupidity only by means of a genuine "inner liberation," which is acquired by leading a "responsible life before God." Only by leading such a life, he asserts, can one gain "inner independence and wisdom," and thus effectively oppose worldly powers wishing to take advantage of stupidity. [12]

You Can't Fix Stupid

Many people are familiar with Ron White, the cigar-smoking, scotch-drinking stand-up comedian from the Blue Collar Comedy phenomenon, who through hilarious stories, presents a lot of truth.

He has always been a storyteller relaying stories from the time he was a boy growing up in a small town in the middle of Texas oil country to selling windows for a living in Arlington, Texas to performing in sold-out theaters and arenas as a headliner comedian all across the country.

I put Ron White right up there with George Carlin, Winston Churchill, Robin Williams, Jonathan Winters, Mark Twain, Will Rogers, George Burns, and my granddaddy J. A. Meadows, Sr., all great raconteurs. The only difference is, last time I checked, Ron White was still alive.

His "You can't fix stupid" series, is just plain funny. However…

I believe you *can* fix stupid!

You can't THINK what you don't know. We are commanded to "stop being stupid" in Eph. 5:17. In this context, who then is a "foolish Christian"? The believer who remains in the state of carnality and ignorant of Biblical Doctrine and the ministry of the Holy Spirit cannot be spiritual or grow spiritually. A Christian is either carnal or spiritual. Carnality is caused by sin.

I have been asked many times, about comments that I have made, "Where did you get that?" My reply, sometimes, is "from Bible Doctrine." I then often hear, "I didn't know you were religious." To which I would most often reply, "I'm not religious." That would often open up some interesting conversations. Or, I might say, "I'm not religious, I'm a Christian." This often opens even more discussion on "Just what is Christianity?"

Christianity Is not a Religion

Dinesh D'Souza writes, "There are two types of people who allege that all religions are the same. The first group is made up of religious believers, although not the fervent kind. These well-meaning folks insist that all religions are equal pathways to heaven—a position that only one major religion, Hinduism, actually endorses. But there is widespread sentiment in the West that religions are similar in that they are all human pathways to the divine. By this measure it doesn't really matter very much which religion you subscribe to, and to go around trying to persuade others to adopt your religion is a mark of impoliteness, if not fanaticism.

"The second group that considers all religions to be the same is atheists. This group views all religions as equally false…"[13]

Every Christian should know this…

Christianity has one key difference which separates it from religions and other belief systems. It is found in one word: *relationship*. By simple definition, religion is man-centered, and based upon man's works. Most all religions are similar in that they stand, conceptually, on the pretense that man reaches higher power or being, based on his own efforts. Man is the aggressor and the deity benefits off man's efforts of good deeds. Even man sacrificing something, in religion, has man being rewarded for adhering to whatever the religion calls for, with man doing something.

In Christianity, the aggressor is God and man benefits (Romans 8:3). The Bible states clearly that man can do nothing to make himself right with God (Isaiah 53:6, 64:6; Rom. 3:23, 6:23). In Christianity, God did for us what we cannot do for ourselves (Col. 2:13; 2 Cor. 5:21). Sin is what separates us from God's presence (Rom. 6:23; Matt. 10:28, 23:33). Because of God's love, He took our punishment upon Himself and all we must do is accept God's gift of salvation, through faith in Jesus Christ (Eph. 2:8-9; 2 Cor. 5:21).

God's Policy is Grace; the Authority is the Sovereignty of God and the Purpose of God's system is the Glorification of Jesus Christ. Therefore, the graced-based relationship between God and man is the very foundation of Christianity and the antithesis of religion.

The Bible is so vastly misinterpreted and therefore misunderstood. Religion (again, Christianity is not a religion) rationalizes and twists phrases and modifies translation into "feel good theology," "prosperity theology," and, therefore, so many Christians are thinking totally in Human Viewpoint.

We Christians are commanded to study. "The Word of God is alive and powerful, sharper than any two-edged sword, piercing even to the dividing asunder of the soul and the spirit, and of the joints and the marrow, and is the critic of thoughts and intents of the heart." (Heb. 4:12, R.B. Thieme, Jr. corrected translation)

"All Scripture is God-breathed and is profitable for doctrine, for reproof, for correction, for instruction in righteousness; that the man of God might be mature, thoroughly furnished unto all good works." (2 Tim. 3:16-17)

"Study to show thyself approved unto God, a workman that needeth not to be ashamed, rightly dividing the word of truth." (2 Tim. 2:15)

How I Study the Bible

Why not just pick up the Bible and let my thumb run along the edges of the pages, stop, open it up and with my eyes closed simply put my finger down and start on that verse, as a sign that God wants me to read this, right here and now.

My answer is: There is no hocus-pocus with God. This creates foolish mistakes and incorrect interpretation. What happens, with such random selection, is this: Ideas and different topics come up and there will be so much to process that confusion arises on how to put it all together.

Why not just pick up a Bible, start at Genesis 1:1 and begin reading the whole book from start to finish? If you are serving a life sentence in a prison, this might be OK, but while living your life, and reading the Bible, you will quickly come to a point when you wonder what the Bible says about this subject, or that subject, while you first started with interest in something else. What about the Trinity, the second coming, sin, being filled with the Holy Spirit, etc.? So, starting at the beginning of the Bible could make it a long time before you get to the topic of your interest.

It is called Systematic Theology, which I found back in 1969 and discovered the Bible has been taught to Christians in this manner for centuries. For me, Systematic Theology gives me confidence that I know what the Bible wants me to believe and how I grow in my faith. I can understand and grow in my relationship with God and with other people.

The Work of the Holy Spirit

You don't grow spiritually by works, fellowship with people, or what you do for God but by the knowledge of God's Word and the execution of God's Word in your life. Only the ministry of God the Holy Spirit can execute the Christian way of life.

We are all born with an Old Sin Nature. There are three categories of sin, which is another important doctrinal study.

There are a) Mental Attitude sins (pride, jealousy, hatred, guilt, anxiety, implacability, fear, worry, self-pity, nit-picking, bitterness, vindictiveness, irritability, self-righteousness, boredom, and the like), b) Sins of the tongue (included on the list are lying, maligning gossip, judging…), and c) Overt sins: (including murder, theft, adultery….).

You might be surprised to learn which category is the worst. (Hint: Mental Attitude sins)

There are many overt things that are not sins and religious people are hung up on them. Personality, being happy or sad, and intense or relaxed are not sins. Obnoxiousness in its overt character is not sin, either.

Many things happen for the new believer at the point of salvation, but God never touches or changes the Old Sin Nature. Thieme compiled a Biblical list of some 40 things (benefits/assets) which are given to every believer at the moment of salvation; among these is the power system God designed for the execution of his plan for each Christian's time on earth.

I, definitely being a "systems-oriented person" want to learn and grow in Systematic Theology. I found that God's system can only accelerate spiritual growth.

"Rebound"[14] is a key to understanding *being spiritual.*

In our time on earth, every Christian will sin again and again because the Old Sin Nature (OSN) stays with us. The first thing Christians must learn is how to get out of control of the OSN, which is the believer's enemy.

Here it is… God's grace provision for spiritual recovery is one of the most glorious and wonderful promises from God.

Let's start first with humans at birth. We are born with an underdeveloped soul, made up of *an undeveloped self-consciousness, mentality* (which must be developed by the learning of words so we can have a vocabulary to think), *volition* which at birth is tied to physiology (i.e. when we are hungry, we scream… or, as my Grandmoney said, "pitch a conniption fit"), and some sort of *emotion which develops norms and standards, a conscious* (which like teeth…) aren't there yet, either.

We are all born spiritually dead (Eph. 2:1; Rom. 5:12). When we are born, we have done nothing good or bad, but in God's viewpoint we are physically alive but spiritually dead. In terms of divine viewpoint… we are unpleasing to God.

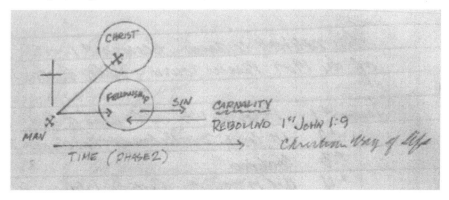

Rebound diagram, from my personal Bible study notes of 1969 Basics, are the same today as it ever was… in the Christian way of life. Top and Bottom Circles – original diagram attributed to R. B. Thieme, Jr.

Man will come to the Cross and make a decision, positive volition or negative volition, to the salvation message.

At the moment of positive volition, accepting Christ as Savior, the believer is placed in the top circle forever, in union with Christ, eternal relationship (Rom. 8:38-39), which is an Eternal Security, and the believer is placed in a Temporary Fellowship, the bottom circle, filled with the Holy Spirit.

Temporary, because through time every one of us sins: Mental Attitude Sin, Sins of the Tongue, Overt Sin. Yes, we all sin, even sinning in the same way a non-believer sins (***shocking, I know***). Because of our sins, we are out of fellowship with God and removed from the bottom circle, being a carnal Christian and out of fellowship with God, unable to grow spiritually.

Eternal Security

Many Christians do not understand eternal security, thinking that they can lose salvation, because of sin. Being out of fellowship for some time, even years, they think they must believe in Christ again. Not the case. There are no "rededication gimmicks."

God, of course, knew in eternity past that we all were going to sin again. Therefore God, in his grace, provided a means for us to return into the bottom circle and back in fellowship with Him. My Pastor-Teachers, Theologians, and Seminary attendees all teach the principles of Rebound.

Rebound reveals the majestic grace of God. Rebound is never a work on the part of the believer. God does all the work. God requires no emotional purging, agonizing, godly sorrow, penance, only our faith. Recovery from sin and regaining fellowship with God results only when the believer follows the gracious mandate of 1 John 1:9.

Sin makes us carnal and places us out of fellowship with God. Sin is the barrier between man and God and separates us from spirituality. There is no Christian who achieves sinless perfection in time.

The mechanics of rebound come through confession of sin. The Scripture says, in 1 John 1:9, that "If we confess [simply name] our sin, He is faithful and righteous to forgive us [cancel] our sins and to cleanse [purify] us from all unrighteousness" (NASB).

In my Rebound study notes from Bible class, in understanding the original language of the New Testament, an important word is the Greek word used for confess: ὁμολογέω, *homologeo,* "to name, cite, admit, acknowledge." The word means simply to acknowledge or name your sins to God. "Homologeo does not mean to feel sorry for sins, to publicly announce sins, or to suffer a guilty conscience; there is no emotional connotation involved."[15]

So the basic principle is to address God in his essence of Righteousness and Justice, which He always is, and claim the promise of 1 John 1:9, confess sin, and return to the bottom circle. We are to confess it, forget it, and move on.

You will exit the bottom circle again and again for sure, but the more you are aware of what sin is, the more faithful you will be, through the use of God's promise of 1 John 1:9, and Rebound.

Again, this requires the study of sin and the three categories of sin: Mental Attitude Sin, Sins of the Tongue, and Overt Sins.

Rebound Technique

Every believer must know this technique, first and foremost. This promise of God to Christians is found in 1 John 1:9, "If we confess our sins, He is faithful and just to forgive all our sins and cleanse us from all unrighteousness."

Does God keep His promises?

The Bible is a promise book in many ways. In our study of the Doctrine of Inspiration you will find that the Bible is the inspired, inerrant, infallible Word of God. So, we can conclude that God's promises can be trusted because the promises that are in the Word of God are inspired of God. They express God's will, purpose, and plan for our lives. The promises in the Word of God can be trusted because of who and what God is in reviewing the essence of God. We can trust the promises of the Word of God because of the perfect virtue and integrity of the author of these promises. We can trust in the promises of God because of the divine essence, God is veracity, He is also immutable; therefore, God can never lie.

A biblical worldview is one's total conception of the world from a biblical standpoint. It's a Christian's basic belief system about the meaning of life, the nature of God, the source of truth, and other foundational concepts. Yet many Christians' worldview is not biblically consistent. They may approach some issues from a biblical viewpoint, but not every issue.

Here is a very good question: *Why, then, do so many Christians not have a consistently biblical world view?*

We are now living in the Information Age (Computer Age, Digital Age, New Media Age) and that creates one big issue for most Christians.

When we pick up and read the Bible, it takes us back thousands of years, someplace in the near Eastern World, back to a primitive, unmechanized and barbaric world. To a place totally unfamiliar with life and our world today!

So we ask ourselves this: *How does the Bible of that world fit into my world, today?* We are living in the Information Age, so how does the Bible fit into my world? It is difficult to see how there is any application to us. Many Christians, therefore, fall off, become lukewarm, and never seek the personal and direct dealing that God has for all of us.

He is not a different God, but the same. From eternity past and for eternity future, He is the same. His character has never changed nor will it ever. The Truth has not changed. God's ways have never changed. His purpose, policy and authority remain constant. Jesus Christ is "the same yesterday, and today and forever." (Heb. 13:8)

Man is constantly trying to change God to fit man's need. God is immutable. He is neither capable nor susceptible to change. We must come to realize that we can trust in his word, live by faith, believing in every promise of God and discover that the realities of the Old and New Testament believers are ours, too.

The answer is found in God Himself. Go back a few pages and see the essence of God, again. The God of the Bible and God of thousands of years ago is the very same God for us today. He's the same God because he is Immutable!

No wonder some Christians fail to have a consistently biblical worldview.

We say we believe the Bible because we really want to know God. But, when we read, it isn't telling us anything about what we want to know today… and we really *do* want to know.

It's just so far away, this human viewpoint dilemma. I know, for I have experienced it, too. We are ignorant of what the Bible says. We do not know the Word. For those who are ignorant, education is the key.

They reject what the Bible says on certain issues. If a professed Christian does not believe what the Bible says, it will be impossible for him or her to have an authentic biblical worldview.

They are more concerned with what the world thinks of them than what God thinks. "Fear of man will prove to be a snare." (Proverbs 29:25)

A believer who views the world from a biblical standpoint recognizes that he is not of the world. Jesus said, "If you belonged to the world, it would love you as its own. As it is, you do not belong to the world, but I have chosen you out of the world. That is why the world hates you." (John 15:19;17:14)

When a believer starts making compromises within the world's way of thinking, he loses focus on God's perspective.

They are lukewarm in their commitment to Christ. Like the church of Laodicea, they are "neither cold nor hot" (Revelation 3:15), unwilling to take a stand for Christ. For the lukewarm, *commitment* is the key.

They are influenced by the lies of the world. From the time of Adam and Eve, Satan has used his ability to deceive and confuse (Genesis 3:1-6; Revelation 12:9). A powerful tool in Satan's arsenal is the idea that the Bible is a book of myths, that it's full of errors and not to be trusted. Satan wishes to convince people that the Bible is no longer relevant; its laws and principles are obsolete. Many in the church have been influenced by such thinking.

They are swayed by their circumstances and doubt God's promises.

Who's in the pulpit?

We most likely check out the credentials of plumbers more carefully than the guy standing behind the pulpit of a church, where lies are often fed.

You do not grow spiritually by works, the Mosaic Law, fellowship with other people, giving of your money, or by what you do for God, but by your knowledge of God's Word and the execution of that in your life.

As opposed to discussion groups or coffee chats, with a lot of confusion and without any scholars in Theology present and teaching, I highly recommend Bible study conducted in monologue from a teacher who has the gift of Pastor-Teacher and who has devoted himself to the study and teaching of Biblical Doctrine, and not one who is communicating a feel good theology, prosperity theology, or how "God wants to be your best friend" theology.

Your Pastor-Teacher should be academically trained in the Hebrew and Greek languages.

Today's Pastors are mistakenly moving away from Scripture and are into subjective decision making. To them, feelings are more important than truth and reason and the creature, not The Creator, has the final say on what is right and wrong. Sincerity has become more important than truth and more important than reason.

Yes, *Sincerity* has become the standard for being successful in life, even a standard for being spiritual. As it has been said: "Sincerity is the key to success, because once you can fake that (sincerity) you've got it made."

I hope you're laughing at that one!

Choosing the Right Pastor-Teacher

- His life should be devoted to the study and communication of Bible Doctrine.

- He has ability and authority to teach via Monologue, not a discussion group.

- He communicates the Word of God to the congregation who make up the classroom.

- He can't be a friend of everyone; yet he loves everyone in impersonal love, for he has no time otherwise.

I highly recommend you ask this question: When and where was the guy you will study under trained for the work to which he has been called?

The right P-T (Pastor-Teacher) for you wants you to grow spiritually and to be equipped to do the work God has for you to do. But for this to become a reality, two things must happen:

1. We must learn the sound doctrines taught in Scripture, not merely study Bible stories.

For example: You can read the story of Adam and Eve and miss the study on the origins of human *total depravity*. You can read the Nativity story and miss the meaning of the *incarnation*. You can read the Easter story, and miss the glorious meaning of *atonement*.

The Bible is not a magical book which one can just open anywhere and find answers to life's problems. The Bible is not literature which simply depicts the history, myths, and legends of a people. The Bible IS *the infallible rule of faith and life.*

2. You must have *Biblically qualified leadership.*

You cannot grow spiritually with a leadership that does not understand what the Bible is—and what it is not. You will not grow spiritually if the Bible is taught incorrectly.

My Pastor-Teacher R. B. Thieme's methodology was based on a system he called **ICE**.

Isagogically – Historical Introductions

Categorically – Divisions/Classifications of principles of understanding

Exegetically – Critical Interpretations

And…

Etymologically – linguistics that study the derivation of the words

A Bible-based church must have Biblically qualified leadership. When congregations use *all* these criteria for choosing their leadership, they will have *Biblically qualified* leaders. They will have leaders who can teach the sound doctrines taught in Scripture and equip the saints to grow spiritually and be ready and able for God's work.

To have a consistently biblical worldview we must go back to the Bible and take hold of the promises God has made to us, for the world offers us nothing. (Luke 9:25; John 12:25; Matthew 6:19) There is no better way to learn each of the fundamentals of the Christ-centered life than with the ongoing guidance and encouragement of the right Biblical Pastor-Teacher.

The Christian Way of Life

What exactly is the Christian life? Is it going to church? Is it doing good works? Is it developing and regularly using a holy language? Do you stop hanging out with your old friends? What exactly is Christianity, what is the Christian life and exactly what do you do as a Christian?

The present trend today among many Christians is to emphasize experience and interaction with people. This is understandable from the human viewpoint, since all you see are people; you rub elbows with people all the time. Therefore, it is inevitable that you will be people-conscious. This sets aside the number one priority of relationship with God, which can only be fulfilled through the perception and application of doctrine.

But to assign number one priority to God and relationship with Him requires the perception of Bible doctrine.

God is so completely different—holy—from us that the only way we can know Him is if He openly reveals Himself to us. This He has done in two ways: through Creation and through the divinely inspired books of the Bible.

It is, therefore, important that we make sure that our belief system about God is rooted in God's revelation of Himself and not on human speculation about God. There are extensive scholarly writings which have much to offer to us in understanding and communicating our Christian Faith. But the 66 books of the Bible are the only writings which are God breathed.

Most of us think that we are limited to just our physical body and state of affairs, including your gender, race, family, job, and status in life… but spirituality comes in and says "there is more than this."

As I've quoted before and as Dad said, "There is an absolute science to all things spiritual and it isn't mysterious at all. It is only mysterious according to the level of awareness we have. The higher our level of awareness, the more the mystery is resolved and the more truth you have."

Finding Wisdom and Truths: The Pursuit of Happiness

We all want to be happy, but how do we define happiness? It certainly, means different things to different people. For most people, it seems, happiness is based on circumstance. It's a state of mind, a feeling or pleasant sensation of the mind. Circumstances make us feel happy.

Pleasant circumstances mean happiness… unpleasant circumstances means unhappiness. Pleasant circumstances derived from pleasant experiences, is a helpless world view (human viewpoint) of happiness. In our human viewpoint we are always in what I call the FSH & PCP, The Frantic Search for Happiness which comes with a Perpetual Car Payment.

If you do not accept or believe in God then all you can have is your human imagination, your own creativity, and you cannot seek joy in a God who may or may not exist. Your happiness is determined by circumstance or happenstance, which is fleeting and is only determined by the details of life… like wealth, power, sex, drugs, rock 'n' roll, fame, etc.

Unhappy people complain constantly. Hence, the arrogance of unhappiness assumes that people, success, prosperity, promotion, romance, marriage, friendship, or getting attention can make them happy.

"Beware of Destination Addiction—a preoccupation with the idea that happiness is in the next place, the next job and with the next partner. Until you give up the idea that happiness is somewhere else, it will never be where you are," advised Robert Holden, psychologist and motivational speaker.

This is the myth of marriage, sex, success, prosperity, wealth, and social status.

People think of marriage as a state of happiness. Idiots get married because someone promises to make them happy forever or because they want to leave the environment of an unhappy home and transfer that unhappiness into their own unhappiness. This is the "both sides of the fence" syndrome. This happens with the poor and the rich, the single and the married. All are unhappy, looking to the other side for happiness. The reality is you take your unhappiness with you, even when you cross the fence.

Happiness is not something that is made or manufactured by you, and no one can make you happy. Most of us are often confused about happiness, as it is so fleeting. We place so much importance to various stimuli of life which are the "enjoyables for the moment," but which have no ability to sustain us in our day-to-day living. Happiness by stimuli of life is happiness for all the wrong reasons.

Contentment comes closer to describing what we all should seek along with a RMA, relaxed mental attitude, a tranquility for every circumstance that comes our way. But no, we get caught up in things such as "the grass is always greener on the other side of the fence" syndrome. Troubles in life come when we believe the myth. We are taken over by envy, believing that other people have all the good stuff, and then we get feelings of depression, anxiety, and self-persecution by the belief that we have so little.

Along with this comes the mental attitude sins of jealousy, bitterness, and on and on.

Young people, for the most part, think only in the moment. I remember actually creating my own self-induced misery as a teenager. I would be in one place, *here*, and worry about missing out on something, yet I had no clue of what was going on somewhere else...*over there*. And I didn't even know where *over there* was. It's got to be even greater today, with approbation lust and the search for constant approval, praise, acknowledgment, living to please others, and all those constant "dad-blamed new-fangled notions" of technology in front of us.

God has perfect happiness, has always had perfect happiness (in eternity past), will always have perfect happiness (in eternity future) and wants you to have His happiness, during your lifetime. And get this: You can't make God unhappy (this might be a blow to your ego... and all this time you thought *you* were making God unhappy). God can make you happy, but you cannot make God unhappy. What a deal!

Contentment and Holiness

The holier we are, the more contentment in any and all circumstances we will have. If you want to be more content, you must become knowledgeable of God's plan for your life as revealed from Bible doctrine.

Only your volition can retard the execution of the Plan of God in your life.

CHAPTER SEVEN

Go with God and The Hybrid.
What Is in a Name?

Hybrid systems, as the name suggests, are systems combining two or more modes of power.

Everyone knows that there are hybrid cars with electric/gasoline/diesel power systems and hybrid beings in Greek mythology. Hybrid is something made by combining different elements. In golf there are hybrid clubs. Ultimately, though, there is but one pure and perfect hybrid…

For me, The Hybrid Christ arises out of the theological understanding that Jesus Christ is simultaneously divine and human in nature. He is neither purely one nor purely the other. Jesus Christ is simultaneously both God and human, and yet he is not two, but The One Christ.

The Absolute Uniqueness of One Person

The Lord Jesus Christ is unique in the universe. He lived a sinless, perfect life. He is The God-Man having all the attributes of God. The human nature of Christ, in union as the God-Man, had to depend entirely upon the plan of God the Father and the power of the Holy Spirit. He is not only God, but true humanity. Therefore, a Christian should desire to know all about HIM. Everything you know about HIM makes HIM unique and The HYBRID.

God Himself is the Ultimate Hybrid for He is Triune. The Trinity is a doctrine unique to Christianity. No other faith, religion, sect, or philosophy that advocates one God also proclaims that there are three who are God. This apparent paradox does not mean there are three gods in one, but that one God exists in three distinct persons who are coequal, co-infinite, and co-eternal, all possessing the same essential nature. God in one essence, but in three persons.

"The Trinity is not abstract theology, but a practical doctrine that is important to comprehend. Your understanding of the plan God the Father has designed for your destiny in time and eternity is critical for your spiritual growth. Your understanding of the person and work of Jesus Christ so illuminates the greatness of your quest for salvation. Your understanding of the Holy Spirit affects your concept of living the Christian life. Only by perceiving the true biblical perspective of the Trinity can you come to love God, grow spiritually, and fulfill your very own spiritual life."[16]

What about life and its purpose? For Christians, I suggest you get the Manual and a Mentor—The Bible and the Right Pastor who is teaching **Systematic Theology.**[17]

Systematic Theology is any study that answers the question, "What does the whole Bible teach us today?" on any given topic.

A doctrine is what the whole Bible teaches us today about a particular topic. "*Systematic Theology* summarizes each doctrine as it should be understood and *applied* by present-day Christians."[18]

Here is my personal life plan, going forward

To continue building confidence under all circumstances through the rough or fairway…

Create stability in adversity or prosperity, with double bogies or birdies…

Gain greater inner happiness, producing greater capacity in life, love, blessings…

Develop the relaxed mental attitude while living in the cosmic system…

See God's purpose for my life… requiring me to mentally separate myself unto Him, not separation from the world.

Grow in Grace and Knowledge of our Lord Jesus Christ…

Renew my mind with the mind of Christ and advance in spirituality, knowing that…

Advance in Biblical Doctrine which means advancing in spirituality, Advancing in the Plan of God, for the purpose of Glorifying the Lord Jesus Christ.

Grow with God as my power source requires me to the study of the Word of God, in Systematic Theology, The Mind of Christ… Biblical Doctrine—The unique HYBRID of the universe.

I, in faith, am going to…

**Go with God,
Hogan
and The Hybrid**

AFTERWORD

I had often heard, *"J. Mike, you should write a book."* This came from those who enjoyed the funny stories of my experiences, viewpoints, business adventures, travels and especially stories about golf and all those Screen Door Open Golf Championships.

The big question: *Could I write a book of my own stories and experiences?* I liked the challenge I found in the writing itself. There is a system and process to it and lots to learn. *I tell you what… writing ain't for wimps!* You need a lot of help from others along the way.

Here's some of what I didn't know. I didn't know how the review of my own life and writing about it would give me more self-clarity and affirmation in regard to my life's purpose. I, for sure, didn't have any idea that I would be so naked in my self-expressions about the things that matter most to me.

This book is not only about some hilarious experiences but is also about my fundamental beliefs and essential parts of the systems under which I was raised, educated, and continue to live. The fundamentals of life and faith systems sustain me.

Readers will have some laughs and may even be reminded of similar personal circumstances. Others will be as passionate as I am, in some of the things that really matter to me. Hopefully, some will have their lives touched in a meaningful way.

Please feel free to let me know.

Within these pages, therefore, I believe I've pretty much answered my own questions of *Well, how did I get here? Why am I here? And where am I going?* It is my hope that you find enlightenment and joy in your own journey.

I like "process" much more than goals. And for me ***the getting there*** can be more fun than ***the there*** you seek.

EXCELLENCE is *not* a destination.

– J. Michael Meadows

MORE OF J. MIKE'S PERSONAL
GOLF EXPERIENCES

1968 PGA Championship,
inside the ropes and a friendly Gardner Dickinson

I had an assignment with IBM Sports Network, working the 50th Annual PGA Championship at Pecan Valley in San Antonio, TX. I will never forget Gardner Dickinson, a Ben Hogan protégé, yelling at me, "Hey, we're trying to play some golf out here. Think you could hold it down, please?"

My picture appeared in the *San Antonio Light* newspaper sports section. It was a picture of Sam Snead chipping onto the first green at Pecan Valley, during that PGA Championship, with me prominently standing in the background. The following day I took the paper to Pecan Valley in hopes of getting an autograph from Snead. I got it along with a very sour look from the Slammer.

The last day of the PGA Championship, I was assigned to follow Arnold Palmer inside the ropes with my walkie talkie, relaying scores and info back to the IBM scoreboard mobile trailer.

1973 Texas Open
Phil Rodgers, Gentle Ben Crenshaw and Ben's Bunnies

Woodlake Country Club, San Antonio...my first ever pro-am. Phil Rodgers was the PGA Professional in my group. I remember Phil as being from California and a super talented amateur golfer who played college golf at the University of Houston. I was impressed with his short game and putting. He became the creator of the Trusty Rusty wedges, and a great teacher of the short game, helping Jack Nicklaus in the '80s with his game.

The '73 Texas Open was won by a very impressive Ben Crenshaw (aka Gentle Ben) winning his first-ever PGA start. But more impressive to me were all those young'uns, affectionately called Ben's Bunnies.

1976 Champions Golf Club and Jimmy Demaret

An IBM friend of mine, Dan Shackleford from New Orleans, and I had the opportunity to play Champions Cypress Golf Course in Houston, Texas, site of the '69 US Open, won by Orville "Sarge" Moody. And we took it!

All of a sudden, while we were playing the great Champions golf course, another three-wheel golf cart came our way, down the middle of the fairway. It was Jimmy Demaret himself (the first three-time Masters Champion). Mr. Demaret stopped and asked, "How you boys doing?" "Just great!" was the reply... and "Oh, Mr. Demaret, could we get a picture?" We waved down a couple of golfers from another fairway who took the picture with my camera. Then Mr. Demaret said, "You fellas come in for a drink, now, when you're finished playing. OK?" We surely did. The Men's locker room and bar at Champions Cypress is one of finest locker rooms and drinking establishments I have ever enjoyed.

Me, Jimmy Demaret, and Dan

1984 The Masters Tournament
Augusta, Georgia

Dick Taylor, a friend and business associate at Xerox Corp., living in Houston back then, and a member of Houston Country Club, called me in Dallas on the evening of Tuesday April 10, 1984. "Hey, what are you doing?" he asked. His question was met with some typical response from me like, "Not much, what's up?" Then he said, "No, no, it doesn't matter what you're doing, Meadows. Stop whatever it is and get on a plane now to Houston, because tomorrow we leave from here to Augusta." Dick told me that a fellow member of HCC had his tickets to the Masters, as he did every year, but something had come up and he couldn't go this year. The member was asking around the club if anyone wanted to go to the Masters, which started the next day with the Par-Three Tournament. Can you believe it? He was having trouble giving away tickets to the Masters?

There were two tickets available with a house, car arrangements, etc., all of which had previously been planned and arranged. The other two people going were Dick Harmon, professional at River Oaks Country Club, and Charlie Epps, professional at Houston Country Club. Dick Taylor said, "When the HCC member turned to me, and before he spoke a word, I said, "Yes! And all I have to do is just make one phone call for the other guy to take that last place on the trip."

This was my first time to The Augusta National Golf Club and a Masters Championship.

Hord W. Hardin, Chairman, said of the 1984 Masters: "This year marks the 50th Anniversary of the first Masters. However, we chose not to recognize the occasion in any formal way. It has always been our feeling that every Masters is worthy of equal recognition. And yet, it is somehow appropriate that our Champion in this 50th year is a modest, immensely likeable young man whose natural talent is unquestioned and whose love of golf is boundless. Truly Ben Crenshaw is a Champion in the tradition of Bob Jones."

I have yet to read anything as perfectly descriptive as the four following paragraphs from my 1984 Masters Annual. These are words, I believe, that paint a portrait:

SUNDAY

"Silently, deep in the lush cathedral of hole number 10, Ben Crenshaw surveyed his sternest challenge of the afternoon.

He had putted well all day, well enough to birdie the previous two holes. But what faced him now was more than a putt. It was one of the longest, most torturous assignments the Augusta National could impose. His dearest hope was for two putts and a par.

In the shadows of the dogwood, in the gaze of a thousand hopeful eyes, Crenshaw completed his research and settled into his stance. Then with the long, lazy pendulum stroke that is his trademark, he sent the ball on its way.

At the midpoint of its 60-foot journey, the putt gathered speed, and for an instant it seemed too strong. But then, with less than 10 feet to go, the ball climbed a subtle rise, slowed to perfect pace, and fixed its final path, curling, as if magnetized into the diametric center of the hole."

Gentle Ben then took command of the tournament. He won... and I was there!

July 6, 1991 The Dan Jenkins Partnership & Goat Hills Glory Game Reprise

My playing partner that date in July was Mike Hyatt from the Screen Door Open and OSU days.

I've talked about Dan Jenkins earlier in this book. He is an American author and sportswriter who often wrote for *Sports Illustrated*. Jenkins was born and raised in Fort Worth, Texas, where he attended R. L. Paschal High School and Texas Christian University.

Mike and I are huge Dan Jenkins fans and have every one of his books and most are autographed by the author. Mike Hyatt, except for a little time in the U.S. Armed Forces, lived his adult life in Ft. Worth, Texas.

One of Dan Jenkins' early novels, *The Dogged Victims of Inexorable Fate,* was about a cast of characters, having a love-hate relationship with the game of golf, who played in *The Glory Game* at Goat Hills and is the funniest chapter ever written about golf (in my opinion).

On that oven-baked day, July 6, 1991 in Ft. Worth, The American Golf Corporation presented "The Dan Jenkins Partnership & Goat Hills Glory Game Reprise" benefitting the Bob Bolen Scholarship Fund. My friend Mike Hyatt somehow got us in and registered as participants of the two-man best-ball golf tournament. I remember Dan Jenkins along with Chris Schenkel, American Sportscaster, Ed Sneed, PGA professional, and a lot more notables… in addition to Mike and myself.

Food and drink, along with the standard goodies: golf tees, balls, towels etc. And prizes were provided… well, not really. On the second hole, a par three measuring 165 yards, yours truly two-hopped a seven iron, right into the hole. My first ever hole-in-one! It wouldn't be until after the round that I found out that there was *no* hole-in-one prize, which normally would be a car, a trip to Juárez, a $25 gift certificate… *something*!!! Devastating news for a 44-year-old up-and-comer!

After turning in our scorecard, at the end of the event, I asked for my scorecard back. After all, it showed the first ACE of my life. I then took the card and found Dan Jenkins and said something to the effect of, "Dan, I had my first hole-in-one in this tournament and there's no hole-in-one prize. How about signing my card, could you do that?"

He wrote on the back of my scorecard: "To J Period, F*^K your hole-in-one, Dan Jenkins."

Oh great, Dan, I can hardly wait to show this to my daughters.

1992 - Thousand Oaks, California

Wayne Gretzky, hockey superstar known as The Great One, invited me on a Tuesday to play on Thursday. He said, "You bring a friend, and I'll get one, too—we'll have a foursome." I called Jim Rankin, Club Champion at Ridglea Country Club in Ft. Worth, who stopped whatever he was doing and flew out for the match. Jim and I each lost $58 to Gretzky, a 15 handicap. I don't think so!

Me, Wayne and Jim

June 22, 2000 – Golf in the Kingdom Tour

The 2000 Golf in the Kingdom Tour included The Old Course, St. Andrews, Scotland, and Carnoustie, site of the Open Championship nine times: 1931, '37, '53, '68, '75, '99, 2007 '09 and '18... and several other Jewels in the Crown of Scottish golf...

At Carnoustie, on June 22, 2000, I played with Gary Penn, Cameron Goldston and Lee Roy Pearson... all "good ole boys" from Ft. Worth.

Number 16 is a 248 yard, par three hole of sheer terror, with an uphill front to back green, surrounded by gigantic and very deep bunkers. Our foursome finished with a total combined score of "8". Yes, you read that correctly... an aggregate "8"! When we walked off the green the caddies said that they had just witnessed the absolute best foursome total score ever recorded on the hole.

Here's how it "went down." Into a swirling and gusty wind, I hit my driver left of the green. The ball was left of the left greenside bunker. Gary and "Cammy" drove the green with "bump and run" drivers. Nice! Lee Roy "Saw My Leg Off" Pearson hit his new Ping Eye 2 one iron, (like a rocket boring a hole into the wind) which hit the green and rolled uphill, right into the hole… for an ACE! Holy crap! A hole-in-one on arguably one of the finest finishing holes in all of golf. It was a one-iron, folks!

When all the hoopla (caddies included) of screaming and jumping up and down subsided, we approached the green. I headed left and pitched the ball over the bunker onto the green. Then the putting began. All three long putts found their way into the bottom of the hole. Yes, siree!

That's one ace, two birdies and my par, which still adds up to a total score of "8" for the foursome. Wow! And the total number of putts for the group was 3. Unbelievable, but true!

Thursday, July 10th, 2003 – Carnoustie, Angus, Scotland

I nicked the flag off of #6 Carnoustie Golf Links

While sitting in the bar area, known as Hogan's Alley, at the Glencoe Hotel in Carnoustie Scotland with owner Joe McClory, I asked him about the Open Championship of 1953. He had gone to the bar to retrieve a bottle of single-malt whisky and returned with it along with a bit of history on the 1953 Open. We soon discovered that we were sitting there alone, on the very date of Hogan's Open victory 50 years earlier. We sat there, overlooking the Carnoustie Championship course that evening, while the sky was still light, as it can stay light over there until 11:00 pm, or even later in July. No one was on the course. Why wasn't there a 50-year celebration going on?

I felt compelled to go for an evening walk, so I excused myself. I walked directly across the street, Links Parade, and another 100 yards to the first tee. I strolled down the first fairway, imagining what it was like back in '53. I had seen, even took pictures of pictures, of Hogan playing in the 1953 Open. I have this one of Frank Sinatra who came across the ocean to watch Mr. Hogan in the Championship.

Sinatra at Carnoustie and the 1953 Open championship
…look closely, left, standing with his hands crossed in front

I had played Carnoustie many times and have many times since. I was there watching the great debacle of Jean van de Velde in 1999, but now I was thinking of Hogan in 1953 (I was six years old at that time). Walking down the first fairway, I was thinking how Hogan must have kept his drive down the left side, giving him sight of the first green on this 406-yard hole named Cup. After walking to the first green, I turned left to the second tee, and walked down its fairway. It was a very calm and quiet evening and finding myself lost in thought made it somewhat surreal. I thought: *Hogan was right here…* as I turned and walked up to the #3 tee, right across it through some rough and on to #5 fairway, going toward the green. I walked off the other side of the fifth green to the 6th tee. There is a plaque on the championship tee of the sixth hole.

Yours truly… on July 28, 2018
playing Carnoustie six days after the 147th Open Championship

I was there! The #6 hole is now known as Hogan's Alley. A 578-yard, par 5 demands one of the bravest tee shots in all of golf. The out of bounds extends down the entire left side, and players must carry a tee shot 310 yards to take the fairway bunkers out of play. Challenging the left side can lead to an easier second shot—or disaster—while going to the right makes hitting the green very difficult because the hole normally plays into the wind. Every caddy at Carnoustie can show you the exact spot where Hogan hit his drive during each round of the '53 Open, even though not one of them had been around back then. A drainage ditch pinches the fairway 80 yards short of the green, so the lay-up is tricky, too. The 6th green is heavily contoured and protected by bunkers at the front and back.

The flagstick that evening had a golden flag gently flowing in the breeze with green lettering: Ben Hogan 50th Anniversary. Again, I was a thief, and took that flag right off the flagstick. When I got back to the Glencoe Hotel, I showed Joe the flag that I had "nicked" (taken without permission). Joe said: "You could have got one of those right here; we sell those same bloody flags right here." "Yeah," I said, "but this was the only one flying on No.6 today, 50 years to the day!"

There is a plaque on the back of that framed flag now that reads: "On July 10, 2003 this flag, which was on the No. 6-hole flagstick at Carnoustie, 50 years to the day of Ben Hogan's Open Championship, was presented to J. Michael Meadows in memory of the occasion."

September 28, 2017 Phoenix Country Club

While playing with my 72-year-old friend Zane Bell, I watched him birdie every par three (four of them), for an aggregate score of eight on the par threes at Phoenix Country Club. The yardage of each hole was: 137 yards, 171 yards, 167 yards and 156 yards. I am now 72 years of age and having 63 of these years being involved in golf...I have only seen this once.

There are still many 'never befores' in golf and in life to be experienced!

I certainly know that I am a blessed man. I have friends all over the world who are or have been in every imaginable endeavor of life, many still working, some retired. My friends are an eclectic mix from the financial world, the legal profession, mail carriers, insurance brokers, builders, developers, investors, entrepreneurs, tradesmen, scientists, doctors, truck drivers, restaurateurs, surgeons, politicians, and some serving proudly in the Armed Forces. My friends and I are not just bonded... we are welded together!

And the common denominator is golf. Most of my friends are golfers, people who have traveled the world in planes, trains, ferries, and cruise lines and are all seasoned globetrotters, going somewhere, with golf clubs inside of travel cases, just to launch a little white sphere in a game called golf. We've traveled to play the great courses and most all the other golf gems of the world. I have played on five different continents: North America, Africa, Europe, Asia, and Australia.

Today, I play golf with friends in their 80s—both in age and in score—as well as a few, like me in their 70s. There are also many in their 50s and 60s, several in their 20s, 30s, and 40s... and even a couple of high school kids. And, *I tell you what*: a 72-year-old golfer who hits a tee shot 220 yards (sometimes) can beat a 20-year-old that can drive it 320 yards... and they both know it!

J. MIKE'S TOP 10 GOLF COURSES...
AND WHY

#1 The Meridian Golf Course – Oklahoma City, Oklahoma where in 1956, I first played and practiced golf...and, where I learned about a legendary cast of characters— from Tom Haney, (Malcolm's dad) to Stormy Williams, "Long Thumb" Kelly, "Whiskey Nose" Wilson, and a few more (of an elite group of old codgers.)

#2 Twin Hills Country Club – Oklahoma City, where in 1959, Arnold Palmer won the Oklahoma City Open.

#3 Lakeside Golf Course – Stillwater, Oklahoma 1965, where the OSU golf team played and where Glenda Fite [The Kappa Sigma Dream Girl] and I would park some nights, in my '57 Chevy Convertible.

#4 Pecan Valley Golf Club, (my first golf club membership) San Antonio, Texas, where during July 18 - 21, 1968 I was inside the ropes, working for IBM Sports Network, during the 50th PGA Championship. Me, with Arnold Palmer and a walkie-talkie. Here, I saw, on the last day, last hole, his incredible three wood shot from the left rough, after getting relief from the TV cables. It was an uphill, 230-yard shot, to an elevated, two-tier green. Palmer smashed the three wood to within eight feet of the hole. He missed the putt on the high-side and lost the PGA Championship by one shot to Julius Boros. Arnold Palmer won the other three majors, but he never won the PGA Championship.

#5 Tenison Park Golf – East Course, Dallas, Texas, 1978, birthplace of the Screen Door Open, where after we played the 1st hole, par five, we always drove our carts across the street, Tenison Pkwy, to the package store and loaded up on beer. Texas Taxis, Hot Air Balloons, Harley-Davidsons and a bad-ass biker gang.

#6 Goat Hills - "Z Boaz" – Ft. Worth, Texas, where on Sept. 6, 1991 on the 2nd hole, of 150-yard par three, while playing in The Dan Jenkins Partnership & Glory Game Reprise, with Mike Hyatt, I "two-hopped" a 7 iron into the hole… for my first ever, hole-in-one (check that one on the Bucket List). "What do you mean, there's no hole-in-one Prize?" There are all kinds of prizes, but there is no hole-in-one price. I asked Dan Jenkins if he would sign the back of "my No-Hole-In-One prize scorecard." He signed the back of the score card with "F*^k Your Hole-In-One J Period." That's what he called me: "J Period."

#7 Sherwood Country Club – Thousand Oaks, California, where, in 1992, Wayne Gretzky, the Great One, invited me on a Tuesday, to play on the next day, Wednesday. He said, "You bring a friend, and I'll get one, too—we'll have a foursome." I called Jim Rankin, Club Champion at Ridglea Country Club, Ft. Worth, who stopped whatever he was doing and flew out for the match. Jim and I both lost $58 to Gretzky, a 15 handicap… I don't think so!

#8 Ojai Valley Inn and Country Club – Ojai, California 1993 and the GTE Seniors Tournament
It was here that I talked a complete stranger into letting me caddie for him. He was an amateur who was paired with Arnold Palmer in the GTE Seniors Pro-Am. I walked the 18 holes with the King, Arnold Palmer, and at one point, in conversation, told him "I was there, at the 1968 PGA and saw your second shot, on #18, in the final round." Mr. Palmer said, "You were there?" I said, "Yes, sir!" Mr. Palmer then told me, "Son, that was the best three-wood I ever hit." (Confirmed by Doc Giffin, Palmer's personal assistant.)

#9 The Old Course, St. Andrews, Scotland – 1997 and the 20th United States Screen Door Open International-Invitational Golf Championship. A 75 is my best score on the Old Course.

#10 Phoenix Country Club – Phoenix, Arizona where I shot my lowest score ever, a 71, on January 9, 2014 and where, in the same year, I won the SideWinder Member-Guest with Pat Gallagher of Glen Eagles Golf Club, Texas. Still on my bucket list is to shoot my age. Phoenix CC is where I have had two of my five hole-in-ones, on #2 and #8. And, in 2010, the Member-Member Club Championship I won with my partner, B.J. Bohne, also member at Butler National Golf Club, Oak Brook, Illinois.

ACKNOWLEDGMENTS

I would like to acknowledge and thank…

My Advisors
Patrick A. Meadows, M.A., PhD., Princeton University
James E. Tuckett, PhD., Princeton Theological Seminary

My Friends
Sam Casano, who read many pages before they became chapters
J. Malcolm Haney, who reminded me of our many shared experiences
Mike Swartz, PGA Professional, Encanto Golf & Yacht Club, Phoenix, Arizona
All SDO brothers and friendships I have been blessed to have through golf and life
The Board, Members, and Staff of Phoenix Country Club

My Pastor-Teachers
R.B. Thieme, Jr., Bible Ministries, Houston, Texas
Herman Mattox, Spring Valley Bible Church Dallas, Texas

For all those who teach Truth and for those who seek to fill their soul with
doctrine and the filling of knowledge for spiritual wisdom and growth

My Editors/Publisher
Mona Gambetta (Brisance Books Group), for coordinating all efforts and
details contributing to the final product… for her teams' intelligence and
insights, putting in countless hours in thorough editing of this book—
while keeping me on timeline… almost

I wish to pay tribute to my Diane, who was also instrumental in the editing
of this book, whose patience and encouragement helped me concentrate on
putting the stories, experiences, and thoughts in writing
Thank you all

My Supporters
Thanks to all who provided their Praise and Endorsements for this book

ENDNOTES

1   Ben Carson, *What We Can All Do to Save America's Future ONE NATION*, (NY, NY, Penguin Random House, 2014)

2   Michael Murphy, *Golf in the Kingdom*, (NY, NY, Viking Adult, 1972)

3   R. B. Thieme, Jr., *Mental Attitude Dynamics*, (Houston, Texas, R. B. Thieme, Jr. Bible Ministries, © 2000, 1974, 1970)

4   Kerry Graham, *The Power of Mental Golf*, (Phoenix, Arizona, Learning Zone, Imprint of Brisance Publishing, 2016)

5   Ben Stein, American writer, lawyer, actor. Recited by him in 2005 on CBS Sunday Morning Commentary

6   J. I. Packer, *Knowing God*, (Downers Grove, Illinois, IVP Books, Imprint of Intervarsity Press, 1973, 1993)
     J.I. Packer is a British-born Canadian Christian theologian. Education: University of Oxford Corpus Christi College, Oxford, Trinity College, Bristol, Wycliffe Hall, Oxford

7   C. H. Spurgeon, quoted by J.I. Packer in *Knowing God*, p.18

8   Dinesh D'Souza, *One Nation, What We Can All Do To Save America's Future*, (New York, New York, Penguin Group, LLC, 2014)

9   R. B. Thieme, Jr., *Old Sin Nature vs. God The Holy Spirit*, (Houston TX, R. B. Thieme, Jr. Bible Ministries, 2013, First Edition 1973, Fourth Edition 1976)

10   Ibid.

11   J. Michael Meadows' Study Notes in Bible Doctrine with Pastor-Teacher, R. B. Thieme, Jr., 1969 - 2018

12 Patrick A. Meadows, M.A., PhD., Princeton University
Has taught at Princeton, Hamilton College, Université Paris IV –
Sorbonne, and Indiana University. Since 2006, on faculty as Professor at
Georgetown University School of Foreign Services, Qatar.

13 D' Souza, *One Nation, What We Can All Do To Save America's Future.*

14 R. B. Thieme, Jr., *Rebound and Keep Moving!* (Houston: R. B. Thieme, Jr.,
Bible Ministries, 1993)

15 J. Michael Meadows' Study Notes in Bible Doctrine with Pastor-Teacher,
R. B. Thieme, Jr., 1969 - 2018

16 Ibid.

17 Wayne Grudem, *Systematic Theology* (Grand Rapids, MI, Zondervan,1994)

18 Ibid.

ABOUT THE AUTHOR

J. MICHAEL MEADOWS

J. Mike is an avid 10-handicap golfer, member of Phoenix Country Club in Phoenix, Arizona and The St. Andrews Golf Club, Scotland. Golf and business have taken Meadows around the world and helped create his interfaces with famous golfers like Ben Hogan, Arnold Palmer, Jack Nicklaus and others. *Go with God, Hogan, and The Hybrid* is Meadows' first book and shares the truths and wisdom of the experiences that have shaped his life.

He is President of two organizations based in Phoenix, Arizona: Golf in the Kingdom, Inc. creates custom golf tours to Scotland (and elsewhere), allowing golfers to experience the history and traditions of the birthplace of golf and golf around the world, and ProFund, Inc., an innovative system of fundraising for not-for-profit organizations that Meadows developed and which has raised hundreds of millions of dollars for charities across the country.

J. Michael Meadows was born in Oklahoma City, OK in 1946. After completing high school there, he attended Oklahoma State University and received a Bachelor of Science Degree in Economics in 1968. He has served as senior marketing representative, IBM Corporation; district programs manager and national sales training specialist, Xerox Corp.;

marketing manager Exxon Corporation and director of sales training, Exxon Office Systems Division, United Kingdom and the Netherlands.

Since 1992 J. Mike has been President of Golf In the Kingdom, Inc. and ProFundWest.

Golf in the Kingdom is a golf tour organization experienced in organizing and delivery of customized golf tours (China, South Africa, and primarily, throughout all of Scotland).

ProFund is a national financial development organization assisting non-profits and worthy causes in ways to be more effective and efficient at raising dollars for their causes.

J. Mike can be reached through his websites:

www.godhoganhybrid.com

www.profundwest.com

www.scotlandgolf-gik.com